Start Your Own

INFORMATION

MARKETING

BUSINESS

Additional titles in *Entrepreneur's **Startup Series***

Start Your Own

Arts and Crafts Business

Bar and Club

Bed & Breakfast

Business on eBay

Business Support Service

Car Wash

Child Care Service

Cleaning Service

Clothing Store

Coin-Operated Laundry

Consulting

e-Business

e-Learning Business

Event Planning Business

Executive Recruiting Service

Freight Brokerage Business

Gift Basket Service

Grant-Writing Business

Home Inspection Service

Import/Export Business

Information Consultant Business

Law Practice

Lawn Care Business

Mail Order Business

Medical Claims Billing Service

Personal Concierge Service

Personal Training Business

Pet-Sitting Business

Restaurant and Five Other Food Businesses

Self-Publishing Business

Seminar Production Business

Specialty Travel & Tour Business

Staffing Service

Successful Retail Business

Vending Business

Wedding Consultant Business

Wholesale Distribution Business

Entrepreneur
MAGAZINE'S

startup

Start Your Own

INFORMATION MARKETING BUSINESS

Your Step-by-Step Guide to Success

Entrepreneur Press and Robert Skrob

EP
Entrepreneur.
Press

Jere L. Calmes, Publisher
Managing Editor: Marla Markman
Cover Design: Beth Hansen-Winter
Production and Composition: Eliot House Productions

This publication is designed to provide accurate and authoritative information in regard to the subject matter covered. It is sold with the understanding that the publisher is not engaged in rendering legal, accounting or other professional services. If legal advice or other expert assistance is required, the services of a competent professional person should be sought.

Library of Congress Cataloging-in-Publication Data
Skrob, Robert.
    Start your own information marketing business/by Entrepreneur Press and Robert Skrob.
        p.   cm.
    ISBN-13: 978-1-59918-174-5 (alk. paper)
        1. Information services industry—Management. 2. New business enterprises—Management. 3. Information services—Marketing. 4. Small business—Management. I. Glazer, Bill. II. Skrob, Robert. III. Entrepreneur Press. IV. Title.
    HD9999.I492K463 2008
    025.5'20681—dc22   2008004715

Printed in Canada

13 12 11 10 09 08   10 9 8 7 6 5 4 3 2 1

Contents

Chapter 3

Financing Your Info-Marketing Business

Chapter 8

Maximizing Online Info-Product Sales, Generate More Money from Your Business by Bob Regnerus

Chapter 9

Using Ezines as a Fast and Practically Free Way to Sell More Info-Products Online by Alexandria Brown

Preface

It's Not What You *Know*, It's What You *Learn*

by Robert Skrob, President
Information Marketing Association
www.Info-Marketing.org

Over the last 12 years I've marketed products, newsletters, and seminars to 32 different business and professional occupations. I generate millions of dollars a year in subscription income and meeting registrations each year. You can learn more about me from my blog at www.RobertSkrob.com.

In 2004, I worked with a group of info-marketers to create the Information Marketing Association, the trade association for our industry. Each month, the *Info-Marketing Insiders'*

Journal profiles two or three successful info-marketers and gives our members details about how they built their business, obtain their customers, and where they generate their best profits. No where else are million-dollar businesses dissected and outlined in such detail. I conduct these profiles personally. This gives me access to what's working in the information marketing business today.

The material in this book is the result of hundreds of conversations to find out what beginning info-marketers need to launch their business and get started quickly. The book walks you step-by-step, through the startup of your information marketing business. It's arranged in such a way so you can create your business as you proceed through the book from incorporating your company to delegating the work necessary to launching your business quickly.

Also, within this book you learn everything you need to know to prevent mistakes. This book is a launch guide for your business.

Rather than limit this book to my experience and my knowledge, each chapter is written by a specific expert. Each expert provides their best information about a particular aspect of launching a successful information marketing business. This way, you get 100 years of combined experience in the information marketing business.

Chapter 1: Escape Hours for Dollars: Do the Work Once and Get Paid Many Times. I wrote this chapter to give you a better explanation of the information marketing business. This way you have a better understanding of your opportunities.

Chapter 2: Protecting Your Information Marketing Business. The author, Scott Letourneau, is a great corporate attorney from Nevada. He has a lot of great advice for you to build your business on a solid foundation. Every business you create has risk. However, with the tools Scott provides in this chapter, it's easy to manage that risk.

Chapter 3: Financing Your Info-Marketing Business. The investment to buy a McDonalds or even a Subway franchise is out of reach for most people. Most information marketers get started with $5,000.00 or less. Even though the investment is minimal, it's critical that you establish credit for your business. Gerri Detweiler and Garrett Sutton give the secrets you need to finance your startup business in the best way.

Chapter 4: Simple and Easy Strategies for Creating Products You Can Sell for Years. Kendall SummerHawk created dozens of products for herself and she works with clients to develop their own. In this chapter, she reveals her secrets for creating hot-selling products in a short time. Once you have your own information product, you can sell it many times without additional work.

Chapter 5: The Five Keys to Effectively Marketing Your Business. The only way to sell your products is to put yourself and your products in front of people who are likely customers. Diane Conklin has sold dozens of products, filled seminars, and created coaching programs for several info-marketers. Her insights in this chapter will help you create a sales machine for your business.

Chapter 6: How to SELL Your Information Product Online or Offline. As you promote your product you are going to need to write e-mails, articles, and sales letters. Whether it's sales letters for your product or sales letters to potential partners, you have to be convincing. Michele PW, a professional sales copywriter, tells you how to create persuasive sales materials.

Chapter 7: Getting the Lifestyle and Income of Your Dreams by Using Joint Ventures. If you are new to the information marketing business it may surprise you to learn that info-marketers often sell each other's products. In this chapter, Larry Conn reveals the business model he used to generate customers without any marketing investment by offering other info-marketers content and a revenue share from sales.

Chapter 8: Maximizing Online Info-Product Sales, Generate More Money from Your Business. There is a standard formula for creating successful info-marketing websites. For ten years Bob Regnerus has been creating winning websites for information marketers. He's tested hundreds of formats and reveals everything he's learned within this chapter. This is a huge shortcut for you as you build your information marketing website.

Chapter 9: Using Ezines as a Fast and Practically Free Way to Sell More Info-Products Online. As a perfect complement to Bob's chapter, Alexandria Brown teaches you how to build a relationship with individuals who visit your website. Alexandria's ezine secrets will teach you how to keep in contact with your customers so they buy from you over and over again.

Chapter 10: An Alternative to Professional Publishers. Authoring a book is a great way to build your credibility. And, with the secrets Jordan McAuley reveals in this chapter, it can be a lot easier than you'd think. For years after you publish your book using Jordan's secrets, this book can serve as a customer acquisition tool, get you speaking engagements, and generate publicity opportunities.

Chapter 11: Build a Coaching Program from Scratch, $2 Million a Year within 18 Months. Today, nothing is hotter than coaching programs. Individuals within all economic levels and all types of businesses are hiring coaches to help them achieve their goals more quickly. Within this chapter, Scott Tucker reveals the strategies he used to launch his million-dollar coaching program in a few short months.

Chapter 12: A Coaching Program Making Millions with No Affinity, No Money and No Experience in Info-Marketing. Are you saying that you don't know anyone? Are you concerned that you don't have any contacts and you've never done info-marketing before? In this chapter, Ethan Kap and Brett Kitchen reveal how they built their business without any knowledge of the industry, no contacts, and no prior knowledge. This is a great shortcut for anyone.

Chapter 13: Speed Implementation: How to Get Your Info-Marketing Business Up, Running, and Profitable Quickly. Especially if you are building this as a second business, getting everything done can be frustrating. While you are generating your income elsewhere, you are also trying to get a brand new business launched. Melanie Benson Strick gives you the strategies you need to manage your business, delegate, and use virtual assistants to get everything done.

Within this book you have the accumulated knowledge of over 100 years in the information marketing business. You have the best secrets of 13 different experts.

Now, what are you going to do with them? Are you going to act and build a business now? Or, are you going to put this off for next week, next month, or next year?

Within the cover of this book, you have everything you need to get started and begin making money in your information marketing business. Don't put it off. Launch your business today.

Escape Hours for Dollars

Do the Work Once and Get Paid Many Times

by Robert Skrob, President
Information Marketing Association
www.Info-Marketing.org

There have never been greater, more diverse, more lucrative opportunities for everyone—from very experienced, successful entrepreneurs to rank beginners—in the field of information marketing. As the president of the Information Marketing Association, I thought I'd begin with defining information marketing, a bit of personal background, and a quick preview of what you can expect in the rest of this book.

Information marketing is responsive to and fueled by the ever-increasing pressure on people's time. Businesspeople and consumers alike need information provided to them in convenient forms, and in some cases, need an extension of it; methods and strategies that might merely have been taught to them ten years ago are now done for them. The information industry encompasses products such as traditional books, audio programs, videos, or DVDs that you might buy in a store, from a catalog, or online; magazines; newsletters; ebooks; membership websites; teleseminars and webinars; telecoaching programs; and seminars and conferences—and combinations thereof. The possible topics are almost endless. People are buying information on every imaginable topic, from better sex, to teaching parrots to talk, to gardening, to investing in real estate foreclosures, to running businesses. Information marketing, then, is about identifying a responsive market with high interest in a particular group of topics and expertise, packaging information products and services matching that interest (written and/or assembled by you, by others, or by both), and devising ways to sell and deliver it. If you can name it, somebody is packaging and profitably selling information about it.

It'll be instructive to give you a random list of topics and markets these businesses cover, and then some more detailed examples. The random list of subjects: yoga for golfers, investing in tax lien certificates, extreme fitness, persuasive voice skills for business, how to get women to approach you, how to make money on eBay, how to learn gunsmithing at home as a hobby or a business. Business niches include: marketing systems, management, or finance information for restaurant owners, dentists, chiropractors, auto repair shop owners, real estate agents, insurance agents, menswear retailers, jewelry store owners, pest control operators, or even professional magicians.

As an example from a business niche, consider IMA member Rory Fatt, who owns Restaurant Marketing Systems. Rory has more than 100 restaurant owners each paying $10,000.00 yearly to be in his top-level coaching program; nearly 4,000 buying and using his advertising, marketing, and business kits—information products ranging in price from a few hundred to a few thousand dollars—and subscribing to his newsletter; and nearly 500 attend his annual multiday conference. He also provides prefab websites, a loyalty points program (like a frequent flyer program), new mover mailings done for them, and other products and services. These products are sold using print ads in trade journals, direct mail, websites and e-mail, and teleseminars. It is a multi-million-dollar a year business built from scratch in about five years. Rory has only two employees, and he works from home most of the time, takes a lot of time off to be with his family, and goes on at least two extended vacations a year. And maybe what's most significant is this: Rory has never owned, operated, or managed a restaurant.

Quickly, a few other examples from the IMA's membership: Gene Kelly made more than $1 million this year selling gunsmithing and related home-study courses to hobbyists. Scott Tucker (see Chapter 11), who only 18 months after creating his information businesses from scratch, is bringing in as much as $2 million a year, while still working full time as a mortgage broker. Ron and Jill Wolforth have a similar income selling information on baseball hitting to parents of Little League players. I could go on and on and on.

In the last 30 years, information marketing has gone from mail-order to the much bigger, broader, and hugely profitable arena of opportunities it is today. People now routinely go from zero to $10,000.00 to even $100,000.00 a month and more, in just a matter of months.

Information marketers do not have any special talent, secret knowledge, or remarkable skill. Everything you need to get started is between the covers of the book you are holding right now.

I got started in information marketing because I was tired of working harder as a consultant and continuing to fall behind. During the summer of 2001, I completely changed my consulting business. I reduced the number of clients I served by one-third, reduced the number of employees from 20 to 2, and over the next year, I tripled my fees. Also, I charged any client with a Saturday work meeting an extra $6,000.00 (and some even paid the fee to have me attend).

In the beginning of 2004, I realized I had not accomplished enough. I was making more money than ever. Every week, I was banking money for savings and charitable giving. I was working about 30 to 35 hours a week and spending the rest of the time on hobbies or with my family. However, I realized I was topped out. There was no way I could double my income without taking on a lot more work or employees.

In a consulting business, people pay you for your services. To double the amount of income, you have to double your fees or double the amount of services you provide. When you've maxed out your fees, your only choice is to work more hours or to hire employees to work those hours. Either way, you increase your headaches.

For many years, I had watched the world of information marketers. There were people who created an audio program with six cassette tapes and a manual. They could create that program once and sell it many times for years. All they had to do was advertise their product, and new orders came in.

What's better, they could set up systems, so products got shipped by a vendor. They could be making sales, with money deposited directly into their checking accounts, and they could be anywhere in the world on vacation. This was something I had to investigate.

I began creating products. At first, some manuals and an audio program. Over time, I created more complicated products, and I have created dozens of products on a joint venture basis with other info-marketers. They have the reputation, and I use my marketing/product creation knowledge to help get the business started.

Now, I make money from products I created four years ago. Yes, in 2004, I had to sit in front of a computer and a microphone and create something. I spent 31 hours over three weekends to create a manual on selling sponsorships. However, three years later, I still get money from that weekend of work I did three years ago. Can you imagine a job where you work really hard for a month, and then people pay you extra money for years?

In the information marketing business, you do the work once and then get paid many times because your marketing systems generate sales. The best part is, each time I create a new product revenue stream, that stream gets added to the streams I have already created. I begin each year with assets that will generate sales whether I work a day or not. Then, any profit I generate from work I do is stacked on top of what comes in without work.

In 2006, a group of info-marketers and I were talking. While there is a lot of info-marketing knowledge out there, it's in too many places. They suggested that I work with Dan Kennedy and Bill Glazer to create the Information Marketing Association. The association could serve as a central repository for industry knowledge.

The core mission of the Information Marketing Association is to make it easy to start and operate information marketing businesses. An important part of that mission is to separate the promises from the reality.

In this book, you'll learn from many successful Information Marketing Association members. They will teach you the strategies they used to create successful businesses for themselves. Study their techniques; they work. Plus, they will be valuable in your marketing efforts, even if you never create a full-scale info-business.

Within information marketing, your raw material is knowledge. Personally, I read about 26 books a year and more than 40 magazines a month. The reason? Reading is the way I stay ahead, the way I stay in touch with what's going on, the way I excel. I've seen patterns in another industry, so I can teach others what they need to know to become successful.

If I had to give you the single most important info-marketing strategy, it would be to *invest in your personal education through observations, reading, and testing*.

Before I explain *how* to create your own information marketing business, let's talk about *why* you'd want to build one of these unique moneymakers.

There are six advantages of an information marketing business:

1. Replaces manual labor by "multiplying yourself" and leveraging what you know.

2. Buyers of your information products will buy more.

3. Little or no interaction with buyers is possible.

4. Few staff members are required.

5. Only a small investment is needed to get started.

6. Large profit potential exists.

So, let's talk about these advantages.

1. Replaces Manual Labor by "Multiplying Yourself" and Leveraging What You Know

How does the information marketing business replace manual labor by "multiplying yourself" and leveraging what you know? (*Leveraging* is just a one-word way to say "makes what you know do the work for you.")

Whether you're working for someone else or you're a professional selling your services by the hour or by the job, you are being paid for what you produce. The moment you stop producing, you stop getting paid. This is true for everyone, even for professionals such as attorneys, doctors, CPAs, and businesspeople who have large incomes. Trying to multiply yourself by hiring employees to increase the amount of product you can sell is full of hassles. You have the employee who leaves and takes clients with him. You have training issues. You have liability issues, even if the employee does a good job. There are hundreds of ways an employee can get the business owner into trouble. The work and the aggravation never end.

With an information marketing business, you create a product once, and you're done. It takes a lot of work to create the product, but you can sell it many times, often over a period of several years, without having to do any additional work. Creating an information marketing business is a terrific way to multiply yourself. Few other businesses allow you to duplicate yourself in this way. With an information marketing business, you take information you already know and create a product.

You might think you have to be a genius and invent a newfangled device or identify a trend before it happens. You might worry that if you create a product, you won't know how to protect it through the trademark and patent process. You might not have any idea how to find a manufacturing and distribution company to put your product on the market.

With an information marketing business, everything you need to create a new product is already inside *you*. You don't need dozens of experts. You don't need newfangled distribution methods. An information marketing business allows you to take the information, the secrets, the techniques, *the things that you already know*, and leverage them. That's the easy way to "multiply yourself."

You may have a hobby and find yourself answering other peoples' questions about what you do in online chat rooms on Google or Yahoo!. If that's true, you can be sure there are plenty of people who have not discovered those online discussion groups. You can package what you know into an information product and make money with your own information marketing business.

Or you may have developed great ways to perform services in a particular business. You can leverage that knowledge by creating a product to show others how to do what you do. By creating your product one time, you provide that business solution over and over again instead of performing the service yourself each time. That's how you multiply yourself and leverage what you know!

2. Buyers of Your Information Products Will Buy More

People ask me, "I'm already a consultant. If I create an information product that explains my entire process, won't people just do it themselves and stop hiring me to do work for them?" Absolutely not.

People who buy your information products are much more likely to hire you to perform services than any other customer you market to. Quite simply, having your own published information product makes you the obvious expert. It shows the customer the complexity of the services and the special ability you have to perform them. The only possible conclusion for the buyer is that he should hire you when he needs additional help with his business or hobby. Publishing your own information product will only increase the services you're currently providing and expand your business far beyond what you're doing now.

In addition, the people who buy your information product will buy other information products from you, whether they are products you create yourself or products you license from others. You can also partner with other information marketers to sell your products or pay them to create products for you. Once you find a customer who wants information about a particular subject, that customer will continue to buy information from you on that subject.

Encouraging repeat business helps you further leverage yourself. You spend a certain amount up front to identify potential customers and to sell them your information product. That first product can then be used to sell them other information products. Once you've gotten a customer, you're going to be able to sell that customer many things in the future, for as long as you continue to provide high-quality information at a good price.

3. Little or No Interaction with Buyers Is Possible

One of the best things about the information marketing business is that very few customers will insist on coming to your business location to buy your products. This means you can work at home with your computer in a closet or build your information product on your kitchen table. You don't have to worry about customers showing up at your door to buy your new book. You can create products and sell them online from your beach home or as you vacation across the world. As long as you've got a way to create a product, you don't have to be in any particular location for people to buy it.

Not only is this exceptionally convenient, but it also helps you get into this business with very little overhead expense.

4. Few Staff Members Are Required

The information marketing business is a terrific business because you don't need a lot of people to run it. Many info-marketers have no employees, and instead pay an independent contractor to help maintain the customer database, ship products, and handle customers' questions. This is known as *outsourcing*. You can literally operate a business that makes well over $1 million a year with very little staff and very little operating overhead.

5. Only a Small Investment Is Needed to Get Started

The information marketing business does not require a lot of equipment. It doesn't require fancy offices, furniture, or multiple computers. It doesn't require special licenses (in most cases). And it doesn't require special education or degrees. You just need to leverage the information you already know. How? By 1) identifying a market of people who are excited about the information you have; 2) creating a product those people want; and 3) offering it to them in a persuasive way.

That's why you can get into the information marketing business with a relatively low startup budget. One word of caution: Many info-marketers do not invest enough in their marketing and end up with a very slow start. Investing a little money in marketing up front will increase revenue more quickly. You can take a stair-step approach by investing a small amount in your first campaign and reinvesting your sales revenues into the next campaign. You can increase your marketing investments as you continue to have success in selling your product. That way, you can start with a very modest investment, but by continuing to reinvest profits into making new sales and getting new customers, you can build your business.

Just remember, you don't have to go to school for 12 years, you don't have to pass any exams, you don't have to buy special equipment, and you don't have to have huge facilities. But you must be willing to put *some* money on the table to find potential customers and to market your product to them. If you try to do this business without any investment at all, you're certain to fail.

Even the smallest franchise has an initial investment of $10,000.00 to $15,000.00, and there are continuing fees. You should not be fooled into thinking you can start an information marketing business with no investment. Some think the moment they create a product and put a sales page on a website that people are going to suddenly flood that site and buy their products. That is a myth. Don't believe it.

But don't be discouraged! This is a very easy business. This is a business with a lot of profitability, but you will not create a business that generates more than $1 million a year by investing nothing. You must be willing to test a marketing strategy to find new customers (known in the business as a *front-end marketing funnel*) and test it until it produces positive results. When you get positive results, you must invest in expanding that marketing campaign and growing your customer base.

6. Large Profit Potential Exists

Many info-marketers are making million-dollar incomes through their information marketing businesses. One day, without any products, without any customers, they went out and gave it a shot. They researched potential customers, they found out what those customers wanted the most, they offered it to them in a compelling way, and then they continued to sell their products until they were making a lot of money. Some info-marketers have $50-million to $100-million businesses. Some info-marketers are making in the high single-digit millions and have 5 to 10 staff. Other info-marketers are making a half-million dollars with one or two staff people. This is a business that is completely scalable, that is, you can make it as small or as large as you want.

▲ ▲ ▲

But don't think an information business doesn't require work. It does. You will have to work hard, just like any other entrepreneur does. Just like you see entrepreneurs working hard in the mall, in a retail store, or in a new restaurant they've created, you should plan on working hard on your information marketing business. The good news is, if you build an information marketing business and put in the necessary work, you can eventually replace your manual labor by multiplying yourself and leveraging what you know to create new products. Your customers are going to buy more from you in the future. You can run your business with little interaction with your customers. You can be successful using a very small staff. It takes a small investment, and the payoff can be huge—if you stick with it and continue to develop your business.

2

Protecting Your Information Marketing Business

by Scott Letourneau
Nevada Corporate Planners
www.NVinc.com

*S*tep one in creating your info-marketing business is the corporate structure. Building this right gives your business a solid foundation for creating a million-dollar business. One structure isn't the best for everyone. This chapter includes everything you need to choose the best structure for you.

▲ ▲ ▲

▲

First, let's look at the basic question at hand: Why bother with incorporation at all?

If you're like many small business owners, right now you're operating as a sole proprietorship. That's probably not because you've chosen to do so, but because you don't consider your business large enough or sophisticated enough to need to incorporate—or maybe you've never thought about it at all. If you're lucky, you'll never have to pay the price for putting off that crucial next step . . . but that's a very dangerous "if."

Sole Proprietors Are Rolling the Dice

In today's ultra-competitive and dangerously litigious business climate, you can't afford to throw the dice with your most valuable asset. Your exposure is far greater than you may think, both personally and professionally. As a sole proprietor without incorporating, regardless of the size of your business, you personally have *unlimited liability* if your company is sued. You could actually *lose your personal assets*.

Sharon McNair is a CPA and member of the Nevada State Board of Accountancy. She tells us that her fellow CPAs often advise their clients that they don't have to incorporate until they reach a certain profit level—say, $30,000.00. She thinks this is madness, and we couldn't agree more. Think about it, just being *involved* in a lawsuit is so very, very costly, regardless of whether you win or lose the case. It's pretty twisted logic to think that a small business can absorb that financial blow better than a larger one.

Even worse, most people are naively unaware of what can happen to them, both professionally and personally, if their business is hit with even a frivolous lawsuit.

Here are just a few things you will struggle with or be completely unable to do if your business is sued:

> **Smart Tip**
>
> Tip...
>
> As a business owner, you have two choices regarding a business name. You can use your legal name, such as "Paul Fredrickson Info-Marketing," or you can make up a name, such as, "Action Business Resources." If you choose to use a name other than your legal name, you must apply for a DBA name with your state corporate office.

1. You may *not* be able to get a loan for a new home, refinance, or take a second mortgage on your current home. (We'll explain why in a moment.) At best, you would have to pay a much higher interest rate because you're now considered a higher risk to the lending institution—*through no fault of your own.*

2. You may not be able to finance a new car.

3. You may not be able to lease office space.

Beware!
Even if you incorporate or form an LLC, you must operate it as a separate legal entity; otherwise, you still risk losing your assets!

Why are loans so difficult to obtain for people who have pending lawsuits? If you haven't recently applied for a home loan, a second mortgage, or financing for a car, you may not be aware of how times have changed. Five years ago, financial forms asked, "Do you have any judgments against you?" That meant, "Have you been sued, lost the suit, and had a judgment levied against you?" However, financial institutions have gotten smarter. They've tightened up the system they use to rate levels of risk for loan applicants. Today's loan applications ask a very different question: "Are you *currently involved* in a lawsuit?" That means that if anyone tries to sue you *for any reason*, frivolous or not, at the very least you'll be rated as a much higher risk. (Remember, that's before the lawsuit is even decided.) And that translates to a lot of money out of your pocket! The result, you may be financially paralyzed!

Are you willing to forego that dream home or that new car because someone tripped on a pavement crack in your business's parking lot? And just imagine what being unable to lease office space could do to your business. Creating a legal entity separates the business from you and your personal assets, so that any legal action can only affect that entity—and not you personally!

This is by far the biggest reason to incorporate or form an LLC. It makes no sense to have a sole proprietorship unless you have no assets or future assets coming . . . in which case, you shouldn't—and wouldn't—be in business at all.

Smart Tip *Tip...*
Consider incorporating in Nevada first to help protect your corporate veil. Keep in mind that your corporation or LLC will still need to register to do business in your home state.

Be Sure to Play by the Rules

It's essential to do things properly when you incorporate. Remember, when your company incorporated, you created a legal entity separate from yourself. It's imperative that your corporation is treated as such. If the corporation is sued and there aren't enough assets or insurance to cover the liability, the plaintiff may decide to go beyond the corporation and after you personally to recover alleged losses. This is called *piercing the corporate/LLC veil*, and the consequences to you can be devastating. You are essentially a sole proprietorship again, financially paralyzed, with a lawsuit against you personally!

How do you keep this from happening? Your new corporate entity:

1. *Must follow corporate formalities*, keeping recorded minutes and resolutions;

2. *Must have proper capitalization*, which is the amount of money you put into the corporation to get it started; and

3. *Must not co-mingle funds* with your personal account. Under no circumstances can you use corporate money to pay for your personal expenses.

Let's take a closer look at how these three requirements can be breached or compromised.

1. *Lack of corporate formalities*. Here's an example: When an officer of the corporation goes on a business trip, the corporation must have a meeting to authorize that trip. This is hard for some to understand, especially if you're a one-person corporation and you wear all the hats. Still, you must show in your corporate meeting minutes that the trip was approved, because the corporation is NOT YOU. It must be treated as a separate legal entity. Some people will tell you that an LLC doesn't have to perform the same formalities as an S or a C corporation. (Actually, the main reason that CPAs sometimes recommend an LLC is because of lack of formalities.) While this is somewhat true, it is changing. We've discovered recent court cases involving piercing the LLC veil where the judge looked at corporate cases for guidance, particularly with regard to formalities. Accordingly, use of the term *piercing the corporate veil* has evolved to "piercing the entity veil" or "piercing the LLC veil."

2. *Lack of proper capitalization*. When you form a corporation, it has to be capitalized. That usually means money is put into a corporate checking account, and stock for the corporation is issued to whomever capitalized it (usually an individual, but it could be another entity). There are certain guidelines in each state that ask, "Did you capitalize the corporation with enough money/assets, or was it too thinly capitalized?" But what exactly is "too thinly capitalized?" Lately, an unfortunate trend has been taking place in the courts. In some situations, they have adopted a sort of "20/20 hindsight," and companies in high-liability sectors like manufacturing are especially at risk.

   For example, let's say you're a widget maker with five employees, and you're capitalized at $50,000.00 and have a $1-million insurance policy, which is appropriate because widgets are cheap and you don't sell many. Then one day, Joe Employee cuts off a hand with the box cutter and saddles you with a $3-million lawsuit. The court says, "Mr. Business Owner, when you formed this company, you should have known that Joe would slice off a hand someday, and you should have known that your insurance would cover only $1 million of the $3 million he'd want. Since you only have $50,000.00 in capitalization, we're going to consider your company too thinly capitalized. Therefore, we're going to allow for piercing your corporate veil to recover the rest." Crazy? Of course. But true.

3. *Co-mingling of funds.* As a sole proprietor, you no doubt have a company bank account. You can use that money for your business or personal expenses. At the end of the year, your CPA will help you determine which part of that money was deductible for business expenses and which portion was for personal expenses. Often, your CPA will find that you spent a lot of money on personal items that are not deductible business expenses. Still, the only consequence to you is that your net profit is higher than you thought, so you owe more in taxes than you expected.

It's very different in a corporation. There must be a separate checking account used for business purposes only. Using that money for personal reasons is called *co-mingling of funds*, and the consequences are dire. A judge may actually set aside the corporate veil because you ignored the fact that the corporation is a separate legal entity from yourself, leaving you totally exposed.

Choice of Entity Comparisons

You have multiple choices when it comes to structuring your business; these are called entities. Entity is just a fancy word for saying "the way a business is structured." We will cover five of the most common choices of entities you can choose from including the sole proprietorship, general partnership, C corporation, S corporation, and a limited liability company. Here is a profile of each entity, so you can choose the right structure for your company.

Sole Proprietorship

A sole proprietorship is the simplest form of business. It is not a separate entity. Instead, as a sole proprietor, you own the business and are directly responsible for its debts. Just remember that whenever you do something the "simplest" way, it is typical for your results to be directly proportional to the effort required.

Management and Control

As the business owner and sole proprietor, you retain complete management and control over your company. However, the price you pay for total management and control is near total risk for personal liability incurred through the acts of your agents or employees.

No Formalities

With the exception of complying with applicable licensing requirements, you'll find no formalities required of a sole proprietorship. However, when you conduct business under a name that does not show your surname or that implies the existence of additional owners, your state may require that you file a fictitious business name statement and publish notice. If your name is Joe Smith and your business is called "Joe Smith's Services," you may not have to file. If you name your business "Joe's Services," "Smith's Services," or "Smith and Sons," chances are good that you will have to file. And if you want to deduct your expenses, you'll still have to log them into a diary format on a timely and consistent basis—no matter which entity form you choose.

Beware!

Simple vs. asset protection. Although the sole proprietorship is the easiest and most simple form of business operation, it also has the risk associated with losing your current and future assets. One lawsuit can wipe you out!

Transferability

As the owner of a sole proprietorship, you can sell your business at will.

Duration

The sole proprietorship remains in existence for as long as you are willing or able to stay in business.

For more details, go to www.NVInc.com/IMAresources.

General Partnership

A general partnership is a business entity in which two or more co-owners engage in business for profit. For the most part, the partners own the business assets together and are personally liable for business debts.

Liability for a Co-Partner's Debts

Each general partner is deemed the agent of the partnership. Therefore, if you, as a partner, are apparently carrying on partnership business, all of your general partners can be held liable for your dealings with third parties.

Liability for a Co-Partner's Wrong Doing

Each partner may be held jointly and severally liable for a co-partner's wrong doing or tortuous act (e.g., the misapplication of another person's money or property).

Sharing Profits

If you don't have a formal partnership agreement, profits are shared equally among partners. A partnership agreement, however, usually provides for the manner in which you and your partners will share profits and losses.

C Corporation

The label C corporation refers to a regular, state-formed corporation. To form a corporation, you must file articles of incorporation and pay the requisite state fees and prepaid taxes with the appropriate state agency (usually the secretary of state).

Beware!

Simple vs. asset protection. Although the general partnership is the easiest and most simple form of business operation when two people are involved, it also has the risk of losing the current and future assets of both partners. One lawsuit can wipe both of you out!

Management and Control in Corporations

Normally, a corporation's management and control are vested in the board of directors, which is elected by its shareholders. Directors generally make policy and major decisions regarding the corporation, but do not individually represent the corporation when dealing with third persons. Instead, officers and employees, to whom directors delegate authority, conduct all dealings with third persons.

Board of Directors

The board of directors is responsible for the corporation's management and policy decisions. There are, however, a few instances when the shareholders are required to approve the actions of the board of directors, such as an amendment to the articles of incorporation, the sale of substantially all corporate assets, or the merger or dissolution of the corporation.

Corporate Officers

Corporate officers, elected by the board of directors, are responsible for the day-to-day operational activities of the corporation. Corporate officers usually consist of a president, vice president, secretary, and treasurer.

Number of Persons Required

In most states, one or more persons may form and operate a corporation. Some states, however, require that the number of persons managing a corporation be at least equal to the number of owners. For example, in certain states, if your corporation has two shareholders, it must also have a minimum of two directors.

Beware!

Most who file C corporations do not fit the model from a taxation point of view (capital intensive). Be cautious of companies that promote a C corporation to help save you business taxes in year one without consideration of your business over the next three to five years.

Fringe Benefits

Corporations may offer employees unique, and deductible, fringe benefits. Although, a C corporation employer can deduct the cost of a qualified educational assistance program, and employees can exclude up to $5,250.00 of such benefits from taxable income each year, there is a restriction on this benefit. Be sure to check with your CPA for C corporation fringe benefits that may apply to your business.

Lower Marginal Tax Rates

C corporations have overall lower tax rates than pass-through entities like partnerships and S corporations. Even at higher levels of taxable income, the current tax cost of operating as a C corporation is generally lower than the tax cost of operating the same business in the form of a pass-through entity. Specifically, a C corporation will pay 15 percent federal tax on $50,000.00 in profit, which is much less tax than you would pay if that same level of profit flowed through a pass-through entity to your personal tax return. The key is to avoid or to reduce double taxation, which must be taken into account if you're considering a C corporation. Also, some businesses, if formed as a C corporation, may be viewed as Personal Service Corporations, which pay a flat 35 percent tax rate from the first dollar in profits, or Personal Holding Corporations, which pay 15 percent tax on any undistributed profits of the C corporation. Check with your planning professional to make sure your business won't fall under one of these definitions.

Corporate Formalities

If you want to retain the corporate existence, limited liability benefits, and special tax treatment, you must observe corporate formalities. If you're the owner of a one-person corporation, you will find that you must wear different hats depending on the occasion. For example, as a one-person corporation, you will be responsible for being the sole shareholder, director, and officer of the corporation. You will be required to hold annual meetings, take (and keep) corporate minutes of the meetings, appoint officers, and issue shares to yourself.

Bright Idea

If you go from a sole proprietorship to a corporation or an LLC and you have a DBA name, make sure to refile it linked to the corporation or the LLC as the filer vs. you individually. If you keep the DBA filed by you and form a corporation or an LLC, you are still operating the DBA as a sole proprietorship until you make this change.

Duration of a Corporation

As a separate legal entity, a corporation continues indefinitely. Its existence is not affected by death or incapacity of its shareholders, officers, or directors, or by transfer of its shares from one person to another.

S Corporation

Generally, S corporations may have a maximum of 100 shareholders, and those shareholders must be individuals, although certain types of trusts and estates may qualify as a shareholder. Once your corporation makes the Subchapter S election to become an S corporation, profits and losses are passed through and reported on the individual shareholders' tax returns. This is the same basic pass-through treatment afforded partnerships and LLCs. The key distinction of the S corporation is that profits and losses are not taxed at the corporate/business level like they are if the business operates as a C corporation.

IRS Filing

The S corporation must complete and file IRS Form 1120S to report its annual income to the IRS each year.

> ## Beware!
> Do not violate the S corporation shareholder rules. Remember to file Form 2553; otherwise, your corporation will be taxed as a C corporation.

General Shareholder Requirements

ALL shareholders of the S corporation must be U.S. citizens or have U.S. residency status. If for any reason S corporation shares are sold or transferred (even if by will, divorce, or other means) to a shareholder who is a foreign national, the corporation will lose its S corporation status and will be treated as a C corporation. This also means that C corporations, foreigners, or LLCs taxed as limited partnerships cannot be owners of an S corporation. This is important to know because it may affect your future investment options should your business require additional investors.

Only One Class of Stock

S corporations may issue only one class of stock, which becomes a problem when you need investors.

Limited Partnership

In a limited partnership, one or more "general" partners manage the business, while "limited" partners contribute capital and share in the profits but take no part in

Beware!

If you form a limited partnership for your business, the general partner has UNLIMITED liability. You must at least consider a separate entity to act as the general partner.

running the business. General partners are personally liable for partnership debts, while limited partners incur no liability with respect to partnership obligations beyond their capital contributions. One way to reduce the personal liability of a general partner is to form a second entity to serve as the general partner of a limited partnership. Typically, you can use an S corporation or an LLC as the general partner. When that happens, the amount that the general partner can lose is limited to the value of the assets in the S corporation or the LLC. This method brings more operating expense to the limited partnership, but that can be overcome with an LLC taxed as a limited partnership. The purpose of a limited partnership is to encourage investors who will be risking no more than the capital they have contributed.

Another potential problem with the limited partnership is that limited partners can lose their limited liability protection if they become too actively involved in managing the business. This potential means that limited partnerships are not suitable for activities where all of the partners are heavily involved in the business.

Duration

Death, disability, or withdrawal of a general partner dissolves the partnership unless the partnership agreement provides otherwise, or unless all partners agree in writing to substitute a general partner. Note that the death or incompetence of a limited partner has no effect on the partnership.

Formalities

You will find that setting up and operating a limited partnership brings with it the same formalities as when you're starting a small, for-profit corporation. Most states require that you file a certificate with the secretary of state, who applies restrictions on the use and availability of partnership names and sets forth statutory requirements that dictate how you add new limited partners and replace general partners.

Limited Liability Company

Limited liability companies (LLCs) are a relatively new business form in the United States, although they have a longstanding history in Europe. LLCs were first formed in the United States in 1977, and were granted pass-through tax status by the Internal Revenue Service in 1988. As a result, LLCs can elect to be taxed like partnerships, with tax incurred only at the individual level when profits are paid as dividends.

Any Person or Entity Can Own an Interest in an LLC

Generally, any legally recognized "person" may own an interest in an LLC, except a professional LLC where ownership rules are restricted to licensed practitioners. The question is, then, what is the definition of a "person"? The definition may be slightly different from state to state but includes the following: individuals, partnerships, domestic or foreign corporations, trusts, business trusts, real estate investment trusts, estates, and other associations or business entities.

Number of People Needed to Form an LLC

You can be the sole owner of your LLC in all states except Massachusetts, which requires two people to form one.

Ownership Structure of an LLC

An LLC's owners are called *members*. A member's interest in an LLC is represented by interest certificates. An LLC can be managed by managers or by members. An LLC is managed by its members, with each having control commensurate to his percentage of ownership, unless the members hire managers to operate the business. If the members hire managers to operate the business, the members can dictate the amount of control the managers will have.

Differences Between an LLC and an S Corporation

Some differences between LLCs and S corporations are:

- *"Memberships" vs. stock issuance.* LLCs cannot issue stock, but rather, they offer "memberships." S corporations, on the other hand, can issue stock and are owned by the shareholders.

- *Management.* S corporations are managed by the directors and officers, while LLCs are managed directly by the members unless they hire managers.

- *Restrictions.* S corporations have some restrictions that are not applied to LLCs. For example, S corporations are limited to 100 shareholders, while the number of members in an LLC is not subject to any restriction.

- *Taxation.* S corporation shareholders potentially will save self-employment taxes (15.3 percent) on distributions, whereas, with an LLC taxed as a partnership, generally the distributions are subject to self-employment taxes (exception is for passive members).

- *Liability.* If an LLC member is sued for someone or something unrelated to the operating business, the creditor will be limited to a "charging order," which in most states allows the creditor to gain access only to the "economic interests" or profits distributed vs. the ownership of the LLC. In an S corporation, the creditor can take control of the S corporation stock and, therefore, the S corporation itself, with more ease. That is why an LLC taxed as an S corporation offers more protection vs. a regular S corporation.

LLC Taxation

An LLC may be treated as a partnership or a corporation for federal income tax purposes. An LLC is treated as a partnership for tax purposes if it elects to be taxed as a partnership under the "check-the-box" regulations.

A business entity with only one owner is classified as a corporation or is disregarded; if the entity is disregarded, its activities are treated in the same manner as a sole proprietorship, a branch, or a division of the owner. As of January 1, 1997, a business entity with two or more members may elect to be classified for federal tax purposes as either a corporation or a partnership.

Beware!

Are LLC formalities required? Many incorporating companies will tell you that operating as an LLC is easier than operating as a corporation because the LLC does not require the same formalities as a corporation. This is NOT TRUE based on our research. We recommend that you also do formalities for an LLC, even a single-member LLC disregarded for tax purposes.

The Default Rules

A newly formed domestic entity will automatically be classified as a partnership for tax purposes if it has two or more members unless an election Form 8832 is filed to classify the entity as an association (and thus taxable as a corporation). If the entity has a single member, it will not be treated as an entity separate from its owners for federal tax purposes unless an election form is filed to classify that organization as an association.

The Federal Tax Identification Number

Each new entity requires a new Federal Tax Identification Number (also known as an Employer Identification Number, or EIN) to identify the entity for taxation purposes. What a social security number is to an individual, the Federal Tax ID Number is to the corporation. Generally, any corporation doing business within the United States is required to have an EIN. In fact, the EIN is necessary when filing tax returns and for establishing bank accounts.

In conclusion, if you have two partners, the LLC will be taxed as a partnership. If you have two members and you want the LLC to be taxed as an S corporation, you must first file Form 2553 to make the federal S election. If you have a single member LLC, the default rule is to be taxed as a disregarded entity, like a sole proprietorship. If you want the single member LLC to be taxed like an S corporation, then you would file Form 2553. In all of these cases, please consult a tax professional regarding your individual situation.

For more details, go to www.NVinc.com/IMAresources.

Factors Affecting Your Entity Choice

Here are ten factors to consider when you chose the best entity for your information marketing business.

1. What Do You Expect Your Business to Do in Gross Sales During the First and Second Years?

Gross revenue and question 2 on net profits, will greatly impact whether a regular corporation or a flow-through entity like an LLC or an S corporation would be best for you overall. The more net profit your business will have (with low overhead and expenses), the more likely your business could be a flow-through entity. An internet business that is purely online may fit this model. Flow-through entities include

1. S corporations;
2. LLCs taxed as single member disregarded, S corporations, or partnerships; and
3. Limited partnerships.

2. What Will Be Your Business Expenses and Net Profit During the First and Second Years?

Net profit is key to determining what you will do with the profit. Will you reinvest it into your business, or take the profits and purchase other assets like real estate? Typically, real estate would be helpful in a separate entity, and you would want the profits from your main business to flow through and use that for a down payment for real estate.

3. Do You Have a Partner for Your Business?

This affects your ability to have an LLC taxed as a partnership. A spouse counts as a partner.

4. What Is Your Personal Income Level (Aside from this New Business)?

This will help determine the potential savings linked to self-employment (SE) taxes. In 2008, SE taxes are 15.3 percent on earned income up to $102,000.00. An S corporation puts you in a position to potentially save on SE taxes. If you are already maxed out with your full-time job or another company, the above is a key component to know.

5. Will Your Business Develop a Net Worth?

Meaning, will it develop systems and have a net value over time? Or is it based solely on your efforts, and the day you stop working is the day your company stops generating revenue?

- This mainly affects the difference between having an LLC or a corporation. An LLC has more protection if the owner is sued and loses for something unrelated to the operating business. For example, if you get in a car accident and are sued personally and your insurance provider does not cover all of it, you are personally responsible. If one of your assets is the stock in your corporation and you own that personally, potentially you could lose control of your corporation (and business) from a personal lawsuit.

- An LLC has an extra layer of protection called the *charging order* that makes it more difficult for a creditor to gain control of your ownership interest.

- If on the day you stop working there is no value in your business, then if you are sued and lose control of the company, it is not a major concern because without you as the major asset and income producer, there really is no value. For example, you may be a consultant with a contract with a client, in which case an S corporation may be OK to have. You may not be as concerned about losing control of your S corporation stock from a personal lawsuit because there is really no value in your business if you are not a part of it.

6. Is the Goal to Sell the Business Soon?

This is important if you are considering becoming a C corporation because when you sell the business, you may experience double taxation. In this situation, typically at the sale of a business, the buyer will purchase the assets from your current company. This would mean that the C corporation would have income. When you shut down your C corporation, the corporation would pay taxes and you would pay taxes on the money taken out of the C corporation, which is double taxation. As an option in this situation, a flow-through entity like an LLC, taxed as an S corporation, may have been a better solution.

7. Will Your Entity Keep Profits as Retained Earnings for Future Growth and Expansion? *(Important if you're considering a C corporation)*

If this is the case, you may want to consider a C corporation. If you plan to sell the business, a C corporation may not be the best choice. It is important to check with your CPA or a tax professional from a tax planning point of view.

8. Are You Looking for Investors for Your Company?

This mostly will affect an S corporation or an LLC taxed as an S corporation. An S corporation or an LLC taxed as an S corporation has restrictions as to who can become shareholders. If your investor wants to invest in your company through his C corporation, LLC taxed as a partnership, or limited partnership, or is a foreigner, he CANNOT be a shareholder in an S corporation (or an LLC taxed as an S corporation). You do not have this problem with a C corporation, LLC taxed as a partnership, or taxed as a C corporation, or limited partnership.

9. Do You Have Other C Corporations?

If you currently have a C corporation and you want to form a new entity, which also becomes a C corporation, you have formed a control group according to the IRS, which means instead of two federal tax brackets on the C corporations, you may only have one. For liability purposes, you still have two separate entities. This is an advanced subject, and if you fall into this situation, you need to speak to a tax professional who has experience in this area. In some situations, it may be to your advantage for the C corporations to be considered part of a control group, but not usually.

10. Are You a U.S. Citizen or a Resident Alien?

This is an important S corporation question because nonresident aliens cannot own S corporations. If you are going to have a partner,

> **⚠ Beware!**
> Companies that promote C corporations do not take into account if you have other C corporations and the ramifications of the control group status.

Why Do I Get Different Input From My Attorney and CPA?

Many business owners get frustrated when their attorney gives them advice that is the opposite of what they received from their CPA. It's important to know that each professional has a different perspective. Here's some advice for understanding these perspectives and getting them both working together for you.

- ○ *Tax perspective.* One of the biggest challenges in business is conflicting information, especially from your professionals. The key is to understand their roles and why you are getting particular advice from each professional. For example, if you go to your CPA to ask if you should incorporate your business, he is going to give you advice from a taxation point of view, which is what he should do. He may recommend you remain a sole proprietorship because your business may not make enough profits to justify (from his point of view) setting up a corporation (usually an S corporation) to save you taxes. On the surface, this may seem to make sense, but what about the liability perspective and the marketing perspective?

- ○ *Liability (legal) perspective.* If you went to your attorney, he would typically say, yes, you must form a separate legal entity and an LLC provides the most protection. Of course, the attorney—unless you ask—will probably not discuss the fact that an LLC can be taxed in four different ways: a disregarded entity, a C corporation, an S corporation, or a partnership. That is typically something you discover later on, once you meet with your CPA, which, of course, creates challenges after the fact. The attorney typically will not recommend you continue your business as a sole proprietorship because you will have unlimited personal liability. Even if you have insurance, you may still lose your personal assets. Why didn't your CPA mention this part? That is not the advice CPAs give.

- ○ *Marketing perspective.* Many times, the CPA will have a benchmark in his mind at what level of profits you will save on taxes before you should consider incorporating. Generally, that benchmark is around $40,000.00 in net profits (after all expenses). In this situation, an S corporation would put you in a position to save on SE (self-employment) taxes, which is 15.3 percent on earned income up to $102,000.00 in 2008. If your CPA recommends you do NOT incorporate because your company does not make enough profits and you decide to continue to operate as a sole proprietorship, what is the

Why Do I Get Different Input From My Attorney and CPA?, continued

marketing message you are sending to the world? "Hey, I am not profitable. That is why I am still a sole proprietorship, but would you like to do a joint venture with me anyway?" That makes no sense and may not be in your best interest. If fact, you may lose business without knowing it by operating as a sole proprietorship. You never know who will say to themselves, "He or she is not successful. I am not sure I want to do business with him or her." This may be the difference between being in or out of the game!

and the partner is a foreigner, you cannot form an S corporation unless your partner is considered a resident alien. Or if your partner wants to have ownership in your new company as a C corporation, you cannot be an S corporation because the C corporation cannot own stock in the C corporation! FYI, a living trust can be an owner of an S corporation.

Disclaimer: The above comments are only suggestions. It is recommended that you speak with a professional about the best entity for your situation.

For more details, go to www.NVinc.com/IMAresources.

Best of Both Worlds

Be aware of where the advice is coming from when you meet with your CPA or attorney. Typically, an LLC has the best *liability* advantage, and in many cases, an S corporation has the best *tax* advantages. What to do? How about an LLC taxed as an S corporation? That may be the best of both worlds for you (liability protection plus tax savings). The LLC has an extra layer of protection that is not available with an S corporation. This is called a charging order.

For more details, go to www.NVInc.com/IMAresources.

Choosing a Place to Incorporate

Which state offers the most benefits? Is it Nevada, Delaware, or your home state? Many small businesses prefer to incorporate or to form an LLC in their home states. In general, it is less complicated and more cost effective to incorporate in the state where you're planning to operate your business. Unfortunately, keeping things simple and asset protection are inversely related. In many situations, Delaware and Nevada do offer advantages that may be appropriate for your business.

If you incorporate outside your home state, however, you still may be required to qualify to do business in your home state. The cost of a local incorporation is usually less than incorporating in another state and then qualifying to do business in your home state as a "foreign" (out-of-state) corporation.

If you have a partner and/or business activity in more than one state, you'll have to decide where to domicile your corporation or LLC and again, register as a foreign corporation or LLC doing business in the state where the activity occurs. That decision should be based on multistate taxation rules and registration requirements, which vary from state to state.

Delaware and Nevada are often cited as the best states in which to domicile (or form) your new business. Both states have advantages, but not all may apply to your situation.

Action List

1. Define your passion and goals personally and financially over the next three years. Focus on your outcome and what you want to accomplish.

2. Develop your business startup to-do list and put in priority order with timelines to complete.

3. Develop a budget for your business startup, plus capital required during the first 90 days.

4. Speak to your professionals concerning what entity may be best for you.

5. Call NCP at (888) 627-7007 for a free 30-minute consultation for the startup of your business, fees, and timeframe, a $200.00 value!

6. Before you sign any contracts or leases or open a bank account or obtain a business license, form a separate legal entity for your business. Do not operate as a sole proprietorship!

7. Go to www.NVInc.com/IMAresources to review the information to help you stay on track!

8. Take care of your mental and physical health. Focus on what is working, what is great about today! Get in shape, eat better, and work out. You will need the energy to produce results and get off to a fast start.

Resources

www.FastBusinessCredit.com for establishing business credit

www.BusinessLicenses.com for obtaining the forms for your business license

www.GoDaddy.com for reserving your domain name

www.GrowThink.com for business plan information

www.INCnationwide.com for incorporating in all 50 states

www.IRS.gov for tax forms and questions

www.NVinc.com/IMAresources.htm for complete information on incorporating and starting your business

www.TMexpress.com for information for obtaining a trademark

▲ ▲ ▲

Scott Letourneau is the CEO of NCP Inc. and an authority in helping people form entities, grow their businesses, and protect the assets of those businesses. His Top 5% Club is highly acclaimed by business experts around the country. Visit www.NVinc.com to receive your free guide, *Costly Mistakes to Avoid When Incorporating in Nevada!* Contact Nevada Corporate Planners Inc. at (888) 627-7007 for information and fees for us to help your information marketing business get off to a fast start! Or e-mail us at NCP@NVinc.com.

Financing Your Info-Marketing Business

by Gerri Detweiler and Garrett Sutton, Esquire
www.BusinessCreditSuccess.com

After you establish the legal structure for your company, it's time to consider startup financing. Whether you are putting your own money into the business or borrowing your startup capital, it's important that you create a plan for generating revenue and paying those debts. Also, here are some tips on minimizing this risk of creating your own business.

▲ ▲ ▲

When Melanie Benson Strick started her coaching and info-marketing business, Success Connections Inc., corporate credit was the last thing on her mind: "The first two years of my business, I had no idea how much money it would take to become profitable. Flying by the seat of my pants, I used two strategies: borrow from my credit cards and borrow from my father. Unfortunately, it wasn't until I was up to my ears in debt that I knew about other forms of capital, and by then it was too late."

Benson Strick, who is now a successful million-dollar lifestyle coach and seasoned info-marketer, says there was an upside to her early struggles: "The positive by-product of looking for a capital infusion was that I became proactive about revenue projections. I learned how to identify what was going out, what was projected to come in, and create strong strategies to pay off the debt, including using low-interest credit cards. There is no way you can stick your head in the sand and become financially profitable," she advises.

According to the Small Business Administration, more than three out of five small enterprises will borrow to start or grow their ventures, frequently using credit cards, home equity loans, and loans from friends and family to get started.

Many entrepreneurs rely heavily on their personal credit to get started, but find it creates problems:

1. Mixing business and personal funds can create headaches at tax time.
2. Personal guarantees put their personal assets at risk.
3. Their credit scores often sink due to the level of debt they are carrying for the business.

A smarter approach is to create a business financing strategy, just as you would a marketing or business plan. Even if you don't intend to borrow, having access to capital when you need it will allow you to pursue opportunities when they arise.

Where Will You Find the Money to Start Your Info-Business?

Stat Fact
There were 21 million small business loans totaling $601 billion reported to the Small Business Administration (SBA) by financial institutions as of June 2005. Small business credit card loans had grown by 25 percent from the year before, to a total of $19 billion.

Information marketing businesses can be started on a shoestring. With just a computer, for example, you can create an ebook and market it online. Or you may already have a successful business and want to develop another revenue stream. Karyn Greenstreet, founder of Passion For Business LLC, started her info-marketing business with revenues from her already successful coaching practice. She already owned a computer and office equipment, and had an established website. For her, creating and selling info-products was a logical expansion of her business, one that allowed her to reach many more small business owners than she could solely through coaching.

But most successful information marketers find that in this business, it takes money to make money. See the table for common startup expenses. A combination of capital and credit is needed for product production, online promotion, direct mail marketing, advertising, travel, support staff, etc. You can look to a number of sources for any necessary money.

Common Info-Marketing Startup Expenses

Computer, Office Equipment, Supplies	Cost
Computer system with printer/copier/scanner	$1,000–4,500
Digital camera	$100–700
Digital video recorder	$300–1,000
Business phone with features such as hold and three-way calling	$75–200
Microphone for computer	$25–200
Voice mail	$8–25/month
E-mail hosting	$0–25/month
Website design	$500–5,000
Website hosting	$50–500/month
Online shopping cart	$50–250/month
Customer relationship management (CRM) software	$600–10,000
Uninterruptible power supply	$125–250
Hard-drive backup	$150–300
Surge protector	$15–250
Calculator	$10–25
Desk	$200–600
Desk chair	$50–250
File cabinet(s)	$25–100

▲

Common Info-Marketing Startup Expenses, continued

Computer, Office Equipment, Supplies	Cost
Bookcase	$50–100
Computer/copier paper	$25–50
Logo design	$150–300
Business cards	$10–50
Letterhead, paper, and envelopes	$50–125
Printer cartridges	$25–80
Miscellaneous office supplies	$100–150

Product Development/Production	Cost
Graphic design for book cover, CD labels, and/or product cover design	$50–500
Recording and/or editing of audio program	$100–1,000
CD or DVD duplication and labeling (outsourced)	$1–3 each
CD duplicator (do-it-yourself)	$200–1,000
Audio album for multiple CD programs	$1–3 each
Printing: labels, covers, CD inserts, etc.	$.50–3 each

Professional Services	Cost
Full-service entity formation (incorporation)	$600–2,000
Trademark registration	$325–1,000
Copyright registration	$35–100
Business license (if required)	$25–500

Shipping, Equipment, and Supplies	Cost
Hand truck	$55–125
High-speed tape dispenser	$16–25
Carton stapler	$200–500
Electronic scale	$50–700
Paper shredder	$25–150
Sealing tape	$5–8
Shipping boxes, tubes, or cardboard mailers	$.14–4 each
Miscellaneous shipping supplies (bubble wrap, labels)	$20–100

Friends and Family

A handshake is not enough if you are asking friends and family members to lend money to your business or to invest in your startup. A legal agreement will spare both of you from misunderstandings, and may provide tax benefits. If you are not able to pay back a loan, for example, your lender may be able to deduct the loss if there is a written loan agreement. That may not be the case for informal loans. In addition, a well-prepared loan or investment proposal and professional agreement may loosen the purse strings faster than a personal plea for money.

Virgin Money (formerly CircleLending.com) is a popular resource for facilitating business loans between individuals. You approach people from whom you want to borrow money and with the help of Virgin Money's service, present a professional proposal and loan request. If your lender agrees, Virgin Money handles the details, including loan documents, payment processing, reminder e-mails, and year-end statements, etc. See Financing Resources at the end of the chapter for more information.

Bank Loans

It can be tough to get bank financing for a young startup business unless you are willing to pledge collateral (such as home equity) and have a strong personal credit score. It is still a good idea, however, to meet with a loan officer from a local bank or credit union active in small business lending. Ask the loan officer to review your business and financing plans. While you may not be ready or able to get a loan, your banker can provide you with valuable advice and help you position your business for a loan when you need it.

MaryAnn Shank had two websites under her belt when she decided to become a full-time info-marketer and website consultant. She successfully landed a loan from her bank to help her start up YourSBIcoach.com. "The track record I established with my previous two sites helped convince them I was likely to be successful with the new one," says MaryAnn. With financing, MaryAnn was able to quit her day job and work full time in her new business.

Business Credit Cards

It can be surprisingly easy to get credit cards in the name of your business. There is a distinct advantage to using business credit cards rather than personal ones. Many of these cards will not be reported on your personal credit report, which helps protect your credit rating from the damage that may be created by maxing out one or more cards. Some will also report to the business credit rating agencies, which helps you build a business credit rating. Finally, the rewards programs offered on business credit cards can be very rich, allowing you to accumulate free airline miles, earn cash back, or collect other perks.

Your Customers

Pre-sell your product at a discount before it even launches. If you have a strong following already, a joint venture partner with a strong list, or have found a hungry market, you may be able to pre-sell copies of your program or ebook, or seats at your seminar, ahead of time.

Dollar Stretcher

Your personal credit will typically be reviewed for business loans, credit cards, leases, and more. Get your credit report at www.AnnualCreditReport.com and make sure it is accurate. You can get a free credit score review at www.Credit.com.

One author worked with an information marketing group that sold 100,000 copies of his book before it was even published! Those who pre-order often get a significant discount or valuable bonuses, and you get immediate up-front cash flow. Make sure it is clear when the product will be available, and check with your merchant bank to learn whether pre-billing is allowed under your credit card agreement. Another option: Sell a one-hour teleseminar at an attractive cost, and then use the income generated from that program to launch your full kit or seminar.

Private Lenders

In the past, it was difficult to find private lenders and convince them to lend you enough money to get started unless you had a strong track record or stellar connections. But that has changed with peer-to-peer internet lending platforms such as Prosper, Zopa, and LendingClub. With Prosper, for example, you can post your business plan and financing needs, and individuals can bid to lend you money in increments as small as $50.00 up to a total of $25,000.00 The more individuals who bid to fund your loan, the lower your interest rate. Because the risk is usually spread over multiple lenders, it can be easier to raise money than trying to get a larger amount of funding from one source. See the Financing Resources at the end of this chapter for more information.

Terms from Vendors

Borrowing money isn't the only financing strategy available. Getting terms from vendors can be another way to manage cash flow. For example, you may be able to convince a printer to accept half of your payment up front with the rest due in 90 days. You then have time to sell your product to pay the second half of the bill. Just be prepared with a backup plan to cover the cost in case initial sales aren't as brisk as you anticipated.

Case Study: DigitalGolf.TV

Digital Golf began as an information marketing business by showcasing exclusive interactive online video content on golf courses, equipment, and instruction, along with an innovative social networking platform for golfers to communicate and interact with players of all skill levels. It has expanded to offer golfers the opportunity to "test drive" top-brand golf clubs on the golf course or driving range. The test drive service delivers golf clubs directly to a golfer's home or office based on a monthly membership fee, similar to the Netflix business model.

In 2004, Digital Golf was founded by the husband-and-wife team of Scott Walker and Nichole Neal Walker. Shortly after its founding, the company was selected to be a part of a technology incubator in Irvine, California, that promised access to angel and venture capital funding for internet startup companies. The incubator, however, proved ineffective and had a poor track record of providing funding for any company. At that point, the founders of Digital Golf were disappointed, but decided to take the leap and build the company by self-funding (which included a significant amount of personal savings, sweat equity, and a small amount of funding from family). The initial funds were used to develop the entire website and to produce the interactive and online video content featured on the site. As the company has grown and continues to scale nationwide, phase two of the company's growth includes funds from business loans as well as fees generated from customers' online memberships to the site. These funds are being used to acquire and amass a significant inventory of golf clubs and to market Digital Golf's services to the 38 million golfers in the United States.

Barter

Can you exchange services to help preserve cash? If you are selling a marketing program, for example, perhaps you can trade your program and a consultation with a graphic artist who can design your logo, business cards, and product covers. Consider joining a barter network if you need help finding businesses willing to trade. Make sure you put your agreement in writing.

As Michael D. Walker was putting together the joint venture partnerships that were ultimately crucial to the success of his info-business, Zentimental LLC, he found himself facing a welcome, but serious problem. As he added more JV partners each week, the momentum of his success began to explode. As a one-man operation, however, he soon fell behind in putting into place the technical structure needed to handle customer orders, digital download pages, etc. It soon became apparent he needed a skilled webmaster to quickly and efficiently get his system in place, so he could launch his website, www.Zentimental.com. He couldn't afford to hire someone outright, though, so he contacted several of his JV partners and asked who they were using. One name kept coming up: Corey Lewis of EasyTechVideos.com. Walker explained his situation and worked out a barter agreement under which Lewis immediately went to work solving the technical issues for the new site. In return, Walker agreed to promote Lewis's services and provide a testimonial for his website, which he was glad to do after watching how fast Lewis went to work getting Walker's site up and running. "Without the timeless concept of barter and a business partner who was agreeable to a creative solution, my site would not have been ready to launch on time," says Walker.

Lease

Even if your business is brand new, you may be able to preserve startup capital by leasing computers, office equipment, and other pricey items. A lease may offer tax advantages and will not be reported on your personal credit. Be sure to weigh the overall cost of leasing against buying, talk with your tax advisor, and read your lease agreement carefully before signing on the dotted line.

Partner Up

Alexandria Brown, aka "The Ezine Queen," used this strategy to publish her book *Power and Soul: 42 Entrepreneurs Share Their Secrets for Creating the Business and Life Of Your Dreams*. She enlisted 42 of her coaching clients to write a chapter in the book, for a minimum $1,500.00 entry fee. Writers received a case of 132 books and could order additional ones at a discounted cost. Brown was able to publish her book with a strong first-print run, and she had a team of enthusiastic co-authors to help promote it.

If you work with an established partner, negotiate terms carefully, so you each understand your roles and so you can exit the relationship if things do not work out. Get your agreement reviewed by an attorney.

Sell a Contract

Alarm service companies, health clubs, cell phone services, and other businesses sell contracts for specified periods of time. Info-marketers can create membership or coaching programs for an ongoing membership fee. Get creative and see if there is a

Case Study: Fabienne Fredrickson, ClientAttraction.com

The way I financed the startup of my company was to make the transition from my corporate job a slow one. At the time, I didn't have a lot of money saved, but I knew that I wanted to start my own business. So, instead of taking the great leap of faith too early, I strategically paced myself.

While still working in my corporate job, I decided to sign on a few clients from my new venture, speaking to them in the evenings and on weekends. It wasn't easy to do both, and I often didn't have a lot of sleep. But I knew that for me, this would be the only way to leave my job and still secure my future. So I essentially had two different income streams coming in, some from my individual clients, and the rest from the paycheck I was getting every two weeks from my sales job. The additional income I earned from my new clients helped pay for the startup expenses of my venture.

I used a six-month transition period to build my reserves on many different levels: in cash, equipment, supplies, and marketing materials. Slowly and diligently, I began purchasing the costly office equipment, supplies, and software I needed, while still collecting my paycheck. At the same time, I was using the additional income from clients to ramp up my marketing materials, my website, and logo creation, so that when I was ready to quit my job and go into self-employment, I wasn't starting from scratch. I also collected clients along the way, so that when I was ready to quit my job, I was already at a half-full coaching practice, instead of staring at an empty client calendar. Those reserves really made all the difference for me, and without them, I'm not certain I would be in business today, let alone at the top of my game, teaching thousands of entrepreneurs to attract more clients and make more money.

What I see too many times today is people very anxious to leave their income-generating jobs and doing so before they have their ducks in a row financially and marketing-wise. When these new entrepreneurs see the mounting costs of startup expenses and no money coming in, it can really take a toll on their self-confidence and the belief that they can make it in business. Therefore, in my Client Attraction business mentoring, I strongly recommend setting up the foundation of the business before taking the leap into working solo, and not relying solely on credit cards to fund the business. That way, the transition can be a much smoother one, and the chances for success are much higher.

way you can sell programs or contracts that will allow you to collect payments on a regular basis from customers. This can give you predictable cash flow and help you better manage your business finances. Need a quick cash infusion? You may even be able to factor the ongoing payments, which means selling them for a lump sum of cash before they are collected.

Establishing Business Credit

Building a business (aka corporate) credit rating can help you bypass the common financing hurdles encountered by many startups. The first step is to separate credit for your company from your personal credit. When you get credit cards, lines of credit, or trade accounts, apply for them in your business name. Although you will likely have to provide a personal guarantee, at least in the early years, business loans are not generally reported on your personal credit reports unless you default.

While most business owners would like to avoid personal credit checks and personal guarantees, it is still valuable to establish separate company credit accounts because it helps protect your credit rating. If you rely on personal credit cards, your credit score will suffer if you have too many accounts with balances or are too close to your limits on your individual accounts—even if you pay on time.

To separate your business and personal credit, it is essential you set up the proper business structure and take steps to make sure your business is legitimate and stable:

> **Beware!**
> Do not try to hide from a poor personal credit rating by using an Employer Identification Number (EIN) to replace your social security number. The Federal Trade Commission warns that this is an illegal scam.

- Create the proper business structure, whether it is an S corporation, a C corporation, an LLC or other incorporated entity. Sole proprietors cannot effectively build business credit.

- Make sure your business is properly licensed.

- Obtain a business phone line reported in the name of the business to 411 directories.

- Establish a business bank account.

- Create a business plan, even if it is simply a two-page synopsis.

- Secure credit or terms with vendors and financial institutions that report to major commercial reporting agencies such as D&B, Experian, or the Small Business Financial Exchange (SBFE), and pay them on time or, better yet, early.

- Implement accounting systems that allow you to generate financial statements as requested (preferably by a CPA).
- Have the ability to make a persuasive presentation to a lender or an investor.

Finding the Best Business Credit Cards

As soon as your new business becomes official, either by incorporating or obtaining a business license, your mailbox will likely be filled with offers for business credit cards. They'll try to entice you with offers of low-rate balance transfers and loads of perks. But how do you decide which business credit cards are the best for you?

When choosing a business credit card, there are four things you'll want to consider:

1. *Will the card help build my business credit rating?* A few business credit cards report to the business credit reporting agencies, such as D&B or Experian. It is a good idea to choose a business credit card that does report to the corporate credit agencies in order to establish business credit references.

2. *Will the business credit card affect my personal credit rating?* Max out a personal credit card, and your FICO score will suffer. But if you use a business card that does *not* report your activity to the personal credit reporting agencies, you will help protect your personal credit rating.

3. *What's the cost?* Most small business credit cards will hype very low-rate introductory offers and balance transfers. But before you get too excited, read the fine print. Watch out for rates that increase if you miss a payment on either that individual card or any other account that appears on your credit report. (This practice is known as "universal default.") Also, pay attention to the interest rate after the promotional rate ends, if you will carry a balance.

4. *What are the perks?* This is the fun part of choosing a business credit card. Rewards are rich for business credit cards—just make sure you can actually use them. If you will carry a balance, weigh the cost of the card against the benefits you'll earn. For entrepreneurs who carry balances, a low-rate card will usually win out over one with rewards.

For updated information on how to find the best business credit cards, see Financing Resources at the end of this chapter.

> ## Smart Tip *Tip...*
>
> A good corporate credit rating is a business asset. Even if you have plenty of financial resources to start your venture, establishing a strong corporate credit rating will make your info-marketing business more valuable if you decide to sell or expand it in the future.

Help! My Credit Is Bad

If you have poor personal credit and can't qualify for any business credit, you have several options:

- Borrow from friends or family or private lenders who may be more interested in your business or in giving you a hand than in scrutinizing your credit rating.

- Get serious about improving your credit. Barter, lease, or ask for terms from vendors while you work on raising your score.

- Ask the bank where you have your business bank accounts if it reports to D&B, Experian, and/or SBFE. If it does, ask for a secured business loan to establish a payment history. With a secured loan, you will put up a security deposit for the loan.

- Take on a partner with good credit to apply for initial business loans. But be careful before giving someone else ownership in your firm. A solid legal agreement is crucial.

> **Beware!**
> Watch out for companies that encourage you to misrepresent your business status to get loans or payment terms from vendors. Falsifying loan information is illegal and can spell the end of your business.

Accepting Credit Cards

Accepting credit cards for payment is essential for most information marketing businesses today because most of them sell on the internet. To accept credit cards, you must apply for a merchant account, and your terms will depend on the type of risk your business presents. Finding a merchant services company willing to allow you to process credit cards can be frustrating for a new info-marketer. Internet-based information marketing businesses usually fall into the high-risk category, making it challenging to get started. First talk with the bank or credit union where you hold your business account to find out what it can offer, and then compare that offer to other merchant processing services.

Another alternative at the beginning is to use third-party services such as PayPal or Google Checkout. While these payment options are popular, there are many buyers who

Smart Tip
Find financial averages by industry as well as a list of the safest and riskiest businesses at www.BizStats.com.

still would prefer to pay by credit card directly. See Merchant Services at the back of this book in Appendix B, Info-Marketing Resources and Vendors for a list of merchant and payment services.

Know the Numbers

You must have a clear grasp on the bottom-line numbers of your business. These will be essential if you want to go to a financial institution to borrow money, if you want to get investors or angel funding, or if you want to thrive rather than survive! It is essential to:

Hire a Knowledgeable CPA or Tax Professional with Small Business Experience

You must be able to produce financial statements that adhere to industry standards (not to mention the fact that you want to minimize taxes). The financial statements you should prepare on a regular basis (monthly or quarterly) include:

- *Balance sheet.* The balance sheet provides the company's net worth at any given point in time. The balance sheet consists of assets (what the company owns), liabilities (what it owes), and equity (or net worth). A balance sheet must always "balance." In other words, assets must equal liabilities plus shareholder equity.

- *Income statement.* Also known as a *profit and loss statement*, an income statement describes the company's profits or bottom line over a period of time. The income statement typically includes revenue, expenses, and net income (including income before and after taxes, and if applicable, income per share).

- *Personal financial statement.* Your lender may require a personal financial statement, which will be similar to your business financial statement. It will include your income, assets, and liabilities.

- *Set up your bookkeeping system.* Your system can be as simple as a spreadsheet, or you can do it yourself with a program such as Quickbooks, Peachtree, or Microsoft Accounting Express. If you don't have the time or experience to keep good records and update your system, it is a good idea to hire a bookkeeper. Be very careful about choosing someone

> **Beware!**
> Do not try to "buy" good business credit! Some companies will offer to "sell" trade references for a large sum of money. This may result in your company being blacklisted.

who is bonded, insured, and has a good reputation. More than one business owner has lost his business due to embezzlement by a bookkeeper.

No one can protect your company's money like you can. Keep a watchful eye on your assets and liabilities, so you can spot problems quickly. Successful info-marketers monitor these numbers regularly.

Resources

Books

The ABC's of Getting Out of Debt, Garrett Sutton, Esq., Warner Books

Own Your Own Corporation, Garrett Sutton, Esq., Warner Books

Consultants and Other Experts

Melanie Benson Strick, Million Dollar Business & Lifestyle Coach, 14320 Ventura Boulevard, #222, Sherman Oaks, CA 91423, (877) 830-3139, www.Success Connections.com

Alexandria K. Brown, The Ezine Queen, (877) 510-2215, www.AlexandriaBrown.com

Gerri Detweiler, Business Credit Expert, SuccessDNA Credit Center LLC, 2248 Meridian Boulevard, Ste. H, Minden, NV 89423, (888) 227-3158, www.Business CreditSuccess.com (A free business credit audio program is available at www.BusinessCreditSuccess.com/EntrepreneurBook.)

Fabienne Fredrickson, Client Attraction Mentor, P.O. Box 62, Stamford, CT 06904, (866) RAINMAKER, www.ClientAttraction.com

Karyn Greenstreet, President, Passion For Business LLC, P.O. Box 331, Revere, PA 18953, (610) 346-6601, www.PassionForBusiness.com

Jim Reed, CPA, nationwide preparation of taxes and financial statements as well as bookkeeping, (888) 838-6682, www.TetonTax.com

Garrett Sutton, Corporate Attorney and Rich Dad's Advisor, 348 Mill Road, Reno, NV 89501, (800) 600-1760, www.CorporateDirect.com

Corporate Credit Agencies

BizCreditReports, national reseller of Experian credit information, offers affordable credit solutions for small businesses, www.BizCr.com

D&B Small Business Solutions (formerly known as Dunn and Bradstreet), http://small business.dnb.com

Equifax, www.Equifax.com

Experian, www.SmartBusinessReports.com

Small Business Financial Exchange, www.SBFE.org

Internet Resources

Small Business Administration (SBA), www.SBA.gov

BizStats.com, small business financial and risk information, www.BizStats.com

Financing Resources

Business Credit Cards. A free list of the best business credit cards can be found at www.BusinessCreditSuccess.com/card_ratings.php

Online Lending Communities: Prosper, www.Prosper.com; Zopa, www.Zopa.com; Lending Club, www.LendingClub.com

Priority Leasing, leasing for all types of small businesses, (800) 761-2118, ext. 30, www.PriorityLeasing.com

Virgin Money (formerly Circle Lending), facilitates interpersonal loans and offers free guides for business owners seeking loans or investment capital, www.Virgin Money.com

▲ ▲ ▲

Garrett Sutton is a corporate attorney advising small business owners. As one of only three Rich Dad's Advisors, he teaches corporate formation and business finance strategies to thousands of new business owners each year. He has written several best-selling books, including *Own Your Own Corporation* and *How to Buy and Sell a Business*. He also hosts a syndicated internet radio show, Wealth Talk America (WealthTalkAmerica.com). His firm provides asset protection and business-building services to thousands of clients around the country and internationally.

Gerri Detweiler is a sought-after source on credit topics and has authored and co-authored several best-selling books on consumer financial topics, including *The Ultimate Credit Handbook*. She has been interviewed in thousands of news stories, sharing credit advice for consumers and entrepreneurs. Garrett and Gerri are co-founders of BusinessCreditSuccess.com, a service dedicated to helping small business owners successfully establish strong business credit ratings.

Simple and Easy Strategies

for Creating Products You Can Sell for Years

by Kendall SummerHawk
www.KendallSummerHawk.com

Creating products is as easy as typing or talking. With questions of business structure and financing taken care of, now it's time to create your products. And the best part is, with info-marketing, you work to create a product once, and you get paid many times over.

▲ ▲ ▲

W ho hasn't dreamed of owning a business that gives you the luxury of sitting on a sunny beach under an umbrella with nothing but miles of sand and time stretching out before you and money flowing in while you peacefully relax?

Information marketing is one of the few types of businesses that can actually make your dream of enjoying both financial success and an ideal lifestyle come true. The reason is simple. The beauty of information products is that they leverage your time because once created, they live on indefinitely, continually bringing in steady income, new leads, new sales, and new clients for your other information marketing programs and services.

When I first started my business, I thought I was going to be coaching small business owners on marketing. On a lark, I decided to create an audio program on cassette tape of the topics that my clients seemed to struggle with most, just to see if I could sell a few copies every month and make a few extra dollars. Little did I realize I would end up creating a fast-growing information marketing business that now brings in a high six-figure annual income and is quickly approaching the $1-million-a-year mark.

Information products (CDs, DVDs, workbooks, books, ebooks, reports, manuals, etc.) are the heart of positioning yourself as an expert, attracting more clients, and creating ongoing income that flows in, even when you're on vacation, spending time with your family, or sleeping!

And, if you're an entrepreneur who cares about doing well AND doing good, information products help you reach out and touch the lives of a wider audience. It's not unusual for information marketers to have clients around the world, which means you not only get the satisfaction of creating a lucrative business that earns money for you day and night, but you also get to enjoy the personal fulfillment of knowing your information is helping large numbers of people solve a problem or achieve an important goal.

Bright Idea
You can bundle an information product with other services to generate more leads and clients. For an example of this strategy, go to www.KendallSummerHawk.com/success.html.

Information Products You Can Create

An information product is typically written or recorded, and then packaged and delivered either via the internet or by mail. At first glance, the number of different ways you can combine and package your information can look daunting. Take a closer look, and you'll see that each different combination uses just one (or more) of these three simple formats: audio, video, or print. That's it! No matter which format(s) you choose to use, the steps to producing your information product are the same, so once you've made your first product, you'll be able to make your next one even faster.

To help you visualize what an information product looks like, let me summarize 38 different ways you can combine audio, video, or printed information into popular selling products.

> **Tip...**
>
> **Smart Tip**
> People will buy the same information in multiple formats, so you can offer the information on audio, in printed reports and workbooks, and in a video.

38 Different Types of Information Products

Paper

1. *Reports.* 1 to 50 pages, delivering information on a highly focused topic
2. *Tip sheets.* One page, very specialized "how-to" information
3. *Manuals/workbooks.* Typically 50 or more pages published in a three-ring binder or a spiral-bound format
4. *Books*
5. *Boxed sets of books*
6. *Home study course.* Typically includes printed workbook, audio CDs, and even video
7. *Test/assessments.* Self-scoring or computer scoring
8. *Seminar or workshop transcripts*
9. *Newsletters.* Can be printed or online
10. *"Back issues" of newsletters or reports*
11. *Continuity programs.* Such as "book or CD of the month"
12. *Sets of cards.* Reminder cards or study cards, like recipe cards
13. *Forms/checklists.* Detailed, step-by-step information
14. *Posters*
15. *Multi-author publications.* Several authors contribute to one product, and each gets to sell it

Audio and Video

16. *Audio.* Live recorded speeches, seminars, or consulting sessions
17. *Audio.* How-to instructions you can record on your computer or via teleseminar

18. *Audio.* Interviews of respected experts on a specialized topic
19. *Audio.* Interviews of success superstars on how they did it
20. *Audio.* Interviews of YOU as the expert on a specific topic
21. *Audio.* Roundtable discussions
22. *Audio.* Collection of radio broadcasts
23. *Audio.* Subliminal, self-hypnosis, etc.
24. *Video.* Live recorded speeches, seminars, or consulting sessions
25. *Video.* How-to instructions and demonstrations
26. *Video.* Interviews, conversations, roundtable discussions
27. *Video.* Interactive with a workbook

Internet Products

28. *Ebook.* Book delivered in downloadable format over the internet
29. *Downloads.* Clients download manuals or audios over the internet
30. *Membership site.* Clients pay a monthly/regular fee to access information on a password-protected website
31. *Course/lessons.* Clients receive a series of lessons
32. *Online certification courses*

Combination Products

33. *Trainer kits.* Multimedia, used for certification courses
34. *Computer software*
35. *Combination packages.* Mix of different products, offered at a special price
36. *Customized.* Same basic information customized to different markets or different clients
37. *Licensing.* For reproduction
38. *Private-labeled.* For other marketers to brand and sell

If you have a topic you're passionate about or have experience with, then you're already on your way to creating your first information product. Chances are good that if there is a topic YOU are passionate about, then there are plenty of other people who are passionate about it, too.

Popular topics that people always want to learn more about include:

- Business growth/development
- Business marketing
- Sales
- Team building
- Diet

- Health
- Exercise
- Relationships
- Sex
- Cars
- Hobbies
- Sports
- Golf
- Animals
- Real estate investing
- Stocks
- Personal finances

> **Bright Idea**
>
> See a sample of an information product that has sold more than 500 copies at $157.00 each (totaling more than $78,000.00) in just one year at www.Kendall SummerHawk.com/pricing.html.

Within these topic categories are many small subcategories that make excellent material for a surprising number of information products. People are hungry for detailed how-to information on an unlimited number of specialty topics.

For example, let's say you're a golfer, and you've figured out a way to shave two strokes from your golf game. That's a topic that thousands of other golfers would potentially be interested in. Or let's say you are an expert at selling to big corporations. Do you know how many other salespeople would pay (and pay handsomely!) to get their hands on your sales system? Plenty!

Here are just a few ideas for the information products you can quickly and easily create and begin selling:

- *Idea 1*. You can create a number of different, small, subtopic-specific audio and workbook information products, starting with how to give a presentation, how to get the appointment, how to follow up, how to close the sale, or how to get a repeat sale.

- *Idea 2*. Then you can bundle in your personal worksheets, checklists, forms, scripts, and a day-by-day planner to create a high-ticket home-study program.

- *Idea 3*. To maximize the sales of your home-study program, you can offer ongoing monthly support via teleseminars for a fee. (A teleseminar is simply a telephone call on a special telephone line that can accommodate multiple people at once—called a *bridge line*—that you rent by the hour.) This type of program is called a *continuity program*. Your continuity program can include online links to articles, a members-only community forum, and past recordings and transcripts.

- *Idea 4*. But wait, that's not all. Once you've begun making sales and have clients enrolled in your continuity program, you can periodically offer them additional products, services, a high-end personalized coaching program, consulting, or workshops. See what I mean about leveraging your time?

Let's say you're passionate about dog training, only not just your everyday, run-of-the-mill dog training, but agility training. (Agility training is where the dog is taught to quickly and accurately go through a series of obstacles in a timed competition.) You can easily create a how-to audio, workbook, or video guide that spells out how to get started agility training a dog. Better yet, you can create a series of information products, each one specializing in agility training for a particular breed. The information may be nearly the same in each product, but to the individual dog owner, seeing a book that specializes in her breed of dog is a sure bet she'll want to buy it.

One more tip to keep in mind: When choosing your information product topic, it is helpful to select a topic that already has other books, audio programs, and courses written about it. I know this sounds like the opposite of what you might think, but being the first to launch a new topic is a lot riskier than producing information on a topic that people are already known to buy.

> **Smart Tip**
> Once you have the title of your information product, be sure to purchase the matching domain name.

I recommend sticking with delivering specific, detailed, how-to information on a popular topic.

Selling and Delivering Your Information Product Online vs. Offline

You can start out by selling and delivering your information product strictly online, which will save some money when you're first getting started. Online products are also easy to update or modify. However, you'll probably want to quickly move into being able to sell and deliver shippable information products such as CDs, workbooks, and DVDs, for these four reasons:

1. Shippable information products command higher prices because they have a higher perceived value.
2. Shippable information products typically have a lower return rate.
3. Shippable information products give you the opportunity to include additional marketing information in the box or packaging.
4. Shippable information products can be easily displayed and sold at tradeshows, speaking events, or conferences.

If you're starting out with online delivery, then you'll offer your audio information product as an MP3 file download. (An MP3 file is simply a file format that can be downloaded into an iPod or other MP3 player, listened to online directly from your website, or downloaded to your clients' computers for listening later.)

If you're including a companion workbook with your audio (more later on how to quickly and inexpensively do this), then you'll turn your workbook into a downloadable PDF file called an *ebook*.

Create Your Information Product Content Quickly

Now, let me show you a simple way to create the actual content for your information product. You don't have to be a writer or a professional speaker to quickly make your first product because you're already knowledgeable about your subject.

The simplest way to create your information product content is to ask your buying audience what their biggest challenge is. If you already have a database of contacts in your target market, then you can send out an e-mail survey. Your survey can very simply ask your audience this question:

"What is your biggest question (or challenge) about X?" ("X" is your specific topic).

You can use an online survey system such as www.SurveyMonkey.com or www.AskCampaignsThatMakeYouRich.com, which will let you see your survey results tallied by the most popular entries first.

If you don't have a database of contacts, you can still use a survey. You can partner with others who have a list, asking them to send out your survey. What's in it for them? If you offer them your information product to sell for a commission once it's completed, they will be interested in helping you get the information you need to create your product. One other way to find out what the biggest challenge is in your topic area is to simply ask other people you know who are also interested in your topic. You can send them an e-mail or pick up the telephone and conduct an interview to get the information you need.

Now, to finish creating your content, all you need to do is jot down your tips, techniques, strategies, or steps that solve the most popular questions or challenges your target audience

Smart Tip
Aim for completion, not perfection! It's better to have a less-than-perfect product to sell than no product at all.

says it has. Aim for ten specific challenges and three to five tips, strategies, or techniques for each of the ten challenges.

Keep in mind that you don't need to deliver ALL of the information available on your topic. Your clients are simply looking for ways to get started or to get unstuck. Your information will help them do that, and if they need or want more, they can purchase your additional offers of other information products, workshops, consulting, or coaching.

The Type of Information Product to Create First

Keep it simple, so you can get started quickly. For your first information product, I recommend a simple 20- to 50-page report, an audio CD, or a workbook. Let me show you how you can easily record an audio CD, and then use it to create multiple spin-off products with very little extra work.

Stat Fact
One audio CD can hold up to 80 minutes of recording.

One of the quickest (and my favorite) ways to create an information product is to record a teleseminar, and then have the recording transcribed and bound into a workbook. A teleseminar is simply a seminar delivered via the telephone. The reason I like using a recorded teleseminar to create an information product is because you can turn that one call into multiple products in just a few short hours.

For example, with a single, one-hour recorded teleseminar you can:

- Create a CD audio program that you sell.

- Transcribe the call and create a companion workbook that you bundle with your CD, increasing the perceived value and, therefore, the price of your product.

- Print a single section of your workbook as an article that you distribute to online and offline publications to drive traffic to your website.

- Edit one section of your CD into a separate audio file, creating an audio tip that you use as a sample for your website visitors to hear, so they'll want to buy your product.

- Edit sections of your CD into three- to four-minute, separate audio tips that you post on websites such as www.YouTube.com to generate traffic to your website.

- Use your separately edited audio or written sections as a weekly, downloadable course that clients can purchase and receive online.

- Include your separately edited audio or written sections as a bonus with another product you sell or as a bonus with someone else's product.

You can keep repeating this process to quickly create a library of information products people want to buy. Once you have created multiple audio programs, you can bundle them together into a big-ticket kit or home-study course. See the figure below for an example of creating multiple products from one basic product.

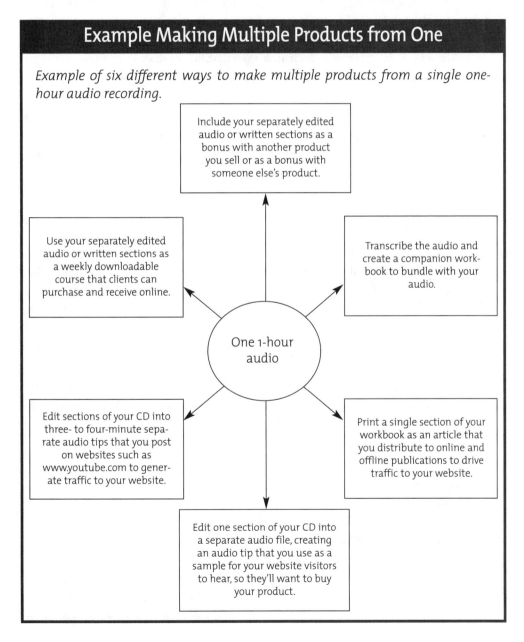

Example Making Multiple Products from One

Example of six different ways to make multiple products from a single one-hour audio recording.

Include your separately edited audio or written sections as a bonus with another product you sell or as a bonus with someone else's product.

Use your separately edited audio or written sections as a weekly downloadable course that clients can purchase and receive online.

Transcribe the audio and create a companion workbook to bundle with your audio.

One 1-hour audio

Edit sections of your CD into three- to four-minute separate audio tips that you post on websites such as www.youtube.com to generate traffic to your website.

Print a single section of your workbook as an article that you distribute to online and offline publications to drive traffic to your website.

Edit one section of your CD into a separate audio file, creating an audio tip that you use as a sample for your website visitors to hear, so they'll want to buy your product.

Use the Telephone to Create Your First Information Product in One Weekend

People like to learn in different ways. Some prefer to read, but given the number of hours people spend in the car or commuting, audio is popular with just about everyone. It's also the fastest, easiest, and least expensive way to create your first information product.

How would you like to create your first information product in just one weekend? It's simple, using a telephone and a few other easily available online resources. Here are the specific steps to follow:

1. *Decide if your recording will be just you or if you prefer to have someone interview you.* Interview-style recordings are great because they sound natural and engaging. Plus, it's often easier to talk about your topic if you're speaking to someone you know.

   You can ask a friend to interview you, or even better, ask someone who is already in your field. Be sure the person has a pleasant sounding voice, does not speak too quickly, and is genuinely interested in your topic.

2. *Next, you'll need a way to record your teleseminar.* One simple way to record your call is with an online service you'll find listed at www.BestInfoProduct Resources.com. For just a few dollars each month, you can record as many calls as you want. They'll store the recordings for you and allow you to easily create links from your website back to the call (very handy for selling your information product online), or you can download the audio file for editing on your computer.

   If you prefer, you can also record a call directly onto your computer, using a digital recorder. Olympus makes several good ones for this purpose. Once the files are recorded, you'll eventually need to upload them to your website if you plan on making your information product available online (which I highly recommend).

3. *Now you're ready to actually record your call.* Don't worry about scripting out your information. To sound natural, don't worry about sounding perfect or about making mistakes. You can edit those out later, if needed. It's normal to have a few "ums" and "ahs" in our speech, and it's more important to sound friendly than it

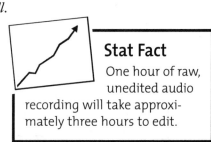

Stat Fact
One hour of raw, unedited audio recording will take approximately three hours to edit.

is to sound canned or stiff. Your clients listening to your audio want to feel they know, like, and trust you, so just be yourself.

4. *You want your finished CD to be about 45 to 60 minutes long.* Usually that means your initial, raw recording will be between 60 and 70 minutes long. Where do the extra minutes go? Onto the cutting room floor when you edit your audio.

5. *Once you have your recording done, it's time to edit out any obvious mistakes or bloopers.* A one-hour, raw recording takes approximately three hours to edit. You can edit the recording yourself, using software like Cool Edit or Sound Forge, or you can hire an audio editor to take care of this for you. You'll find an editing service I've used many times at www.BestInfoProductResources.com.

6. *To finish up your editing, you'll want to record an audio introduction and ending.* It's nice if the introduction is in someone's voice other than yours. If you had someone interview you, then you can ask that person to record your audio intro and ending.

   The introduction welcomes the listener, gives a little bit of information about you, and explains the benefits of listening to the audio. This is an important step because you want to remind your clients why they made a good choice in purchasing your information product.

   Your audio ending thanks your clients for listening, and then tells them about other programs, products, and information they can purchase from your website. Be sure to say your website address, plus spell it out. You can see a sample audio intro and ending script at www.KendallSummerHawk.com/audioscript.html.

Instantly Increase Your Sales Price by Adding a Workbook to Your Audio CD Even If You Hate to Write

Hate to write or don't have the time? No problem. You can create a workbook that looks great and instantly adds value to your audio CD with little effort. Here's how:

- Send your edited audio recording file to a transcription service to have it converted into a written document. I like the service at www.TheAdmin Source.com, or you can use www.Elance.com.

- Add to your workbook transcription any checklists, tip lists, resource lists, or recommend readings that will help your client in using your information. Here's a tip: Use size 12 font (or even larger on pages offering a tip list or checklist) and leave plenty of wide margins on the top, bottom, and sides, plus ample white space between sections. Doing this will make your workbook easier and more appealing to read, plus it will beef up the page count, which increases its perceived value and the price you can charge. It also leaves room for your client to make notes in the margins.

- At the front of your workbook, include a title page, a table of contents, and a short, introductory letter from you, welcoming your reader to the exciting world of learning the information in your workbook and audio.

Dollar Stretcher

You can add professional music to your audio beginning and ending for just a few dollars by purchasing royalty-free music at www.MusicBakery.com.

- At the end of your workbook, add a one-page biography with a photo of yourself, plus a few pages of information on how to contact you, how to either hire you for consulting or coaching, or how to purchase your additional products, services, or programs.

Now you're ready to proofread your workbook (I recommend also having someone else proofread your workbook for you, to catch any typos or mistakes you might have missed) and send it to a local copy shop for printing.

Creating High-End Packaging for Your Information Product on a Tight Budget

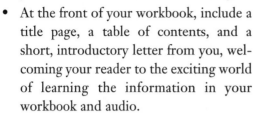

Beware!
Do not print hundreds of copies of your information product workbook or audio CDs just to save a few dollars per copy. It's best to print just a few at a time, so you're not stuck with excess inventory sitting in your garage. The amount of profit you make per copy will more than make up for the difference you'll pay in printing smaller quantities.

Whether you're selling your information product online or offline, you'll need to have a CD label designed, along with a matching cover for your CD case. And if you've created a companion workbook, then you'll need a matching workbook cover and back cover designed as well.

If you're thinking your information product needs to look like a "real" book, then I have good news for you and your wallet—it doesn't. In fact, trying to look too much like an off-the-shelf book is a detriment to charging more for your product. Why? Because books typically sell for less than $50.00, and most are even less than $20.00. Compare that to information products, where, depending on your topic and your audience, you can charge anywhere from

$29.00 to $97.00 for a single CD and workbook combination; $97.00 to $497.00 for information products that include two to six CDs plus a workbook; and as much as $2,000.00 for larger multimedia home-study programs that include multiple CDs, workbooks, samples, and even DVDs.

You can create your own CD labels and covers yourself, using software such as PhotoShop or Illustrator. Or if you shop around a bit, you can have a design made for you for less than $200.00, by hiring a local graphic designer, a design student from your local college, or a designer from one of the resources listed at www.BestInfoProductResources.com.

If you're selling and delivering your information product online, you'll use your designs on your website as a mock CD label and the CD case graphic icon. Remember the phrase "a picture paints a thousand words"? Well, in this case, a picture SELLS a thousand words! You can see samples of online mock CD labels and covers at www.KendallSummerHawk.com/products.html.

If you're creating shippable information products, then you can either burn your own CDs for shipping or use a duplicating service such as the ones recommended at www.BestInfoProductResources.com. You can have a quantity of just 50 CDs burned with a full-color label for less than $2.50 each.

The pages of your companion workbook can be inexpensively printed on regular paper with just black ink (even if there are photos included), but you'll want to print full-color front and back covers. For just a few pennies more than printing on regular paper, I like to have my product workbook covers printed on heavy cardstock paper and then laminated to create a nice, upscale look and feel. The workbook is then completed with spiral binding that looks great and is easy for your client to handle. You can have a 100-page workbook printed for less than $10.00 per copy in small quantities. Ask your local printer for a quote.

The entire CD and workbook package should have an inviting look and feel to it, so your client wants to pick it up, listen to it, or handle it.

If you're planning to sell your information product in bookstores or at conferences or tradeshows, then you'll need to purchase an ISBN. An ISBN is a number used worldwide by booksellers to track inventory. You can purchase a block of ISBNs at www.Bowker.com.

Once you assign your product its individual ISBN, you'll need to have a bar code created that you include on the back cover of your shippable

Quick and Simple Title Tips

Your information product needs a catchy title. Best-selling titles spell out exactly what your clients are going to learn if they purchase your information product. Great title examples are:

How to Charge What You're Worth and Get It!
10 Simple Steps to Increase Your Fees, Starting Today

Secrets to Contacting Celebrities
Get Past the Velvet Rope!

The Official Get Rich Guide to Information Marketing
Build a Million-Dollar Business Within 12 Months

Title Tips
- Long titles are GREAT!
- Use a numeral in your title, not a written number ("5," not "Five").
- Use BENEFIT words and phrases.
- Don't try to be clever—aim for clear.

Two Easy Title Formulas

Formula #1

"How to _____, So You Can _____"

Formula #2

"# Secrets/Strategies/Keys/Skills: How to _____, So You Can _____"

Here are benefit words to include in your title:

Easy	Free	Increase	Decrease	Improve
Reduce	Strategy	Simple	Quick	Fast
Learn	Discover	Learn How	Proven	Discover How
How to	Avoid	Mistakes	Strength	Techniques
Sure-Fire	Tips	Now		

CD case and workbook cover. The bar code includes the ISBN and is what book-sellers use to scan and catalog your product into their computer systems. In addition, many associations and conferences will not allow you to sell a product that does not have an ISBN and a bar code label on it. You can purchase individual bar codes for as little as $25.00 at www.Symbology.com.

Additional Ways to Create High-Priced Information Products

Higher-selling information products typically combine audio or video with printed workbooks, forms, samples, and checklists. These are often called *multimedia* products. Multimedia products have a higher perceived value and, therefore, can command a higher price (often from $997.00 to $2,000.00). They're really not all that complicated to produce either, once you have the basics under your belt.

For example, you can host a live workshop or a seminar and have both the audio and the video digitally recorded. Then, you can turn your recordings, along with your seminar workbook, into a complete home-study program or course.

To fill the seats at your seminar, you can offer registration at a discounted price, telling people it is a special offer because you are recording and filming.

How to Create an Information Product Even If You're Not an Expert on the Topic

You don't have to be an expert on a topic to create your information product. Instead, you can interview experts and create a compilation product. The advantage of using this method is that you often don't have to pay the experts (although they will expect to be able to sell the final product for a substantial commission later), and the experts you interview will often announce and promote the product to their lists, helping you make more sales much faster than you could on your own.

Another advantage to using this method is that you gain instant credibility just by being associated with a stable of stars in your topic area.

If the idea of a compilation, interview-style information product appeals to you, then just

Beware!
Do NOT try to make your information product look like a "real" book. That will lower the amount you can charge.

follow the same step-by-step system already outlined in this chapter. Your project may take a little longer because you will have to coordinate your interview schedule with the schedule of each expert, but you won't have to create any of the content yourself.

Creating an Information Product That You Can Sell Online and Offline Is Really as Simple as It Seems

Sure, there's work to getting started, just like with any business. But there is truly no other business that allows you to make 10 to 20 times (and even more) profit on your product with so little in startup costs. Think about it, no rent to pay or employees to hire. You can make, sell, and deliver your information product completely online if you choose to, and then branch out into selling at conferences, workshops, and seminars when you're ready. You can sell your information product over and over again without any additional work. Plus, you can use your information product as a lead generator for your additional high-ticket products, programs, or services.

The only thing you REALLY need is the desire to create a fun, profitable business with limitless potential and the motivation to get started ... now.

Resources

www.BestInfoProductResources.com for a list of resources to help you create and sell your information products

www.KendallSummerHawk.com/products.html to see samples of what information products can look like

▲　▲　▲

Kendall SummerHawk offers online and in-person membership coaching programs, plus info-products for women entrepreneurs who want to create their own information-marketing business. One program even offers clients the opportunity to travel to Arizona, where Kendall and her horses coach them on reaching new business goals. The horses "tell" the client where she needs to be more decisive and powerful by the way they respond to the client during a series of exercises. Kendall is known as the "Horse Whisperer for Business." She can be reached at (520) 577-6404. For a FREE copy of her special report, "How to Create Multiple Streams of Income in YOUR Business," visit her site at www.KendallSummerHawk.com.

The Five Keys

to Effectively Marketing

Your Business

by Diane Conklin
Complete Marketing Systems LLC
www.InfoBizBuildingBlocks.com

Selling your products is essential for you to make money. Now that you know how to create products, you have to identify a market and sell them. In this chapter, we will show you how to use print and online resources to collect sales leads and convert them into customers.

▲ ▲ ▲

▲

At this point, you've already come up with the topic for your product. It should be in an area you already know something about and have a certain level of experience or expertise in because selling what you know is usually the easiest and fastest way to start your information marketing business.

The fun part of your new adventure is about to happen, as you begin to build your list of prospects, turn them into clients, build your business, and market your products and services, turning new clients into cash and profits for you. Here, we are going to focus on marketing your information marketing products and services.

Is There a Difference Between Marketing and Sales?

One of the first concerns many new information marketers have is they don't like the thought of selling things. "Sales" is a dirty word for most people, but if you think about it, you'll realize that nobody makes any money in this world without somebody buying something.

A tank of gas to power your car, a ticket to see the hot, new movie, a new pair of running shoes, groceries so you can eat—all are examples of things we buy, but we don't really feel like we've been "sold" something when we spend money on them.

The real issue isn't that people don't want to buy; it's that nobody likes to be sold. Everyone *likes* to buy. With the right marketing, with the right product or service to the right people, they will buy and buy and buy. And you'll make money when they do because you're providing them a quality product or service—and you both feel good about it.

So, yes, there's a difference between sales and marketing. One good definition of marketing is *everything you do to create or to put yourself into sales situations*. In other words, marketing is anything and everything you do to create an opportunity and a desire within a prospect or a client to buy your products or services.

Sales, on the other hand, is about getting face-to-face with a prospect or in front of a group of prospects. This is when the money is exchanged. Sales can be made through a sales letter, by getting one-on-one with the prospect

> ## Smart Tip
> Tip...
>
> It's always easier to sell if you offer the fish instead of the fishing pole. Nobody wants to do the work. We all really just want the final outcome. If you can find a way to give people the final product instead of making them do it themselves or work to get it, you'll always sell more.

(but don't worry, this isn't the way you'll be selling), from the platform, or on a tele-seminar or a webinar, just to name a few.

Sales is really about helping people solve their problems. It's providing solutions for people and getting paid to do it. Sales, done right, is always a win-win situation. That's the kind of sales all of us want to be involved in.

Why Marketing Is So Important

Marketing is the most important thing you'll do in your business. Using sound marketing principles, strategies, and techniques will allow you to build a large list, form great relationships with your clients, and provide them with outstanding products and services—things they want, get value from, and that you're proud of.

The marketer always wins because, as a great marketer, you always have the ability to make money, no matter what the economy is doing, whether the housing market is going up or down, when the stock market is soaring or when it's crashing. None of that will matter to you. If you learn good marketing techniques and put them to work in your business, you will be a success.

Where You Start

Now that you have your product idea or topic area, you need to do a little research to make sure there are people to sell your products and services to.

One good place to start is the Standard Rate and Data Service, also known as the SRDS (www.SRDS.com). The SRDS is a catalog of more than 100,000 media sources. It's a great resource to see if your topic has newsletters, magazines, radio stations, and other media dedicated to it. You can also find out how many subscribers the publications have, whether the subscribers have purchased anything and how much they typically spend, where the names were obtained (direct mail, magazine advertisements, etc.), and lots of other information that will help you determine whether you have a viable product, a big enough market, possible joint venture partners, and much more. The SRDS is the first place to get ideas of available lists if you're going to consider renting or purchasing a list.

If you look up your topical area and don't find any publications, this might be a sign that your area of interest isn't one that will be profitable for you. If there aren't people already selling to your target market, there more than likely isn't a market for your product or service, or it might mean the market is very, very small. Either way, you should choose another topic for your product or broaden your topic.

Another way to find out about your topic is to do a search on the keywords of your topic. Use your favorite search engine to do this, like Google (www.Google.com), Yahoo! (www.Yahoo.com), Overture (www.Overture.com), or any of the other engines. If websites come up, you should click through to them to see what they're offering. What kind of products or services do they offer? Is there an offer for something free on the website? Is this a company you could do a joint venture with? Use keyword searches to get a basic feel for the information that's available about your topic.

Keyword Searches

Keyword Selector Tool

Not sure what search terms to bid on?
Enter a term related to your site and we will show you:

- Related searches that include your term
- Estimated number of times that term was searched on last month

Get suggestions for: (may take up to 30 seconds)

marketing

Note: All suggested search terms are subject to our standard editorial review process.

Searches done in January

Count	Search Term
1025908	search engine marketing
224156	marketing
178835	internet marketing
115802	email marketing
112973	marketing agency
40797	business marketing
37534	network marketing
34475	email marketing software
32056	direct marketing
31654	marketing campaign
25234	marketing research
24523	email marketing solution

It's even a good idea to order one or several of the products being sold on a couple of the sites. This will let you look at others' products, see what their follow-up processes are (if any), see examples of sales cycles as they make additional offers to you to buy, and see the different media they use to entice you to buy again.

Using Google is a great way to find websites and companies that are selling products complementary to yours. These are great companies to approach for joint ventures. If the products and services are in direct competition with what you are selling, then it's probably not a match for a joint venture, but you can learn a lot from what they're doing and how they're doing it.

Joint Venture Your Way to Millions

You will hear about, and use, joint ventures a lot as an information marketer. Joint ventures are a great way to make money and a great way to build your prospects list. Due to space limitations, we won't be covering all the details of joint ventures here, but it's important for you to understand how they work and, more importantly, how you can use this strategy successfully in your business.

There are a variety of ways to do joint ventures and several different types of joint ventures. The main ways you'll be doing joint ventures will be for you to go to others and have them market your products and services to their prospects and clients, or for you to market somebody else's existing products and services to your list. A joint venture is just two people working together to market a product or a service, so they both benefit.

No matter how you do a joint venture, it's important for both parties to get what they want out of the relationship. Typically, in a joint venture, both parties want to make a profit, but not always. If your goal for the joint venture is to build your list, you might be willing to give up more of your profit as a way to entice the list owner to do the deal with you.

Again, there are many ways to do joint venture marketing, but in the two ways listed above, it would be typical for each party involved to split the profits on the deal—typically 50/50.

Learn as much as you can about joint venture marketing as your information marketing

Beware!
All joint venture opportunities are NOT created equal. One of you might grow resentful if you feel like the work isn't distributed fairly and the profits are being split 50/50. Make sure your initial agreement is detailed, and keep communications open. It's also a good idea to have a buyout clause in all of your JV agreements.

business grows because it's a great way to make money. There are people who use this strategy to run their entire businesses, and they make millions of dollars every year doing so.

Building Your Herd

Now, you're ready to begin finding people to sell your products and services to. These people are known as *prospects*, *potential clients*, or *leads* until they buy from you. Once they buy, or you convert the sale, they become clients.

You want as many prospects as you can get, but more importantly, they should be qualified prospects. It doesn't make any sense to just have a lot of names on your list; you want names of people who have a genuine interest in your topic. For example, if you're selling dog training and obedience materials and courses, it doesn't do you any good to have a list of 100,000 prospects if all of them are plumbers. Plumbers probably aren't greatly interested in dog training and obedience materials. This example may seem obvious, but you have to think about such things when you start building your list of prospects.

Your goal is to market to people who have an interest in and want what you're selling. So, if you're selling dog training and obedience materials, find people who have just bought a new puppy or who have dogs as pets. You might joint venture with a dog groomer, a dog boarding facility, or a vet to build your list of names. These JVs give you qualified leads that you can pretty easily turn into clients because you have a great message-to-market match.

By looking at the SRDS and doing research with the search engines, you have another opportunity to start building your list of prospects immediately by doing joint ventures with companies that have products and services complementary to yours. You can also use these contacts in other ways. For example, you might place a classified ad (similar to the one on page 67) in their ezines in an effort to get their clients interested in your products and services. Most information marketers are looking for content, so offer to write an article, a series of articles, or a regular column in their online and/or offline newsletters. In return, you simply insert a one-paragraph biography at the end of each article, with your contact information and website listed, and make sure when your articles are used, the bio is always included at the end of the article. This way, readers always have a way to get in touch with you. This is a fair exchange; after all, you're providing the other info-marketers with free content for their newsletters.

You can go to any of the following websites to find listings of ezines you might want to write an article for or place a classified ad in: www.EzineArticles.com,

The 9 Costliest Mistakes All Information Marketers Make and the Secrets You Need to Know to Avoid Them!

To find out how you can avoid these 9 costly mistakes and watch your profits explode by using proven strategies to grow your business, go to www.InfoBizBuildingBlocks.com.

www.DirectoryOfEzines.com, www.EzineFinder.com, or www.EzineSearch.com. Also check your favorite search engine to find additional sources.

A big advantage of using strategies that employ other marketers' lists is that your message comes with an implied endorsement from a person your prospect already has a relationship with. We buy from people we know, like, and trust, and if somebody we already know, like, and trust says we should look at your offer, then it must be good— because they wouldn't have you in their material if you weren't doing good things.

Once you have articles written, you can submit those articles online, always making sure you include your bio with your website address listed. As your articles get used and spread around the internet, you will begin to see an increase in the number of people on your list. Article submission can help your list of qualified prospects grow very quickly. See the sample submission on page 68.

For additional resources on article submission, check out these websites: www.ArticleSubmitterPro.com, www.Articles-Submitter.info, www.SubmitYourArticle.com, and www.ArticlePR.com. You can also do a search for other possible places for submissions—either yourself or by getting help with the process, through automation.

Just as placing classified ads in relevant ezines online is a great way to build your list by using other people's lists, you can also build your list by placing classified ads in newspapers, trade journals, and other offline publications. Of course, you aren't limited to classified ads. You can also place small display ads, half-page ads, or full-page ads in these publications.

When you're first starting out and want to keep your costs low, it makes sense to begin with small classified ads and move your way up to the bigger ads once your classified ads are working. Make sure when you place an ad offline that you ask if your ad also goes into their online publications—many times this can be arranged at little or no additional cost to you, and can be very profitable.

▲

Sample Ad Submission

Why Every Successful Business Owner, Entrepreneur, and Online Marketer Are Using Direct Mail As Part of Every Marketing Campaign, And How Adding It To All of Your Marketing Campaigns Can Add Thousands, Even Hundreds of Thousands of Dollars, To Your Bottom Line Profits Every Time!

A lot of marketers and business owners don't understand the importance of direct mail in their business. A predominant attitude is why should I spend money on mail when I can send my marketing messages out by email – which is free.

First of all, email isn't really free, but we won't debate the details of that here.

There are growing problems with email deliverability, getting through spam filters, getting emails opened, and the latest experts are predicting there will soon be a charge for every email you send – much like putting stamps on the envelopes you mail.

Direct mail is still the best way to market to your prospects and clients.

With the increases in postage that are happening on a regular basis, many business owners are mailing less and less; which gives you a distinct advantage. Mailing when others aren't sending mail increases your response rates and keeps you out of the clutter.

Direct mail works, it always has, and it always will.

Certainly, I'm not recommending you use it, or any other marketing methods, exclusively, but you do need to use it in your marketing plans. Integrated marketing strategies and techniques are the way of business today.

The smart marketer and business owner uses every advantage they have and every advantage they can find, even making their own advantages if they have to. One very big advantage you'll have is using all methods and media available to you in your business – including email marketing, fax blasting (when appropriate and without breaking any of the rules or laws about this), voice broadcast, all types of internet marketing, and direct mail. And, use them every time you put a marketing program together. Use integrated marketing methods for all of your marketing plans and you will be much more successful, and make a lot more money than if you only use one marketing method or media.

If you would like to use this article for your readership, you may do so as long as you include this complete bio with it:

Diane Conklin is an entrepreneur, marketing and business coach, trainer, consultant, event planner, speaker and copywriter. Diane is a direct-response marketing expert who specializes in showing small business owners, entrepreneurs, coaches and consultants how to integrate their marketing methods and, strategies, with their media to get maximum results from their marketing dollars.

For more information, marketing tips and strategies go to www.infobizbuildingblocks.com or www.CompleteMarketingSystems.com.

There are many other ways to build your list. You're only limited by your imagination in the number of ways you can creatively build your herd and sell more and more products and services.

As with most other areas of your business, it makes sense to start with the basics, and as your business grows, continue to add more and more ways to add qualified prospects to your growing herd. A few of these other ways include having your own blog; having a presence on MySpace.com, YouTube.com, and eBay; doing press releases; getting free press through public relations and other means; list rentals, purchases, and swaps; and participating in forums and membership sites.

Direct Response Marketing and Your Money

Now, you have qualified prospects who have an interest in your products and services. How do you convert those qualified leads and prospects into buying customers, clients, and raving fans? You do it with good, solid marketing strategies, by under-promising and overdelivering, by providing good content, by following up, and by continuing to market and sell to these people over and over again.

You're going to get your best marketing results and make the most money by using direct response marketing strategies and techniques. Direct response marketing is not the advertising you typically see on TV, in newspapers and magazines, or anywhere else. That type is called *image advertising*, and it's what all of the big companies use. Companies like Coca-Cola, IBM, Apple, and Nike use image advertising. These companies have millions of dollars to spend to get their names out to you. They do it many times, over and over again, and what they bank on is your remembering their name over somebody else's. That's not the kind of marketing you want to do to grow your business. You can't compete with the big boys, so don't try.

In your local area, you don't have to look any further than the Yellow Pages to see image advertising. The ads all look alike—that's called *me too advertising*. You just do precisely the same thing everybody else is doing. It must work if everybody's doing it, right? Wrong! None of them are measuring results, so they don't know if their ads are working or not. All of those advertisers in the Yellow Pages have businesses, but they don't know what to do. So, they do what the Yellow Pages rep tells them to do, which is to put a typical ad in there with the company's name, location, hours of operation, and phone number.

The successful direct response marketer asks this question about any ad he places anywhere, really about any marketing he does: "How will I know how much business I get from this ad?" Then, he places some type of measuring device on the ad. For example, in the Yellow Pages ad, you can make an offer of 10 percent off when customers bring the coupon attached to your ad into the store, or you can offer them a free report by calling your special 800 number (which is set up solely to measure how many calls you get from that one ad), or you can use a host of other ideas. The point is, again, you must be able to measure the response from each specific media, each specific campaign, and each specific ad.

Use marketing methods that are measurable, so you quickly know whether or not your efforts and money are pulling in a return. If they're producing good results, you roll out the plan and do more; if they aren't, you stop and regroup—quickly, so you can make a lot of money in a short period of time.

Direct response marketing is the kind of marketing you do if you want fast, trackable results from your marketing. It's the kind of marketing where you can spend $1.00 and get back $10.00, do it quickly, over and over again, and know what your results are within a few days, hours, or minutes—depending on what media you use to market your product.

If you use traditional image advertising methods, you'll never be able to measure the return on your marketing dollars. There will be no way to measure it because you won't know where your clients are coming from. You just keep spending money on marketing, hoping it's working. If you place the typical image ad, with no measuring device, you could be wasting thousands of dollars every year with no return on your investment and not even know it.

One-Step or Two-Step Response Methods of Marketing

You'll use one or two basic response methods to get people to respond to your offers. They will usually either be a one- or a two-step process.

In the one-step process, the marketing is designed to get an order directly from that step. In other words, the ad is going to ask for the order. Examples of these ads can be seen in most offers you get in the mail. You look at the piece of mail, and if you want what they're offering, you place your order by mailing in the card, calling a phone number, faxing in an order form, or something of that nature. In this example, your client would put all of his contact information and credit card information on the form, you would get the order and fulfill it, and then start your follow-up process. You have a new client or an order from an existing client in one easy step.

The two-step process is disguised a little, in an effort to make the sale a little less obvious. In this instance, the marketing is designed to get action and interest from the prospect or client first, and then make the sale in the second step, after the prospect has raised his hand to say he's interested in what you have to offer. A two-step process is being used when your prospect asks to get something from you; it's usually something free, like a special report, an audio CD, or a DVD, and can be sent by regular mail, e-mail, or possibly downloaded online.

In most instances—not all, but most—you will use the two-step approach when you're trying to build your list and get new prospects, and the one-step approach when you're selling to current clients or to people who already know you and have an established relationship with you.

Multistep, Sequential Marketing Campaigns

One marketing message is almost never going to produce the kind of results you're looking for. You have to employ multistep marketing campaigns, using different media, to get your message out.

For example, let's say you're going to have a workshop or a seminar, and you want to let your clients know about it, so they can register and attend. If all you do is send one e-mail or sales letter, you probably aren't going to get a very good response. People are busy, and there are so many advertisers vying for our attention that many people will miss your message if you only send it once.

Instead, put together an integrated, multistep marketing campaign that might include as many as 6 sales letters that go out in the mail, 12 to 15 e-mails, 2 voice messages or voice blasts, messages in your online ezine every week up to the event, 2 tele-seminars or webinars, and maybe 4 faxes (if you have permission to fax your clients, otherwise you could be in violation of the law).

In this example, there are about 30 contacts, maybe more, depending on the marketing cycle. A marketing cycle refers to the timeframe of your marketing plan, or how long you start marketing prior to an event. Usually you'll need to start marketing for a live event, like a workshop or a seminar, at least three to four months prior to the event. See the example on page 72.

If you're trying to sell one of your products, you still send multiple marketing messages to your clients and prospects to give them multiple opportunities to invest in your program.

Integrated Marketing Systems Through Seven Different Types of Media

Whatever types of media you decide to use to market your information marketing business, you will want to use direct response marketing methods. Direct response marketing is based on direct selling methods, and it is about selling directly to the

Multistep Marketing Campaign

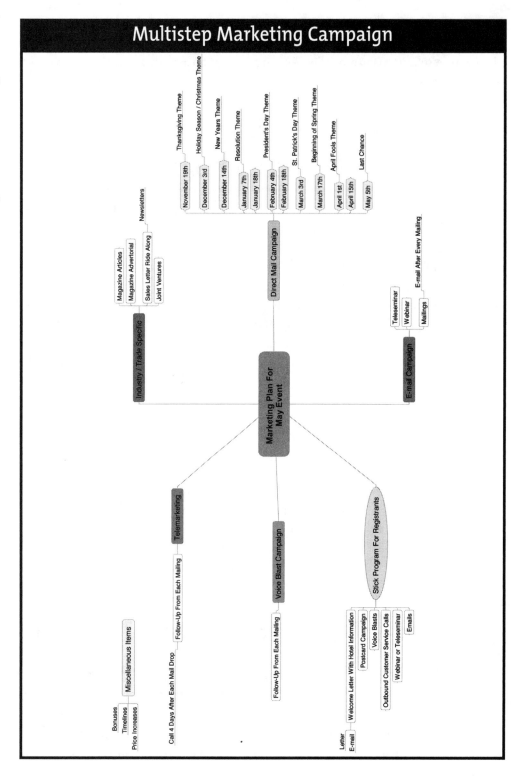

client by using media. Simply put, it's marketing that concentrates on getting clients and making sales, and being able to quickly and accurately measure your results, so you immediately know what kind of return you're getting on your marketing dollars.

Direct response marketing can be used with all of the different media you use in your integrated marketing campaigns. You should be using direct response marketing methods when you advertise in newspapers, magazines, and trade or association journals, in all your direct mail campaigns, and when you're marketing online.

Many people think of the internet as a business. It really isn't a business; it's a type of advertising or marketing media. The internet is just one way to get your message out to the public.

One of the mistakes a lot of information marketers make is that they use only one marketing method. One is always the worst number—in marketing and in business. If something happens to the one stream of income, the one marketing method you're using, the one media type you like, you and your business could be in serious trouble.

If you think about sitting on a stool, you'll quickly get the analogy of one being the worst number. It's pretty tough to balance on a one-legged stool. There isn't any stability, it's wobbly, and without much outside interference, you're going to fall off, just like your business will if you're only using one type of media to market your products and services. A stool with three or four legs is much more stable; it gives you security. You don't really worry about falling off. Your business is the same as the stool. Using a multistep and a multimedia approach will maximize your profits and stability.

The smart marketer uses multistep campaigns and multiple marketing messages via a variety of different media to get her message out. This method allows your message to be picked up and acted upon by more people.

As much as we'd like to think everyone is on the internet, it simply isn't true. If the internet is your only means of marketing, you're missing out on a lot of potential customers. Although more and more people are now reading the newspaper online, there are still people who get the paper delivered to their houses and sit down with their morning coffee to read it.

Another type of marketing media you want to use in your information marketing business is classified advertising. This method is available both online and offline. The offline media where you can place classified ads are numerous. A few of the offline media include newspapers—local newspapers including the penny saver and papers that people get delivered to

Beware!
One is always the worst number in business. You never want to become dependent on only one marketing stream, one lead source, one vendor, or one employee. If that one thing dries up, stops working, or goes away, so does your business. Your business has much more stability if you have three or four sources you're using and getting good results from.

▲

their homes, and national newspapers, like *USA Today*, the *Wall Street Journal*, and others, that might or might not be a fit for your products and services.

Placing classified ads in trade journals for your industry or niche is a great way to grow your herd and market your product and services. There might even be magazines or newsletters applicable to your topical area in which you can place a classified or a display advertisement. To see some of the possibilities, stop by your local bookstore and see what magazines you can find on the shelves or look at a newsstand in the airport the next time you're waiting for a flight.

Always start with a small classified ad as a test, and if that ad pulls, then roll out your marketing campaign to do more and more ads in other places. The other thing to try, once you have a classified ad that works, is to expand up to a small display ad. Again, start with a small test, and then roll out big once you find an ad that pulls in the numbers you need to make money.

Direct mail is one of the best ways to market your products and services. With the right message to the right market, you can send postcards, sales letters, and a variety of offers in the mail and get massive returns on your marketing dollars. This is a tried and true method of marketing your products and services that many marketers underuse, especially today because of the popularity of the internet.

Although television can also be a good media source to market your products and services, it tends to be very expensive. So, television as a media source is probably not the area in which to start out your marketing, but it might be added later as you have the money to do so.

The most common way to see information products sold on television is through infomercials, which are very expensive to make, produce, and make profitable. They are a very effective way to make a lot of money, but they carry with them a lot of risk. So, this is definitely a media to add to your marketing plan once you're established and making money with other, less expensive media.

There are other media in which you can advertise and market your services, including radio, teleseminars and webinars, telemarketing, podcasts, and a host of other online and offline media.

The real issue to concern yourself with is using multiple marketing methods and different media to get the message about your products and services out to your prospects and clients. Use an integrated marketing approach in which you don't become too dependent on any one media or find yourself bringing in new clients in only one way.

There are marketers who try to build their businesses and lists by using only online marketing, and there are others who are getting new clients into their funnels only through speaking on other event promoters' platforms. These are good strategies for your information marketing business, but you don't want to become too dependent on any one method alone. Instead, you want to use all of the methods outlined here in conjunction with one another. If something happens and one of them slows down or dries up completely, you will still have new clients, money, and resources flowing into your company, while you add more and better methods and strategies to your thriving business.

▲ ▲ ▲

Diane Conklin is president of Complete Marketing Systems LLC, which specializes in strategic planning, implementation, and execution of business and marketing systems for information marketers, entrepreneurs, and coaches. Areas of expertise include: direct response marketing (including direct mail); strategic planning; list building and management; business system development; product development; teleseminar planning and implementation; and event marketing, planning, and management. You can find more resources and get a free CD on the 9 Key Building Blocks to Your Information Marketing Business at www.InfoBizBuildingBlocks.com, or call (321) 449-1151.

6

How to SELL Your Information

Product Online or Offline

by Michele PW (Michele Pariza Wacek)
Creative Concepts and Copywriting LLC
www.MichelePW.com

There are hundreds of marketing options found on- and offline, but they all have one thing in common—a powerful sales presentation. You can create great marketing materials by harnessing the powerful "direct response techniques" to sell your information products.

▲   ▲   ▲

Let me tell you about John. John was a busy employee. He had a good salary, decent benefits, but he wasn't happy. He cast about for something else to do, something that would add more meaning to his life, and finally hit upon a business that intrigued him—creating an info-marketing company.

He took a few months to create his first info-product, and because what he really liked about info-marketing was how you can sell things online, he thought he'd start by creating a website. He decided to do it himself and save a few bucks. After all, how hard could it be?

Over a weekend he got a website up. And then he sat back and waited.

Well, a few months passed, and nothing happened. No leads, no sales. Not even a phone call or an e-mail.

Hmm . . . Maybe he was wrong to save a few bucks. Maybe he needed a professional. So, he contacted a company that built websites, and they put together a big, flashy, really cool-looking website.

It cost a pretty penny, but that's OK. You gotta spend money to make money, right? Well . . .

The problem was, that pretty, expensive website wasn't doing any better than his little, cheap, homemade website. Still no leads, sales, or customers. But now he felt even worse because he was out a big wad of money and had nothing to show for it.

I hear stories like John's all the time. And I've made plenty of mistakes myself over the years of being an entrepreneur. But here's the scoop about mistakes entrepreneurs make—there's both a good side and a bad one.

First, the bad. As a new entrepreneur or small business owner, you tend to make a lot of mistakes. Worse, some are quite costly, and by costly I don't mean just financially. They can also cost you a great deal in time (which in some ways is worse—you can always make more money, but you'll never get time back).

But there is a silver lining in that black cloud. And the silver lining is this—everyone tends to make the same mistakes over and over again.

Two Common Mistakes Entrepreneurs Make

1. *They spend thousands of dollars on a pretty site that doesn't sell.* Pretty doesn't sell. Words sell.

2. *They don't respect the power of words.* Just because you know how to write a sentence doesn't mean you should be writing your own promotional copy. Copywriting is a learned skill. Professional copywriters study direct response techniques. To effectively sell with your promotional materials, you either need to study direct response techniques yourself or hire a professional.

Why is that good? Because I have the chance to educate you BEFORE you fall prey to these repeated mistakes.

Avoid Common Website Mistakes

Over the years of working as a professional copywriter and marketing strategist, I've seen two particularly big mistakes entrepreneurs make when creating their promotional materials.

First, they drop a lot of money into a pretty, but ineffective, website. Second, they don't learn about direct response copywriting and how to write it.

Let's start with the first.

I can't tell you how many people I've run into over the years who have told me about spending $5,000.00, $10,000.00, or even more on a website that gets them virtually no response.

No leads. No customers. And no sales.

As soon as I look at it, I know why.

The website is usually very pretty. It has attractive colors, an expensive logo, and probably some sort of Flash introduction. (Flash is what looks like animation on websites.) All of the money went into graphic designers and/or web designers. If they spent any money on the writing, it was probably the cheapest part of the bill.

Unfortunately, pretty doesn't sell. (Neither does Flash. Nor expensive logos.)

Now, if you're one of those unfortunate souls who dropped a bundle on a pretty logo and website, you may be feeling sick to your stomach right now. (But never fear, I'll show you how to fix your problem in a moment.) However, if you haven't spent that money, you should feel like celebrating. After all, I just saved you a big chunk of money!

So, if pretty doesn't sell, what does? Ah, now we come to the second mistake, not understanding direct response copywriting. But I'm getting ahead of myself.

First the definition: Copywriting is writing promotional copy, NOT copyrighting something to protect intellectual property (note the difference in spelling—copywrite/copyright). If you're in the business of copyrighting intellectual property, you either work for the government or you're an attorney. If you're in the business of copywriting, then you're in the business of writing promotional materials to sell products or services.

If you're like many entrepreneurs, when it comes to writing the copy on your website, your first response is, "That's not such a big deal. I can write. Why should I pay someone to do that?"

Well, that's true. I'm sure you can write. But (and this is a big but) can you write words that will persuade people to take action? That will cause people to whip out their wallets in a frenzy because they can't wait to throw money at you?

Oh, you can't?

Well, that's why you need to understand direct response copywriting.

Take junk mail. That's an excellent example of direct response copywriting. Junk mail (also known as *direct mail*) is designed to get a response from the recipients all by its little self. It's like a salesperson, except you don't pay it a salary, benefits, or even need to give it a vacation. It works 24/7/365 with nary a complaint. And as it works, it continually brings in leads, customers, and sales.

The beauty is, the direct mail letter does all of the heavy lifting for you. (That's why it's called *direct response*—because prospects directly respond to the promotional materials.)

But direct response copywriting is not limited to direct mail. You can (and should) use it on your website. When you do, you'll find you end up getting more leads, sales, and customers from your site.

And isn't that the point of a website? To have it be a sales tool?

Better yet, once you master the basics of direct response copywriting, there's no end to where you can use it. Send an e-mail to your prospect list. Place an ad in a trade magazine. Drop your customers a postcard or a letter. You can use direct response to both gain customers and deepen your relationships with them, so they not only buy once from you, but they buy multiple times, *and* they tell all their friends about you.

Five Steps to Get Started Creating Great Sales Letters

Now that you understand direct response is the way to go, where do you begin? Here are five tips to get you started.

Beware!

While it's not a good idea to have too narrow a target market, it's much worse when it's too broad. It's OK to be specific about who you're trying to attract. You'll have much better results if you can niche your target market down to prospects that are easy to identify, find, and communicate with.

1. Know Who You're Talking To

You need to both identify and understand your prospects (also known as your target market). The more specific you are about who you're selling to, the easier it will be to write your promotional materials.

Why is that? Because you're going to know exactly who they are, what their problems are, and exactly how you can help them.

And the more specific you are, the more your prospects will relate to what you're saying.

Another big mistake entrepreneurs make is trying to market to everyone. If I hear anyone say "women are my potential customers" or "anyone with skin is my target market" (yes, that really was a direct quote from someone who sold Mary Kay or Arbonne or something like that), I will send my border collies (all three of them) to your house and force you to play fetch with them until your arm falls off.

Seriously, the quickest way you can end up with the most dismal results imaginable is to try to talk to everyone. Come up with a specific customer—the more specific the better—and make sure your marketing materials speak directly to that customer.

2. Focus on What's Keeping Your Customers Up at Night

This is where understanding who you're talking to helps. Let me give you an example.

Let's say you're a personal trainer and sell workout programs. Everyone needs to exercise, after all. So your target market is everyone . . . right?

Well, not so fast. While I agree that exercise is good for the vast majority of people, the vast majority of people are not going to be your target market. Why? Because of their views and attitudes.

Do you think someone who is training for a marathon views exercise differently from someone who is 20 pounds overweight and has never worked out a day in his life? Does the marathon runner have different issues keeping her up at night vs. someone who is sedentary? Of course. The marathon runner is probably worried about things like "how can I beat my last time?" whereas the sedentary person is probably worried about "I know I need to start working out. I really want to lose these 20 pounds, but I just can't bring myself to exercise." Do you see how differently you would approach each of those potential customers?

So, why do you want to focus on what's keeping your customers up at night? Well, that's what will motivate them to look for a solution. Think of it like this—no one wakes up in the morning and says to themselves, "I am SO happy and fulfilled in my life, but you know what? I think I could be even MORE happy than I already am. I'm going to do a search on the internet for ways to make me even happier."

People do wake up and say, "I'm stressed about my career. I'm scared I'll never find that special person. I'm overwhelmed. I'm in debt. I want to lose 20 pounds. I want to come in first in my age class at my next marathon."

Then, they sit down at the computer and start searching for solutions to those problems.

So, if your copy addresses that problem first thing, right on top, your prospects will know they're on the right website. They'll see you're talking to them, and even more importantly, they'll feel like you understand them. And feeling like you're understood is very powerful and very persuasive.

3. Make Sure You Write Benefits, Not Features

This one is probably the hardest one to "get," but also one of the most critical. People buy benefits, not features, so if you only talk about features, you're just asking for people not to buy what you're selling.

So, what is the difference between features and benefits? Features are a description of a product. For instance, let's say we're talking about a red pen. If you're talking in features, you say "the pen is red." If you're talking in benefits, you say "the pen is red, so if I drop it in my purse, I can find it easily."

There's another example I've started using, and that's diet pills. The feature of a weight-loss pill is that it's a pill. No one says "Wa-hoo! I want to take more pills, so I'm going to take a weight-loss pill." No. People take weight-loss pills because they want to lose weight, and they want it to be easy. The benefit is you want to lose the weight, and you want it to be easy. That's why people take weight-loss pills, NOT because it's a pill.

As much as you possibly can, write about why someone should buy your product. No one buys diet pills because they like taking pills; they buy them to lose weight. Think of the solution your product or service provides and write about that.

So, how do you write features and benefits? Try this exercise: Take a piece of paper. Draw a line down the middle. On the left side, list all of the features of your product or service. Go on. List them all. When you think you've thought of them all, come up with three more.

Now, on the right side, turn all of those features into benefits.

How does this work? Here's an example:

*Cell phones are small and portable, **so** you can easily take them everywhere you want to go.*

The little word "so" (or "so that" if that's easier for you) will naturally get you thinking about benefits.

And keep going deeper. Just keep asking "so." Like this:

*Cell phones are small and portable, **so** you can easily take them everywhere you want to go, so you never worry about missing an important call ever again.*

Ah. Now we're getting into the real benefit. Why would people want to carry cell phones everywhere? Not because they like the idea of carrying one more piece of technology around with them, but because they want to be able to make or receive a phone call wherever they are. And why do they want to do that? Not because they want to always take phone calls, but because they might miss something if they don't have access to a phone.

That's what you need to do. Get as deep as possible into the benefits. Then, once you know what those benefits are, that's what you tell your customers.

4. Overcome Those Objections

This is a biggie. Because the moment you start asking someone for money, objections to giving you money are going to rear their ugly heads.

Think of it as a defensive mechanism. There just isn't enough money in the world to buy every little thing. We need to make choices with our money. There's only so much we can buy. And yes, we can always go out and make more, but again, we have to make that choice that what we want to buy is worth going out and focusing on making more money.

As you can see, it's not personal. It's a defensive mechanism that allows us to function in our society.

So, now that you know this, what do you do about it? You have to overcome those objections in your copy.

The first big objection you need to overcome, no matter what it is you sell, is money. No matter what it costs, there's still going to be an objection. It might be a small objection or a big objection, but it's an objection nevertheless.

What do you do? First, you need to acknowledge it's an objection. Second, you need to show how they're getting so much value for their money that it makes no sense for them NOT to purchase it. Third, compare it to something else, so your price looks good in comparison. For instance, if you're selling a home-study course based on your services, you can tell people how much it would cost them to hire you to do XYZ, so in comparison your product looks inexpensive.

But that's not the only thing you can compare it to. You can also compare your price to X number of Starbucks vanilla lattés and blueberry scones. This works very well because we're now comfortable with spending $6.00 or $7.00 on a cup of coffee and a scone. It doesn't matter if the comparison doesn't make any sense. It only matters if the price is something we're already comfortable spending, then we can transfer that comfort to what you're selling.

Another big objection is time. Now, if you're selling something like shoes, time won't be an objection. But if you're selling a home-study course or a book or a CD or a seminar, time WILL be an issue. Because time is what you need to actually use what you're selling. And if people don't think they have time to get through your product, then they won't purchase it.

So, how do you overcome the time objection? First, by making the time investment look as small as possible. If it takes ten hours to review your materials, tell your audience if they spend just an hour a day, they'll finish it in ten days. Or at 30 minutes a day, they'll be done in less then a month.

Another thing you can do is explain how by investing the time now, you'll be gaining that much more time and/or money down the road, and isn't that a good trade off?

Now, in your particular industry, there will be other specific objections you'll need to overcome. For instance, a health product might have safety concerns. A book on stock tips might raise the concern that if too many people use the tips, the tips will stop working. Whatever the concerns are in your industry, you need to know what the specific objections are and work those into your copy. And if you don't know what they are, you need to ask. Do a survey or even pick up the phone and call a few of your customers. Do some digging. You'll be glad you did.

5. Don't Forget the Call to Action

You've got to tell people what to do next. If you don't tell them what you want them to do, chances are they won't do anything.

Don't assume your potential customers know what you want them to do. They don't. They can't read your mind. Nor do they want to. They're busy people. They don't have the time or the energy to figure things out. Tell them what to do next, or don't be surprised when they don't do anything.

If you want people to buy, you gotta ask for the sale.

Truly, it is that simple. Yet, I can't tell you how many ads, websites, brochures, sales letters, etc., are floating around out there that aren't asking.

So, what is a call to action? It's telling people what action you want them to take. Typical calls to action include:

- Hurry in today.
- Buy now.
- Call now.
- Visit now.
- Click here now.

Nothing terribly sexy, I agree. However, if you want to see an increase in your customers, leads, income, etc., the call to action is an essential component.

You might be thinking, isn't it obvious? Why else would you have a website if you didn't want people to buy what you're selling?

Good question. And it's true, people do know (if they stop to think about it) that you would probably like them to buy from you.

However, the unfortunate truth is, your potential customers aren't going to spend that much time thinking about it. People have too much going on in their lives to spend very much time and energy on your business. If they do read your ad or promotional material, and it doesn't contain a call to action, they'll likely say, "Oh, that's nice" and go on to the next thing.

And even if they were interested in purchasing your offerings, they may not know what their next step should be. Do they pick up the phone? Go to a specific web page? Visit a store? And if they don't know what they should be doing, chances are they won't do anything at all.

So, you need to tell your potential customers what you want them to do. (Remember, people are busy, and if you don't make doing business with you easy, they probably won't do business with you at all.)

So, back to the above calls to action. Did you notice they all had something in common? The word "now" (or in the case of the first one, "today").

If people think they can buy from you any time, they'll say, "Oh, I can do this later." And later rarely comes. You need to give them a reason to buy from you right now, while they're interested. Adding the "now" or some other urgency or scarcity technique (maybe a limited time offer or "few copies left" statement) is a great way to push people into doing what you want them to do right now and not later.

While we're on the topic of calls to action, I want to talk about one other type of advertising campaign where you rarely see calls to action. These are called *branding campaigns*. Typically, they're shown on national television by big corporations (McDonald's, Nike, Tide). In those instances, the businesses are building a brand that will cause you think of their business first when you're interested in purchasing a particular product. For instance, when you're hungry, you think McDonald's. You need new athletic shoes, you think Nike. You need laundry detergent, you think Tide.

While there's nothing wrong with branding campaigns, it is nearly impossible to test if they're working or not. What I'm teaching you, direct response campaigns that include a specific call to action (Sale ends Saturday, Call before Friday to receive your free gift, etc.), is very different.

Without a call to action, you're relying on people to think of you when they need what you're selling. While this is very powerful when it happens, it's very expensive to make it happen. Those top-of-the-mind brands have millions and millions of dollars invested in them over a very long (sometimes decades-long) period of time.

It's actually very difficult to recreate the success that Tide or Nike have had because it's much harder to find places where large numbers of the general population are reading or watching. Thirty years ago, we had three television stations, no internet, and a handful of magazines. The chances of finding Joe Public on one of those three stations was very probable.

▲

What Can You Use Direct Response For?

○ Newspaper ads
○ Magazine ads
○ Yellow Pages ads
○ Classified ads
○ Radio ads
○ Television ads (think infomercials)
○ Postcards
○ Letters
○ Packages
○ Websites
○ E-mails

No more. Now we have a gazillion television stations, another gazillion magazines that are all niched to our particular needs or hobbies, and five gazillion websites to choose from. If it was expensive before to reach a general mass consumer audience, it's now astronomically expensive.

So, what is an entrepreneur to do? Simple. Use direct response copywriting, and always put a call to action on your pieces. That will get people to take action much sooner (and with much less investment) than investing in thousands of brand awareness ads.

Now, branding is still very, very important. As a business owner, you need a good brand, and you need to communicate that brand effectively. And sometimes it makes sense to run a branding campaign.

However, my advice for most situations is to combine branding and direct response. Your brand is clearly communicated in your ads and promotional materials, but you also take advantage of some direct response techniques at the same time.

And whatever you do, make sure you don't forget the call to action.

Write Your Call to Action

Want to include a call to action in your promotional materials, but don't know where to start? Here's an easy step-by-step formula:

1. *Figure out your purpose for the ad or promotional material.* Why are you running this ad, creating this website, printing this brochure? (And no, an acceptable

answer is NOT because everyone else has one.) Is it to generate leads? Get your name out there? Get people to buy? Or what?

2. *Now write it down.*

3. *That's it.* That's your call to action. Whatever the end result you want for the campaign is what you should be asking people to do.

Pulling It All Together

There have been entire books and all-day seminars taught on this subject, so trying to squeeze everything into one chapter just isn't possible. However, I have put together some resources for you. I've created some templates and examples you can download for free at www.BestInfoMarketing.com.

What you can do is take the basics of what I've taught you in this chapter, and then use the templates and examples as ideas to create your own marketing materials.

I'll leave you with a quick overview. All direct response copy has roughly these major segments:

- Headline
- Introduction, which outlines the problem (What's keeping your customers up at night?)
- Solution, which includes features and benefits and overcoming objections
- Testimonials, where you have your customers sell for you
- Call to action

If you follow that format and use the tips I've outlined in this chapter, you should be on your way to writing promotional pieces that land you leads, customers, sales, and MONEY!

Now that you know how important it is to master the art of direct response copywriting, how do you get started mastering it? Here are five tips to get you going:

1. *Study books and resources.* In order to write direct response, it's important to understand it. The way to get started is by reading books and other materials. I would focus on resources that cover direct response copywriting, marketing, and sales techniques. (Direct response copywriting really is salesmanship in print.) Here are a few resources to help you.

   – *The Ultimate Sales Letter* by Dan Kennedy
   – *Advertising Secrets of the Written Word* by Joseph Sugarman
   – *Triggers* by Joseph Sugarman
   – *Influence: The Psychology of Persuasion* by Robert B. Cialdini

   – My home-study course "Sales Letter Secrets: Rev Up Your Business With Copy That Sells!" you can find at www.MichelePW.com/WriteSales Letter.html.

   – I've also put together some resources for you, including templates and examples to get you started. You can download these free at www.BestInfo Marketing.com.

2. *Collect your junk mail.* I'm serious. Junk mail has some of the best examples of direct mail around. Start a swipe file, and collect direct mail, catalogues, post-cards, letters, and even e-mails and online sales letters. Read them, study them, and learn from them.

3. *Copy your junk mail.* Take a sales letter and write it out by hand three times. I know, it will take forever, and it will make your hand hurt in the process. But it's great practice, and it will help you internalize the rhythm of writing direct response . . . and isn't an aching hand worth it if this will teach you how to create million-dollar sales letters? (Note, this is only to help you learn how to write copy; please don't use the copy for your own promotional materials.)

4. *Watch infomercials.* (If you do this, make sure you lock up your credit cards.) Again, infomercials have some of the best direct mail strategies around. You can't read them, but just by studying and watching them, you'll start to absorb the principles.

5. *Write your own sales letters.* There's no better training than to jump in and start writing. Even if you end up writing bad sales letters, just the act of writing will help you eventually write good ones!

▲   ▲   ▲

Michele PW (Michele Pariza Wacek) is your Ka-Ching! marketing strategist and owns Creative Concepts and Copywriting LLC, a direct response copywriting and marketing agency. For more direct response copywriting resources, including easy-to-use, step-by-step PROVEN copywriting templates and examples, visit www.BestInformationMarketing.com.

Getting the Lifestyle and Income of

Your Dreams by Using

Joint Ventures

by Larry Conn
Instant Yellow Page Profits
www.InstantYellowPageProfits.com

*O*nce you have your product and sales materials, working with other info-marketers to sell your products is a great shortcut for generating sales. Learn how a single dad built a business by creating a product other info-marketers could promote to their customers.

▲ ▲ ▲

If you'd like the lifestyle freedom and huge profits available from information marketing, but have little money to invest, then joint ventures may be perfect for you. I have built my information marketing business as a Yellow Pages and print media expert from scratch by using joint ventures exclusively.

In this chapter, you will discover three keys to joint ventures:

1. You will learn how to structure your joint ventures for maximum profit as a win/win for both parties.

2. You will learn where to find joint venture prospects and several successful approaches for key joint venture prospects.

3. You will discover the strategic byproduct of extremely valuable market research, CD interviews, and DVD presentations you can get by doing joint ventures.

My First Interview

In early 2003, my friend and mentor Joe Polish, president of Piranha Marketing, said, "Larry, you know more about Yellow Pages advertising than anybody I know. You should launch an information marketing business as a Yellow Pages media expert. Matter of fact, I'd like to interview you for my Genius Network Interview Series." So, we recorded my first Yellow Pages interview for his Genius Network Interview Series in 2003.

At that time, I had not yet created a product. I promised myself that I would complete my Yellow Page Profits system before my next interview, so I wouldn't be wasting these interview opportunities and generating no sales.

At the first Information Marketing Summit in Cleveland in the fall of 2003, Bill Glazer disclosed that it takes a minimum of $40,000.00 to launch an information marketing business.

That was bad news to me. I did not have that type of money to invest because of my challenging financial situation. I had taken two years off to snow ski at my favorite ski resort during the El Nino years of 1995 to 1997. I knew after living close to my favorite ski resort that I needed a geographically nonspecific business to be able to move there to live the lifestyle of my dreams. I had known for years that information marketing was just that type of business.

Surprise!

But almost immediately after spending all of my savings on this two-year ski vacation, I became the only parent to my daughter, born prematurely, in January 1998. It's a long story that I'll only cover briefly here, but the mother had a history of child abuse and neglect that had been hidden from me. We were not married and had, in fact, dated only two times. So, my daughter went into foster care straight from the hospital.

I learned that I was the only one who would be able to rescue my daughter from foster care, so I went to court six of the first ten days she was in the state's care and was awarded temporary custody. I had no job, no business, and no savings.

Because I had to immediately prove an income to social services and the court, I restarted a carpet cleaning and water damage restoration company on my credit cards. I had built two carpet maintenance businesses with Yellow Pages advertising exclusively before, and I knew I had to take a step back in my business and lifestyle plans to be able to keep my daughter.

I was able to take the skills I had gained from 20 years of Yellow Pages advertising and immediately recreate a business from nothing. I knew that with Yellow Pages advertising, you don't usually get a bill until after the ad is out. I was confident my Yellow Pages ads would be making more than enough to pay for the ads in time to pay the bills. Almost overnight, I had my business line ringing off the hook with new, pre-sold clients from my Yellow Pages advertising.

The pressures of building a business and being a single parent on such short notice contributed to my credit card debt, and I was pretty maxed out when I went to Cleveland to attend the Information Marketing Summit in 2003.

So, when Bill Glazer informed me that it takes $40,000.00 to start an information marketing business, I knew I had to find another way to do it.

Seeking Divine Guidance

Shortly after that, I learned from his informative *No BS Marketing Newsletter* that Dan Kennedy, the "godfather of information marketing," was going to be in Los Angeles and would have 30 minutes to answer questions from his members while he was there.

I met with Dan and asked, "How can I attract the big information marketers to do joint ventures with me?" Dan said, "You've got to make it brain-dead simple for them, Larry. These guys are busy and won't do it unless you have a templated, proven process that they can use that takes zero time for them to implement. You have to do it for them." That advice, like all of Dan's advice to me, was 100-percent correct.

I knew that many of the larger information marketers do monthly interviews that they send to their members on CD. So, I began templating an interview and created trackable order forms, so I could approach my joint venture prospects with an attractive offer.

Since receiving Dan Kennedy's excellent advice to make it brain-dead simple, I have done joint ventures with this simple record-the-interview/mail-the-CD format with many successful information marketers, including Bill Glazer, Brian Sacks, Mathew Gillogly, Ron LeGrand, Rory Fatt, Dr. Tom Orent, Ed O'Keefe, Jerry Jones, Jay Geier, T.J. Rohleder, Dr. Chris Bowman, Chauncey Hutter Jr., Mike Crow, Chet Rowland, Robin Robins, Jimmy Vee, Travis Miller, Ben Glass, and Keith Lee, just to mention the more recognizable names.

I have also presented live at Ed O'Keefe's, Dr. Tom Orent's, and other marketing experts' events. A 60-minute teleseminar and a 60-minute live presentation have generated as much as $135,000.00 in sales of my products and services for a single JV partner.

Many of these highly successful information marketers commented in the process of doing the joint venture that the only reason they even called me back and responded to my joint venture offer was the fact that I had made it brain-dead simple for them. This further proved to me the wisdom in the simple answer that Dan Kennedy had given me.

Develop Your Own, Self-Biased Media

Recording the interviews gives you control of a media to distribute your perfectly delivered million-dollar sales story. My partners and I tested mailing the interview CD alone and the interview CD with it transcribed into a sales letter. The CD without the sales letter outperformed the CD with the sales letter and cost significantly less to mail.

On another JV, we tested putting the interview on a 24-hour hotline, so prospects could reference it anytime. It failed to make a single sale. People really value the ease of the information's delivery by CD.

Another method of delivering the information for a JV was shared with me by my friend Joe Polish at the Information Marketing Summit in Atlanta.

Joe packaged his Bill Phillips interview on CD in the front of a CD-sized book. It is bound with a very nice hardbound cover like a book from any bookstore. The book's content is merely a transcription of the teleseminar on the CD. This is another way of creating your own media about yourself over which you have total control. This makes it very presentable and is another proven JV format.

Recently, I was approached to be part of a book joint venture titled *Gravitational Marketing*. The book highlights different experts' skills and refers readers to a separate website where they have an opportunity to buy the authors' products and services. This book format enables the book's main author to create multiple joint ventures in just one step. It is more difficult to get a book publisher's agreement to publish this type of book. But you could self-publish your joint venture book through one of many self-publishers available on the internet.

Bill Glazer holds two excellent events each year that are great opportunities for meeting possible joint venture partners. I make a point of attending his Super-Conference and Information Marketing Summit every year, not only for what I will learn about cutting-edge new methods to build my information marketing business, but also because of the joint venture partners I will "bump into" at these meetings. Most people know how to reach me away from these events, but there is something magical about seeing prospects in person that gets them to say, "Hey! I'd like to do a joint venture with you." More than half of the joint ventures I have done have been suggested and arranged during one of these events.

If my key joint venture prospects do not approach me, I approach them. I simply ask, "Is Yellow Pages something your members use?" If the answer is no, I end the conversation politely and move on. If they are interested, they'll say, "Hey! You're that Yellow Pages guy. I wanted to speak with you about setting up a joint venture with my group."

Staying in the hotel where the event is held is critical, too. If you stay at the host hotel, you will bump into prospects in the elevator, halls, dining establishments, and common areas. The joint ventures I set up by staying at the hotel more than make up the difference in hotel rates of the cheap hotel down the street every time. Being cheap about this is very expensive in the long run.

Some other joint venture prospects to consider are:

1. *Manufacturers of key products* for your target industry. They have a vested interest in their clients doing better.

2. *DanKennedy.com* has possible joint venture prospects in the "resources" section.

3. *Google your topic* to see who is featured prominently. They could make good joint venture prospects.

4. *Joe Polish joint ventures* with the top trade magazine for his industry for attendance at his annual boot camp and possibly product sales.

The Approach

I have tried several different approaches to possible JV partners with varying degrees of success. Initially, I thought that I could just e-mail or fax my best prospects, and they would respond. That turned out to be wrong.

If you are going to get a busy person's attention, you first must stand out from the clutter. You must send your message by Priority Mail, Federal Express, or UPS carrier at the very least.

Keep in mind that your joint venture prospects will be evaluating your skills and your offer based on the package you send them, so it is a good idea to be creative. I recommend some form of "lumpy mail" approach.

An example of lumpy mail is sending prospects a silver platter with your letter explaining how you are handing them a way to make additional money on a silver platter. You can mail them previous interviews you have done as well as articles or newsletters you have written. You can mail them a letter with a package of two aspirin stapled to the top of the letter stating, "I can get rid of your (fill in the blank) headaches!" You have to convince them that you are an expert at your topic; you must stand out from the clutter they receive, and you need to inform them about the valuable information you have for their members. You also need to point out why your topic will be a perfect match for their audience and the value you will deliver to their audience.

Provide your interview template with the questions they should ask you as well as coded order forms, so they can review the simplicity and trackability of your offer. Including a series of three to five articles you have written is smart marketing, enabling your JV partner to put them in several newsletters prior to your JV sales promotion. This way, his members will recognize you as an expert before they ever listen to your CD interview.

Then I like to close the "approach letter" with a question to open the dialogue. My favorite question serves my prospects' purposes and proves to them that I want to deliver value to their groups. I like to ask, "How can we deliver a ton of value to your group, and what are your top three challenges with Yellow Pages and print advertising?" This tells me what I need to be sure to cover in the interview.

Gathering and Using Your Testimonials

Be sure to use testimonials in your approach. Testimonials from previous JV partners provide social proof that you deliver value to the audience and that you will make a good joint venture partner. And the more joint ventures you do, the more testimonials you will have. Joint ventures are a testimonial gathering shortcut, if you do them correctly.

Getting Great Testimonials Is Easy

The trick to getting a great testimonial from your joint venture partner is to write it into the introduction you should supply for your JV partner to use at the beginning of the interview. If he agrees to say it in the interview, you can just transcribe what he says and ask him to OK your use of it in your marketing materials after the interview is recorded. If he says or writes something else you can use, then that is just a bonus testimonial.

Tricks for Value-Added Bonuses

A trick to building bigger sales numbers is to package several of the group's biggest challenges into bonuses you offer with your products and services. You cover the challenges briefly in the interview. Then you offer the detailed description of how to solve each challenge as a bonus when you present your products at the end of the interview. Frequently, this removes the prospects' biggest objection to buying and opens the gates to a buying frenzy.

Don't go after the Big Fish first. Get some traction and experience on smaller deals to work out any kinks, so your big JVs go smoothly and according to plan.

How to Structure and Pay the Commissions

Offer as high a percentage in commissions as you possibly can to your joint venture partners. I see people get too cheap about this all the time. I can tell you from experience that it takes as much effort to make the sale as it does to fulfill the sale, so both partners should be equally compensated.

I recommend a 50/50 split on product sales. Because I sell both systems and services, I wanted to pay the highest commission possible in a clear and straightforward way. Having different commission structures for different products and services is too confusing. So, I pay 45 percent to my joint venture partners on sales of both the systems and my Kick Ass Ad For You program. Even though designing ads is very time intensive for me, I offer the high percentage of 45 percent to my joint venture partners.

That makes the 45-percent commission on an ad design of $2,997.00 payable at $1,348.65. And the commission on my Gold Mastery system currently selling for $697.00 is $313.65. As you can see, for the right joint venture partner, these can add up to tens of thousands of dollars quickly. And prices are increasing with demand, which builds the commissions simultaneously.

It is critical that you accurately pay your commissions as soon as they are due. Only a fool decreases his JV partners' incentive to do further business with him by stealing or delaying their commissions. The quicker you pay and the larger your commission checks, the more incentive you give your JV partners to sell your programs and products now and in the future. Nothing could make me happier than writing a big check to a JV partner. That means I have tons of sales that wouldn't have happened without my JV partner's influence and actions. I would rather have part of something than all of nothing any day. With successful JVs, you can go back to the same audience at 12- to 24-month intervals with a new offer and do very well.

Processing Orders from Your Joint Venture

I prefer to process all orders myself, so I am not shipping product when there may be a payment problem. Processing orders in my office is essential for the Kick Ass Ad For You program to assure that I do not process an order when the timeframe is too short for me to complete an ad design project prior to a customer's deadline. You do not want to be processing orders you cannot fulfill.

Always ship your orders promptly to reduce refunds. You want customers to receive your information product while they are still "hot." I always ship orders received by 2 P.M. the same day for quick fulfillment and the lowest possible refunds.

Beware!
Merchant service providers for information products get nervous if you suddenly have a lot of sales. Incredibly, this can cause them to freeze your account and balance for up to six months, which can put you in the position of having orders and no way to process them except through a third-party processor at significantly higher fees. The best protection against spikes in sales freezing your account is to have two or more merchant service providers, so you can balance the total sales over several accounts. I know this sounds crazy, but more than one successful information marketer has stories about a spike in sales causing their merchant service providers to freeze their accounts and what's in them for three to six months.

Your Product and Services Price Points

Price points are important, too. If your prices are too low, your joint venture prospect will have difficulty seeing a partnership with you as a lucrative deal in which he should be involved. But your prices should not be overinflated because you will be hurting your partner's credibility with his members.

If there is such a thing as "a perfect price point," I would put it at $1,500.00 at this time. Your product should enable your buyer to quickly get 1,000-percent ROI on what he has invested with you. Over years, they should get 10,000-percent ROI. This way, you are selling dollars for pennies.

With my Gold Mastery system, it is common for my Profits Patrol members to get $60,000.00 to $80,000.00 return on their $700.00 investment within the first 12 months of applying the system. With the Kick Ass Ad For You program, returns of $100,000.00 to $120,000.00 are possible year after year from their $2,997.00 investment. This makes me look good, but more importantly, it makes my JV partner a hero to his members who are looking to him for guidance on how to build their profits.

Your Instant Advertising Agency

In 2006, Bill Glazer advised me, "The real money in your business, Larry, is in doing it for them." He meant that I could sell systems of how to do print and Yellow Pages advertising, but that I would be a lot more successful by offering an advertising agency service to complete the ad copy and layout for customers.

I greatly respect Bill Glazer's advice, so I launched the Kick Ass Ad For You program in the middle of 2006. In this program, customers simply pay me to complete the ad copy and layout for them. This Kick Ass Ad For You program fit perfectly with what the market was already seeking.

Bill Glazer's advice about the real money being in doing it for them was 100 percent correct. It pays to have mentors like Dan Kennedy, Bill Glazer, and Joe Polish who can give you accurate advice. All you have to do is do what they tell you to do next.

I launched the Kick Ass Ad For You program, doubled my business, and tripled my profits in the next year, all while snow skiing 58 days and caring for my daughter alone.

Bill Glazer's advice to do it for them has quadrupled my average sale. It also gave me a reason to go back to all of my partners in my most successful joint ventures to do another interview to offer my new Kick Ass Ad For You design service.

Setting Up a Win/Win Joint Venture

Be sure to compliment your JV partners' contributions to their members' success. It is a wise JV partner that makes a point in each presentation to make his partner "the hero" to his group.

Before beginning your joint venture, you should have a written agreement, signed by both parties, that clearly states the commission structure, which party processes the orders, when the commissions are to be paid, and how returns are to be handled.

Typical returns for my products are about 10 percent, but I know of information marketers with return rates as high as 50 percent. It is highly recommended that you plan how to handle returns and commissions prior to beginning a joint venture.

Always process your refunds through your merchant account. If you send your client a check for the refund, he may request and receive a duplicate refund from his credit card provider. That puts you in the uncomfortable position of having to chase down the customer to get the second, undeserved refund back.

The rights to the recording of the interview should be granted to both parties to use in their own promotions in all media in most cases. When the JV is completed, it is considered good etiquette to send a thank you note or a gift as a show of appreciation to your JV partner.

It's a mistake to offer too low a percentage and/or not provide the marketing materials to make the sale. I was investigating a joint venture with a possible partner. He offered me a small percentage, no marketing materials or testimonials, and an inflated price point. Those are the three reasons I had to decline doing business with him.

He made the mistake of overvaluing what he does and undervaluing my time. I do not have the time to create the marketing materials for him. I'm too busy making money. If he were a better marketer, he would have developed and provided proven marketing materials I could just plug into my audience, and he would have offered a more attractive percentage with a noninflated price.

Priceless Market Research

Doing joint ventures provides a wealth of market research. Some of the market niches you thought were ideal for your product will turn out to be unresponsive. And some markets you would have never targeted will turn out to be highly responsive. For example, joint ventures can show you who is most likely to purchase your information product based upon the state in which they live.

This is priceless money-making research that is not available anywhere at any price. You can receive this key market research for FREE as a natural byproduct of analyzing your response and sales from different niche markets.

Responsiveness of the group is also somewhat dependent upon your JV partner's relationship with his members and groups.

When I went to define who would be my best joint venture prospects, I went to the Yellow Pages. I believed that the top-25 most referenced of 4,200 headings in an average Yellow Pages would be my best prospects because there is already a flood of profitable new clients going to those headings.

To my amazement, I was only about half right. I learned through doing these joint ventures that not all market segments are equally sensitive and responsive to my offers. I did a joint venture with the second most referenced heading in the Yellow Pages, and we only sold six or eight Gold Mastery systems. The businesses that invested in the Gold Mastery system at that time have done extraordinarily well, but that niche was still underresponsive. It is not essential that I know why they were unresponsive, just that they were.

I learned a valuable lesson on this joint venture that wasn't a great success. What would have happened if I had taken all of the money I had to invest and targeted this same market? My promotions would have bombed, and I would not have known why.

Other Joint Venture Resources

Another tremendous resource for joint ventures is the Information Marketing Association. Membership in the Information Marketing Association is one of the best investments any information marketer can make in his business. The Information Marketing Association gives you the shortcuts, guidance, and contacts that you will need to be successful in information marketing. As a member, you can review the website for important information. It even has a special section listing prospects open to JV partnerships.

The association's extremely knowledgeable and capable president is Robert Skrob. Robert helped me when I got into a situation where someone was pirating my system and other big name marketers' intellectual property on eBay. I e-mailed Robert to ask about the best course of action to stop this thief from stealing my intellectual property. Robert quickly e-mailed me back, explaining exactly how to deal with pirates on eBay. I implemented his suggestions, and the thief and his stolen products were removed from eBay within several days. Robert also had great recommendations about how to prevent eBay pirates in the future. The ability to get rid of my first eBay pirate in just days was worth everything I've paid in membership fees to the Information Marketing Association and more!

Avoiding Pitfalls in Your Own Lead Generation

As I continue to build lead generation on my own, I can avoid the markets that my least successful joint ventures have already proven to me are unresponsive. Then I can specifically target the markets that have already proven to be most responsive to my offers. I have interview CDs and presentation DVDs that I got as a strategic byproduct of these joint ventures. These CD interviews and DVDs of presentations I have gathered through joint ventures have proven to be very valuable marketing tools I can use in my own lead generation and promotions.

When I spoke at Dr. Tom Orent's event, he videotaped the entire event with several cameras and then had it professionally edited into a product. It would have cost me tens of thousands of dollars to produce the same event on tape. So, I received the DVD as a strategic byproduct of our joint venture. Dr. Tom Orent made the DVD of my presentation into a product he sells, which is valuable to his members and still continues to generate sales of my specialized Dental Advertising Profits system and Kick Ass Ad For You print advertising design service.

Ongoing Joint Ventures Income

> ### Bright Idea
>
> By doing many joint ventures, I was able to determine not only which markets had potential, but also which markets would be sensitive enough to my offer to buy my information products. And the real beauty was that I was able to determine my most sensitive markets WITHOUT RISKING ANY OF MY OWN MONEY! It is important to point out that I did not waste any of my joint venture partners' money either, for two reasons. One is that many of these partners are paid to deliver content on CD to a list of members monthly, so this filled a month for them. The second reason I did not waste their money was we both entered into the JV arrangement thinking it was going to be successful. In the cases where my products did not sell well, it was a surprise to both of us.

Some of my joint venture partners have chosen to redistribute the same CD interview a year or so later, creating automatic income for both of us. Some JV partners include the Yellow Pages interview as a bonus or part of their primary systems, which triggers system and Kick Ass Ad For You sales automatically when their new members review the CD interview. This is very smart marketing because it is added value to the prospect and added sales for us. I love coming home from having fun and finding orders from previous JVs that have been received by e-mail and fax while I was gone!

Joint ventures took me past guessing at who my best target markets would be, and specifically identified which markets should be my primary target markets based on their past buying behavior. That research can be the difference between success and failure in information marketing.

By completing this "testing" first with joint ventures, I now know which market niches will be worth my time to travel and deliver my "How to Master the Art of Yellow Page and Print Advertising" presentation in person and which markets would be a complete waste of my valuable time.

Priceless Relationships

Another strategic byproduct of joint ventures is the relationships and friendships I've developed with highly successful information marketers. Because of these relationships, my joint venture partners' products and services will always be considered first when I am looking for back-end products to recommend to my Profit Patrol members.

Joint Ventures' Downsides

Up to this point, I've covered most of the upsides of doing joint ventures. Now, I will cover the downsides of joint ventures. The biggest downside for me has been a lack of control of the speed of marketing my products. When you do joint ventures, you do it on your partner's schedule. This puts you in a position of having little control over your sales and income. If your partner has a delay of two to six months, there's not a lot you can do to make your JV happen sooner.

If you do not generate enough joint ventures, then your income and business will dry up. You should reinvest some of your profits from all of your joint ventures into building your own lead generation as soon as possible.

Beware of Intellectual Property Thieves

You may be approached by people who want to steal your intellectual information. These people will disguise themselves as joint venture prospects just to do this. I was approached by "Jim" about a joint venture. We had discussions working out all of the details. Then, at the last minute, he announced that he had decided to offer my Yellow Pages ad design service to his group, using my methods without compensating me. It is because of unscrupulous people, who I believe lack a moral compass, that you should always hold back a key element until the last minute when the joint venture is sure to take place.

Competing against someone like me with 31 years of Yellow Pages advertising experience is a sure way to cause problems with your members. Jim will be in a very uncomfortable position when he promises to do a highly profitable Yellow Pages ad for one of his dentists and that ad has to compete with the ad I have done for another dentist in the same book. It will be obvious to his members that they were sold an inferior product.

I have had other joint venture prospects try to do the Yellow Pages design service for their members. I am always embarrassed for them when I see their poorly designed ads with many obvious defects. And I hear from their clients how these second-rate efforts at advertising bombed and cost their advertisers a whole year of payments with little or no return on their investments.

Double Your Sales!

The best joint ventures are those in which both partners learn something from each other. On a joint venture I did with Jay Geier, he called me up after the deadline and asked if there was anything else we could send to further stimulate sales. This triggered some thoughts, and I told him I would e-mail him something in the next hour. So, I decided to make a promotional page he could fax to his group titled "Oops!!! We Goofed!!!" (See the document on page 103.)

It explained that on some of the CD interviews we mailed, some of the offer was inadvertently cut off. So, we were clarifying the offer and extending the deadline. Jay faxed that single page to his group the following day, clarifying the offer and extending the deadline. Adding that simple step DOUBLED SALES. A lot of the order forms came with handwritten notes saying, "Thanks for reminding me. I had meant to order, but set it aside for a moment."

Learning something that doubles sales on every joint venture has proven very valuable to me and attractive to my potential partners. Now, I encourage all of my JV partners to use this fax follow-up method to extend the offer deadline and potentially double sales from the promotion.

Dr. Tom Orent also shared numerous valuable insights into my business from an objective position when we did our first JV that I valued enough to implement. If you are observant, you can mirror and model what makes each of your JV partners successful and increase the speed of your own success.

Ask People What They Need

Once responsive markets have been identified, quit guessing at your market's greatest challenges in your area of expertise and ask people what they need. Most businesses are guessing at what their clients want and would receive profitable information if they would just ask their clients what they really want and need.

You can do this on a squeeze page for your website by requiring prospects to answer the question to enter the site. You can hold drawings for prizes in which a condition of

Sample Promotional Piece

"Oops!!! We Goofed!!!"

We have had a lot of response and questions at our office about the Instant Yellow Page Profits™ Systems, and how to qualify for the special bonuses offered.

Apparently some of the interviews I did with Yellow Page Expert Larry Conn were edited in a way that cut off the part that explained the offer. So what we've decided to do is **extend the deadline to November 25th[th] to qualify for the special bonuses offered.** If you want to take action and invest NOW in the Instant Yellow Page Profits™ Gold Mastery System, you will receive the best price offered all year long. ($697-**$149.00 off** = only $548 + S&H of $37.00 = $585.00 total)

Remember that the "Dentists" heading is in the top 1% most referenced headings out of over 4200 headings in an average Yellow Pages. **And there's estimated to be about 248,500,000 references to the Dentists heading in the United States EVERY YEAR!**

This is like buying dollars for pennies! Here's what Instant Yellow Page Profits™ system users are saying:

"Your Mastery System is easy to understand and implement. Copious examples reveal common mistakes and how to correct them, or avoid them altogether. My expectation is that my ad will DOMINATE my Yellow Page heading resulting in a significant increase in my Return On Investment." -Dr. Mark Prather, Chiropractor

"The depth and clarity of the content was very organized and detail oriented. Your Mastery System was very helpful in designing a winning Yellow Page ad!" -Dr. Patrick McClusky

"Understanding and using direct response marketing in a Yellow Page ad makes perfect sense! The segment by segment format made for easy reading and understanding. This is the first time I've been confident enough to run a full page ad. I'm excited about my ad and how I will easily stand out from the other Dental ads in the book. Thanks again!" -Dr. Stella's Children's Dentistry

I've included an Action Form on the next page for your convenience;

entry is that they answer the question, "What is your biggest challenge with (your area of expertise)?"

I know of numerous cases where an information marketer has asked his audience their biggest challenge, and the answers his prospects and clients gave him launched another whole area of business that was more profitable than his existing business. He just created a product to fill his clients' stated needs. Talk about easy money. What could be simpler than that?

Doing joint ventures has forced me to quickly learn how to write an effective sales presentation disguised as an informative presentation, how to present to a group by tele-seminar and at live seminar events, how to craft a million-dollar sales story, and how to design effective and trackable "action forms." And it caused me to grow a lot personally.

In summary, I have detailed:

1. How to structure your joint ventures for maximum profit as a win/win for both parties;

2. Several successful approaches for key joint venture prospects; and

3. The strategic byproduct of extremely valuable market research you will get by doing joint ventures.

Joint ventures have many advantages. But for business growth and income stability, joint ventures should be only one of five or more lead generation methods that consistently generate sales for your information marketing business.

Lifestyle and Income Freedom

Because of my geographically nonspecific information marketing business, I now live where I used to only be able to vacation. Thanks to the superior guidance of Joe Polish, Dan Kennedy, Bill Glazer, and Robert Skrob, my daughter and I moved near my favorite ski resort in August 2006. I plan to ski about 80 days this ski season. I now feel like I am retired with a good income and something interesting and productive to do. I am completely debt-free, have no employees, and have the ability to make five- and six-figures per month working only 20 to 30 hours per week.

My friends and family claim, "You are lucky!" But that "luck" is a result of planning and effectively implementing a strategic joint venture plan to build my information marketing business.

▲ ▲ ▲

Leading print and Yellow Pages advertising expert **Larry Conn** has helped thousands of small businesses just like yours create evergreen, automatic marketing systems that get your phones to ring off the hook with new, high-end clients that are PRESOLD on using you before they have ever met or spoken to you. Now, you can go to www.InstantYellowPageProfits.com and get a FREE, 60-point evaluation of your current print or Yellow Pages advertising, and discover the 12 Yellow Page Response Trigger categories Larry uses that are guaranteed to make your advertising message irresistible to your ideal target prospect.

Maximizing Online Info-Product Sales,

Generate More Money from

Your Business

by Bob Regnerus
www.TheLeadsKing.com

A lot of info-marketers sell products online through websites. However, there is a specific way you must structure your website to maximize your sales. Here is the essential information you need to create a site, attract visitors, and sell info-products.

▲ ▲ ▲

When I first got into this business, I didn't give a lot of thought to web traffic. I was a programmer, and I escaped from the corporate world to start my own company, which specialized in setting up e-commerce websites. My clients were large companies that didn't have the time or expertise to build their own online stores, and as internet shopping became more and more common, I found no shortage of clients looking to get in on the action.

Soon after I started my company, something interesting happened. My clients started coming back to me after their websites were up and running. They told me they were happy with the way their sites looked and functioned, but they weren't happy with the number of visitors their sites were getting. Was there anything I could do to help them drive more traffic to their websites?

"Of course I can help," I said, in the spirit of a true entrepreneur. I didn't really know what I was getting myself into, but I accepted the challenge. I started learning everything I could about internet marketing and internet traffic.

That was almost ten years ago. Everything about the internet has changed since then—the number of websites, the way websites look, the way websites function, and the way people access them. One thing hasn't changed, though, and that's the need for website owners to bring the right visitors to their sites. Today, my company has grown beyond my wildest dreams, and I've built my reputation as "The Leads King™" by helping our clients solve that universal problem—how to drive more traffic to their websites and get visitors to take action when they get there.

"I Hate My Website!"

I go through a fairly intense interview process with my prospective clients before I start working with them, and almost always, they begin by telling me that they hate their websites. Some of them actually cringe when they start talking about it. One client, when I told him that I was going to look at his site, said, "OK, just don't say anything about it!"

Why do these business owners hate their websites so much? Because they see them as sources of nothing but frustration. They're frustrated because the sites aren't getting enough traffic. They're frustrated because their sites aren't generating enough sales. They're frustrated because they don't have the time to maintain their websites and because they can't keep up with changes in technology.

Let me point out that I'm not talking about stupid people here. These are highly intelligent business owners, who in many cases are running more than one successful company at a time. They've simply run into obstacles when it comes to doing business online.

Overcoming those obstacles takes time and money, but the benefits far outweigh the costs. One of my clients recently doubled her website responses almost overnight after we made some key changes to her site's front page. She found herself with twice as many potential customers to follow up with, and she cut her cost per lead in half. What if you could get those same results for your company?

If your website isn't doing what it should, you're not only wasting resources, you're also missing out on opportunities to find new customers and build your relationships with existing customers. Here's the good news: Even if you hate your website, the problems can be fixed, and you can turn your site from a source of frustration into a source of traffic and customers. The sooner you make that change, the happier you'll be.

Plan, Build, Advertise

There are three basic phases to a successful web traffic campaign. You need to go through the phases in the proper order, or your efforts will be doomed from the start. If your website isn't ready for visitors, it won't matter how much time or money you spend trying to generate traffic—you simply won't get the results you want.

The first phase of your campaign is to understand exactly what a website can and cannot do for your business, and then develop the strategy that will work best for you. You might feel tempted to skip this step, but take the time and think it through. It's critically important, and in most cases, it's a real eye-opener. You'll learn a lot about every aspect of your business if you approach your planning the right way.

In the second phase of your campaign, you'll either build a new website or change your existing site, so it fits your strategy. The goal here is to make your website as attractive as possible. If your site is attractive, it will be easier for your prospective customers to find, and when they find it, they'll come back more often and tell their friends and business contacts about it as well.

Then, in the third phase of your campaign, you'll use a combination of tactics to drive even more visitors to your site. This includes pay-per-click advertising, search-engine optimization, and other advanced promotional tools.

If this sounds like a lot of work, that's because it is. It's well worth the effort, though, and if you follow these guidelines, you'll be able to see your campaign through to a successful conclusion, whether you're doing it on your own or hiring a consultant to do it for you.

What Is Your Website Supposed to Do?

What is your website supposed to do? It sounds like a simple question, but I've found that most business owners don't really have a good answer. Some of them expect too much, some expect too little, and some have just never thought about it. Before you do anything else, you need to answer that question for yourself. If you don't set the right expectations for your site, you'll probably still get some traffic, but it won't be the *right* traffic. The whole point here is to get the visitors you want, and not waste time on people who will never become your customers.

I advise my clients to think of their websites as tools for generating leads. In most cases, it's not a good idea to expect your website to close sales for you on the first visit. Selling over the internet is difficult for most products, and it's practically impossible for service providers.

Instead, your website should serve as a sales funnel. A sales funnel brings visitors in, lets them decide if they're interested, and then collects contact information from the interested ones. When they provide information, or "opt in," your visitors become sales leads. Once you have your leads, you can send them to an online sales process, close them over the phone, or use other offline methods.

To function as an effective sales funnel, a website needs to do four things:

1. *Establish immediate trust and confidence.* Within seconds of landing on your website, your visitors will decide whether to click away or stick around. A professional-looking, easy-to-read site will make your visitors feel comfortable and encourage them to read what you have to say.

2. *Position you as an expert in your field.* Consumers like to do business with experts, so your site should present you as the go-to authority in your field of expertise.

3. *Reverse the marketing process.* What would you rather do: beg for business or have customers begging you to sell to them?

4. *Get responses.* Few businesses have a need for a branding website, which simply presents information. A direct response website, which engages visitors and collects information from them, will give you the most bang for your buck.

That's just the big picture, of course. Your internet strategy should be tailored to your industry and to your company in particular, and you'll need to ask yourself a lot of questions. How much will your website visitors know about you before they visit your site? How long is your customers' buying cycle: do they spend minutes, days, weeks, or months deciding on a purchase? How many of your competitors will the average customer investigate? What sort of information do you need to collect from your prospective customers?

It's a lot to think about, but believe me, the time you spend answering these questions will not be wasted. If you have a clear understanding of what you should be getting from your website, you'll always know if your site is doing its job.

Making Your Website Attractive

Once you know what your website should be doing for you, it's time to build or update your site to make it as appealing to visitors as it can possibly be. This is where many business owners get pulled in the wrong direction by their marketing staff or web design teams. When it comes to business websites, "attractive" does not mean pretty or exciting. It means easy to understand, interesting, and engaging. Rather than spending your money on high-end graphic design and Flash animation, focus on telling your visitors as clearly and convincingly as possible what you have to offer and why they should be interested.

The Leads King's Rules

Building or redesigning a website can be overwhelming. The possibilities are truly infinite, and everyone you ask will give you different advice. To get the right end result—a website that attracts the right people—you need to focus on a few key goals. My six rules for business websites will help you cut through the chaos and build the most attractive site possible.

Rule 1: Have an Objective

You took the time to plan a strategy for your website, and you know what you want to get out of it. So, before you do anything else, communicate that strategy to your visitors. Make sure that anyone who comes to your website will be able to understand, within seconds, who you are, what you do, and what you want from them.

Rule 2: Sell Your Objective

Tell your visitors what's in it for them. For example, if you're running a martial arts studio, the objective of your website might be to convince people to come in for a free lesson. In that case, your site shouldn't focus on the awards you've won or the classes you offer for advanced students. There may be a place for that information on your site, but the primary focus should be on the free lesson and the reasons your visitors should want it. Then, when you have them in your studio, you'll have the opportunity to sell them on yourself, your philosophy, and your history.

Here's a quick check: If the words "I" and "we" appear more often on your website than the word "you," your site probably isn't doing a great job of selling your objective.

Rule 3: Make Your Site Sticky

You only have a few seconds to convince a visitor to read the front page of your website, but when you've accomplished that, you still have a long way to go. Your goal should be to build a sticky website, one that keeps visitors on the site for a long time and convinces them to come back again.

The key to a sticky website is good content. If you don't give your visitors anything interesting to read, why would they stick around? Adding fresh content is just as important. If you have something new to say every day or every week, your readers will be more likely to come back for an update.

Rule 4: Have Proof

After you convince your potential customers that you do, in fact, sell what they're looking for, you need to convince them that you're a legitimate business and that you can deliver on your promises. Customer testimonials are the single best way to do this. Ask some of your best customers to write or record a paragraph or two about their experiences, and put these testimonials on your site, preferably with a photo of each customer.

If you're a member of an industry group or the Better Business Bureau, point that out as well, and include the appropriate symbol or logo. The same thing applies to certifications you've received or awards you've won.

Rule 5: Give Your Visitors a Reason

If you're collecting information from your website visitors (and you should be), you're asking for something of value, and you need to offer something of value in return. Don't give away spare parts or some PowerPoint presentation you threw together four years ago.

Whatever you decide to offer, be sure to actually sell it to your visitors. You can't assume they'll jump at it just because it doesn't cost them any money. If you appear to value the offer, they'll see value in it as well.

Rule 6: Build a List

What's the point of collecting information from your potential customers if you're not going to use it? Build an e-mail list with the responses you get from your website, and use it to distribute useful information. When you have a new product or service to offer, or you want to announce a special promotion, you can save hundreds or thousands of dollars by sending the information via e-mail instead of regular mail. E-mail might not replace printed materials in every case, but it's a low-cost, high-reward way to maintain contact with your leads.

Your visitors have entrusted you with their e-mail addresses, so don't abuse that trust by filling up their inboxes with useless material. Also—and I hope this goes without saying—don't sell your list to anyone else!

Collecting E-Mail Addresses and Making Sales

A key strategy of information marketers is to collect e-mail addresses of visitors for follow-up. And when a customer is ready to buy, you want a shopping cart page ready for the customer to make that purchase.

I recommend Aweber (www.TheLeadsKingAutoResponder.com) to my clients who are just starting out in information marketing and need an e-mail auto responder. For more robust needs, I suggest 1 Shopping Cart (www.TheLeadsKingShoppingCart.com) if they need the functionality of a shopping cart, order management system, and affiliate program. 1 Shopping Cart:

- *Manages mailing lists.* The software gives you some HTML code that you or your web master simply drops on the web page to make it a landing page, ready to capture contact information.

- *Provides a shopping cart.* This software prompts you through a list of questions to build a page to take orders for your products.

- *Automates an affiliate program.* This system handles all of the details to enable others to sell your products and earn an affiliate commission. Affiliates can come to your site, sign up, and receive their links without any work from you. Now, an affiliate can send an e-mail with its affiliate link to generate sales. The software keeps up with all of the reporting. You pull a report at the end of the month and write checks to affiliates who made sales; it's that easy.

▲

- *Provides tutorials.* There are video tutorials that walk you through every step of the process. Best thing, a trial account is free. It's worth signing up just to go through the tutorials. You'll learn a lot about internet marketing by watching those videos.

Your Landing Page

Some businesses only need one page on their websites, and others need dozens or even hundreds of pages. To determine your own requirements, you'll need to consider the size of your company, the number of products or services you offer, and the amount of information your visitors will expect to find on your site. Whether or not you need pages for product descriptions, frequently asked questions, press releases, or your personal history, one page is a must-have for every website: the landing page.

When someone comes to your site and decides that he may be interested in doing business with you, your landing page is where you want to take him. This is the page that convinces your visitor to opt in: to stop reading and actually do something.

The "something" your visitors do is the objective you chose when you planned your website strategy. You might want your visitor to provide an e-mail address, fill out a profile, complete a survey, or pick up the phone and make a call. Whatever your objective, the landing page is where you either achieve it or miss out on the opportunity. Here's how to ensure that you take full advantage of your landing page:

- *Use a headline.* Give your landing page a good headline. Make it large, easy to read, and strongly worded. It needs to grab your sales prospects' attention and bring their eyes farther down the page.

- *Make an offer.* If you want your visitors to take some sort of action, you need to offer something in return. Your landing page is where you make this offer. Even though no money is changing hands, this is essentially a sale that you're trying to make, so be clear and direct. Tell your visitors what you want, and tell them what you'll give them for it.

- *Elicit action.* Don't make any assumptions about the people who visit your landing page. They may not be comfortable using a computer; they may be nervous about doing business on the internet; or they may be watching TV, eating dinner, and reading your site all at the same time. Tell them, step by step, exactly how to do what you're asking them to do. Give them simple instructions like, "Type your e-mail address in the box below, and then hit the Submit button."

- *Keep it in focus.* Don't do anything to distract your visitors' attention from your objective. Don't clutter up the page with unnecessary graphics, and don't add text that doesn't relate specifically to what you're trying to accomplish on the page.

Case Study: Landing Page Design

Alexandria Brown, the "Ezine Queen," came to me for help with her website's landing page (see Figure 8.1). She was looking for ways to increase her opt-in rate. At the time, only 6 percent to 13 percent of her landing page visitors actually filled out her client registration form. Here's what we did:

○ Replaced a still photo with a video clip in which Alexandria introduces herself, makes her offer, and reminds the visitor to fill out the registration form.

○ Moved the client registration form "above the fold," so that visitors didn't have to scroll down the page to opt in.

○ Cut the headline down from 40 to 18 words, giving it a stronger message, making it easier to read, and making it easier on the eyes.

○ Expanded Alexandria's offer from one item on her old page to three items on the new page, and displayed the offer more prominently on the page.

○ Added several additional testimonials, and added photos of the clients who provided the testimonials.

○ Removed unnecessary text from the page to achieve a cleaner look and focus the message on the offer and objective.

These changes have resulted in an almost immediate increase in Alexandria's opt-in rate from 6 to 13 percent in the old days to 13 to 28 percent today (see Figure 8.2). In other words, she's doubled her opt-in rate and cut her cost per lead in half!

Figure 8.1

Figure 8.2

- *Use video.* It's much easier to add video to a website now than it was just a year or two ago, and video presentations are very effective at getting page visitors to take action. Video is much more attractive to the eye than text, and you can literally point your finger at the space on the page where you want your prospects to type something in.

- *Keep it above the fold.* Try to get all of the elements of your landing page "above the fold," meaning that a visitor can see everything without having to scroll down. You may only have your sales prospects' attention for a few seconds, so you want to make it as easy as possible for them to opt in.

Website Power Checklist

Before you move on to pay-per-click advertising and search engine optimization, let's be sure that your website is up to speed. Use this quick checklist to verify that your website is doing everything it can to attract visitors and that it will use your additional traffic to the best advantage.

○ *Headline.* Does every page on your website have a clear, compelling headline? If you don't want a headline on every page, at least make sure that you put one on your landing page.

○ *Phone number.* Is your phone number prominently displayed on your website? This is especially important if most of your customers will come from the immediate area (within five or ten miles of your location).

○ *Name and e-mail capture.* Does your landing page give your visitors a place to send you their names and e-mail addresses?

○ *Testimonials.* Have you provided testimonials from your satisfied customers? Are the testimonials compelling, and are they accompanied by photos?

○ *Good content.* Is your content good enough to pull visitors deeper into your site? Are you providing interesting, informative text, along with audio and video content? Are you adding fresh content to your site at least once a week?

○ *An offer for every action.* Are you offering something in return for each action you ask your website visitors to take? Is the offer valuable enough to inspire action, and are you doing a good job of selling it?

Bringing in the Crowds

Now that you've developed your internet strategy and built a website that will attract the right people, it's time to start advertising and promoting. Your ability to drive additional traffic to your website is limited only by your imagination—companies invent new ways of doing it every day. However, there are some key tactics you can use as a starting point, which fall into three general categories: pay-per-click advertising, search engine optimization, and promotional campaigns.

You may balk at the cost when you start these campaigns. But remember, as long as your traffic is profitable, it doesn't matter how much you're paying for it. If you find that you're actually losing money, that's when you'll know it's time to try something different.

Pay-Per-Click Advertising

Pay-per-click advertising is exactly what the name suggests: a system in which you pay a fee every time someone gets to your website by clicking an ad on another website. The fee you pay for that click can be anywhere from a few cents to a few dollars. Most pay-per-click operators use an auction system, so the cost depends on how much your competition is willing to pay. Don't waste energy trying to achieve a specific per-click cost. What matters is the result. As long as your campaign is generating profits, you're getting it right.

Google is the biggest name among search engines, and it's the dominant force in internet advertising as well. When you're ready for a pay-per-click campaign, Google's AdWords system is the place to start. You'll be able to show your ads next to search results that are relevant to your business, and you'll have the option of advertising on the sites in Google's content network, which includes other high-profile sites like About.com and *The New York Times'* website.

Google isn't the only player in the game, though. You should also include Yahoo! and MSN in your pay-per-click campaign. They might not generate as many clicks as Google, but their clicks are just as good, and you'll probably pay less for them.

Getting Started on AdWords

You'll be amazed how easy it is to start advertising on Google. You can have your account up and running in less than 20 minutes. Just go to http://Adwords .Google.com, and click on the link "Sign up now." The system will walk you through a simple process:

- *Choose an edition.* If you're doing this on your own, use the Starter Edition at first, then switch over to the Standard Edition once you get the hang of it. Make sure to tell Google that you already have a website.

- *Targeting options.* This is where you choose the language and geographical region in which you want your ad displayed.

- *Write your ad.* Next, it's time to write your ad. You get 25 characters for your headline and two 35-character lines of text. This is also the step where you provide a link to the page you want people to land on when they click your ad.

- *Choose your keywords.* If you haven't done any keyword research ahead of time, Google has a tool that can help you.

- *Account setup.* In the last few steps of the process, you'll provide your target budget and contact info. Once you get an e-mail from Google and confirm with your billing information, your ad will start running.

Keep in mind that Google gives preferential treatment to advertisers whose ads generate a lot of clicks, and it punishes advertisers whose ads have a high bounce rate. (Your bounce rate is the percentage of users who return to Google's search results after clicking your ad and looking at your site.) What does that mean to you? It means you'll get more out of AdWords if you write good ad copy and keep visitors on your site once they get there (see Figure 8.3).

Figure 8.3

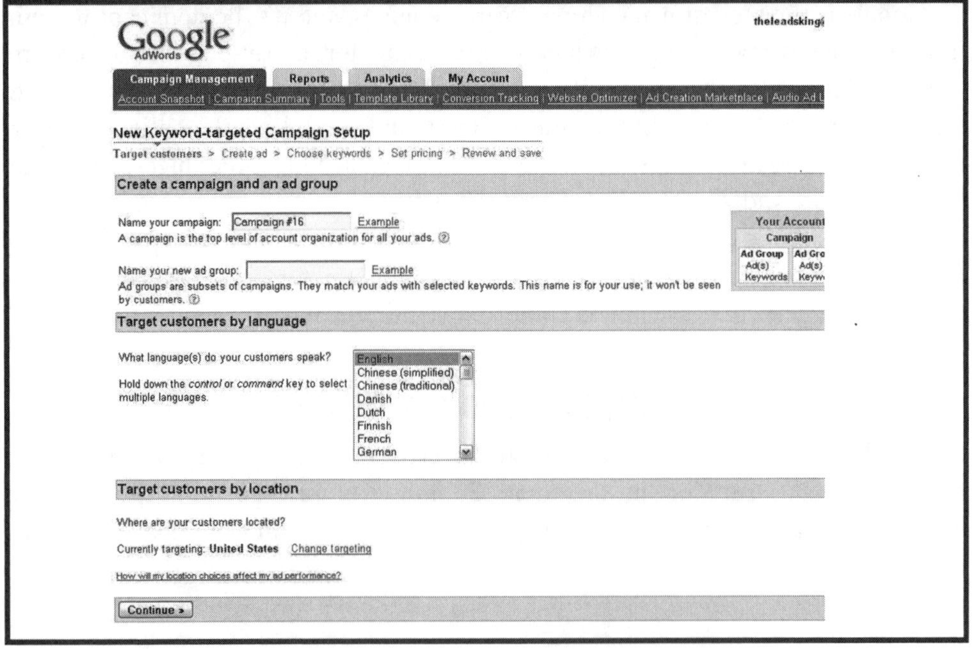

Keywords

You have to bid on the right keywords if you want your pay-per-click campaign to work. Before you start doing keyword research, come up with some ideas on your own. If you know your customers, you'll be able to guess which words they're going to search for. Your sales materials and product descriptions can help you with this. Use your list as a starting point, and then use these resources for additional ideas:

- *Website statistics.* Ask your web administrator to send you a report of the search terms that people are using to find your site.

- *Google Analytics.* Google Analytics is a free tool that can tell you a lot about how people are finding your website and what they're doing on it.

- *Keyword tools.* Most pay-per-click services provide tools that can help you find keywords that are similar to the words you've already selected.

- *Subscription services.* For around $50.00 a month, companies like WordTracker and Keyword Discovery can give you more personalized suggestions.

I usually adopt an aggressive keyword strategy for my clients, which means bidding on some of the most common (and therefore most expensive) keywords in a given market. No matter how you choose your keywords, though, remember that quality is more important that quantity. The vast majority of your traffic will come from just a handful of words (see Figure 8.4).

Figure 8.4

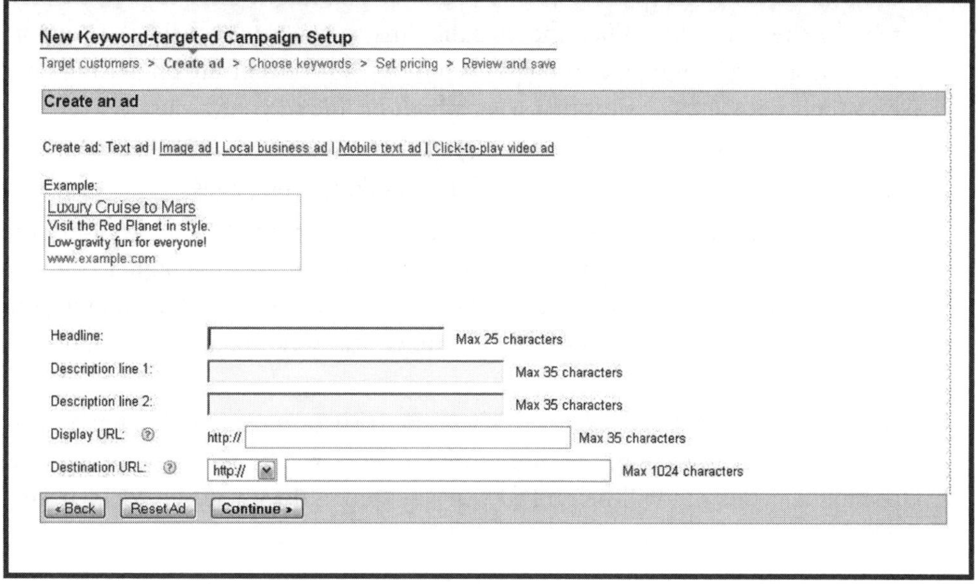

New Keyword-targeted Campaign Setup

Target customers > **Create ad** > Choose keywords > Set pricing > Review and save

Create an ad

Create ad: Text ad | Image ad | Local business ad | Mobile text ad | Click-to-play video ad

Example:

Luxury Cruise to Mars
Visit the Red Planet in style.
Low-gravity fun for everyone!
www.example.com

Headline: ___ Max 25 characters

Description line 1: ___ Max 35 characters

Description line 2: ___ Max 35 characters

Display URL: ⑦ http:// ___ Max 35 characters

Destination URL: ⑦ http:// ▼ ___ Max 1024 characters

[« Back] [Reset Ad] [Continue »]

Search Engine Optimization

You can pay to get better position for your ads that appear alongside Googles' search results, but you can't pay Google to list your website higher within the search results themselves. The same rule applies to Yahoo! and the other search engines. That doesn't mean you can't improve your position within search engine results, though. There are several things you can do to get your website listed higher, some of which are fairly simple and some of which can get pretty complicated. The general name for this collection of strategies is search engine optimization, or SEO for short.

The rules of SEO change all the time because Google and the other search engines are always changing the way they rank websites within their listings. They're all very secretive about their methods, but in every case, the process starts with a program called a *spider* or *crawler*. These programs search the internet constantly, reading websites, exploring links, and looking for changes. The search engines then analyze the information collected by their spiders and decide which web pages are most relevant for a given keyword or internet search term.

How exactly does a search engine decide on those rankings? That's the billion-dollar question. You can spend a lot of money getting advice on how to work the system, but again, because search engines change their formulas all the time, a trick that worked last month might not work next month. Your best bet is to focus on the following three areas, listed in order of importance:

1. *External links.* The more websites link to your website, the more "important" a search engine will think your site is. Do everything you can to convince other website owners to link to your site. You might offer to provide a link back to the other site in return for a link to yours, or you might offer to provide content for the other site. When the sites that link to yours are considered "important" by a search engine, that helps even more, so concentrate on getting links on widely read sites or sites that have a high profile in your industry.

   By the way, this is what first put Google on the map—its search engine was the first one to look at external links when ranking web pages.

2. *Frequent updates.* The more often you add new material to your website, the more often a spider program will come back to read it, and the higher you'll be ranked in the search engine results. This is one reason it's such a good idea to add a blog to your website—blogs are the easiest way to add fresh content to your site.

3. *Keyword density.* Before Google, this was the basis of most search engine rankings. Generally speaking, the more often a keyword appears on your website, the higher your site will be ranked when someone does a search for that keyword.

Warning: search engines have gotten very good at spotting abuse of this rule. A shoe store can't just repeat the word "shoe" on its website a hundred thousand times and expect a good ranking.

Promoting Yourself and Your Business

The real secret to driving more traffic to your site is an effective promotional campaign. Your competitors are all doing pay-per-click advertising and SEO as well, but they may not be promoting their sites with blogs, articles, and press releases. By promoting yourself and your website through these additional channels, you'll increase your visibility, build your reputation, bring more visitors to your site, and make it easier for you to convert those visitors into customers.

Every Website Needs a Blog

Don't think a blog is right for your business or your website? Think again. No matter who you are or what you sell, adding a blog is one of the best things you can do. Start a blog, and update it every day. You'll improve your web traffic with your blog alone, and the addition of new content will improve your search engine results at the same time.

In addition to writing your own blog, visit other blogs and use the "comments" function to respond to what you read. When you leave a comment, always include a link back to your own blog. This is where a lot of the action is, and if your comments are useful and intelligent, you'll build your readership and get people talking about you.

Write Articles

Write articles about issues in your industry and submit them to www.Ezine Articles.com and other websites that serve as article clearinghouses. Again, always include a brief promotional biography of yourself and your web address. If your articles are interesting and relevant, other publishers will pick them up and post them on their own websites. Publishing articles will drive traffic to your site and help you gain a reputation as an expert, which will make it much easier to close sales.

Distribute Press Releases

Get in the habit of sending out a press release whenever you have something new to say about your business. Whether you're opening a new location, adding a new line of products, forming a new partnership, or you've won an industry award, let the press know about it. Sites like www.PRWeb.com provide an online outlet for releases and give you the opportunity to spread the word through traditional news sources.

Starting Your Blog

There's no downside to putting a blog on your website. It will increase your traffic, turn casual visitors into regular visitors, and give you an opportunity to promote yourself to an audience you wouldn't otherwise reach. The dollar cost is minimal, and you'll only need enough time to write a few hundred words per week.

All you need to get started is blog publishing software, and that's easy to find. Avoid free blog-hosting services, though. You don't want someone else's ads next to your content, and you don't want to confuse your visitors by sending them to a different address to read your blog. You can get publishing software from a variety of sources. Just find one you like, and install it on your server.

If you want to use a free service, my recommendation is www.Blogger.com. I prefer www.WordPress.org because it has a lot more features, including syndication built in.

Once you have the software, you're ready to go. Blogging can be a daunting task at first, so don't get ahead of yourself. Write one post of maybe 200 words, and call it a day. The next day, do the same thing. Before long, it will become second nature, and you'll be adding fresh content to your site every day. This will attract attention from search engines and from your customers. People are much more likely to visit a site when they expect to find something new.

Don't worry too much about your writing style. Blogs tend to be more casual, and your visitors won't hold you to a high standard of professionalism here. Just avoid spelling errors, bad grammar, and subject matter that might offend your audience. Common sense will be your guide.

Remember to enable the "comments" function of your blog. When you allow readers to add comments to your blog posts, you'll encourage your customers to talk about you, which means that they can do a lot of your sales work for you. Comments are also a great source of information. They'll let you know what your customers are thinking and what they might be looking for.

I hope I've convinced you that you don't have to be a technological wizard or a marketing genius to generate traffic for your website. All you need is the right three-phase strategy:

Phase 1: Understand what you really need from your website.

Phase 2: Build an attractive site with your objective in mind.

Phase 3: Drive additional traffic through advertising, SEO, and promotion.

Whether you're doing it on your own or hiring a team to do it for you, make sure that you control the process and work toward the goals you set. You know your company and customers better than anyone else, and you have the most to gain from a website that attracts the right traffic.

▲   ▲   ▲

Bob Regnerus, also known as The Leads King,™ is a well-respected speaker, author, publisher, and coach o business owners that want to learn the secrets of growing a business using the internet. Bob would love to offer you his FREE "Internet Success Program" on CD (valued at $197.00) just by visiting his website, www.FreeInternetSuccessCDsEntrepreneur.com.

9

Using Ezines as a Fast and

Practically Free Way to Sell More Info-Products Online

by Alexandria Brown
"The Ezine Queen"
www.EzineQueen.com

*E*ven though you have a fantastic website, you'll still have a lot of visitors who don't buy. It's important to follow-up with your prospects to build trust and familiarity. An ezine is a great way to increase the value of your customers and turn visitors into buyers.

▲ ▲ ▲

Ezines (e-mail newsletters) can prove to be a surprisingly valuable method for marketing your info-products online. If you already distribute to a mailing list or have considered it as an option for your info-product business, you are already well on your way to boosting your sales quickly and easily by using an ezine.

So, what is an ezine? Basically any e-mail publication that your readers subscribe or "opt in" to because they're interested in the information you're sharing. Ideally, you want your ezine to be related to the content in your info-products; that way your subscribers are an ideal message-to-market match for your business.

And you want your ezine to be FREE. Why? Most people are online to search for information, not to buy something. They may end up buying something, but first they'll always look for free information. So, your ezine is the bait. By offering FREE information on the topic of your information product, they will get on your mailing list, hear from you every week or so, and eventually want to buy.

Also, by building a large list of people who are interested in your specific topic of choice, you gain years of future income opportunity. How? Because now you have built-in buyers. And over time, you can introduce new products and services you know they will be interested in. You'll find your list will be the most important asset you'll actually build with your information marketing business. The *who* is actually more important than the *what*.

I started my first ezine several years ago to help promote my marketing and copywriting services when I lived in New York City. (It was called *Straight Shooter Marketing*, and I still publish it today, with more than 24,000 sub-

> ## Bright Idea
> List building, by far, is one of the most effective means of marketing to a selected niche or target audience. Because your subscribers have expressed an interest in your ezine, they will typically also be interested in your information products and services.

scribers.) When I grew tired of working hours for dollars and learned more about info-marketing, I decided to launch my first info-product on a topic I had become knowledgeable about—ezine publishing! (Figure 9.1 shows a recent issue of my ezine today.)

My first ebook was called *Boost Business With Your Own Ezine*, and once I had it ready, along with a simple web page where people could learn more and purchase, I thought, "Gee, I wonder if my ezine readers would be interested in this?" So, I sent them an e-mail about it. WHAM . . . that was the day my life changed forever. As I watched the orders come into my e-mail inbox, one after the other, I realized I wanted to be a full-time information marketer.

Today, I make millions of dollars a year from information marketing, and I think it's the best business in the world! I work out of my beachfront home in Southern

Figure 9.1

The E-Zine Queen's™
Straight Shooter Marketing

Alexandria K. Brown, Publisher

WWW.EZINEQUEEN.COM   ALEXANDRIA@EZINEQUEEN.COM

♦ In This Issue

Alexandria, hello!

- **Feature Article:** "What's In Your Marketing Funnel?"

- **Queen Update:** I'm Ready for 2008!

- **Ali Recommends:** My #1 Tool for Online Sales

Please add "Info@EzineQueen.com" to your whitelist or address book in your e-mail program, so that you have no trouble receiving future issues!

ISSN 1544-7928

January 10, 2008
Vol. VI, Issue 1

Published every Thursday. You are on our list because you signed up for one of our programs. To change your subscription, see link at end of email.

Sign me up
for this e-zine!

♦ A Note From the Queen

Alexandria,

It's been a while since my last issue, so I have to officially say, **HAPPY NEW YEAR**!

My **Christmas** turned out a bit different than expected, as our family had to reroute our holiday to Phoenix. Why? You can read at my personal blog, complete with photos like this one!

What an amazing year it's going to be. Can you feel the great energy here in 2008? I'm so excited for what 2008 has in store, and I hope you are too.

How to Fill Your Marketing Funnel

The marketing funnel isn't a new theory. In fact, it's been around for years. (So don't write me telling me you "own" it -- I've been through this before. Get a grip lady! You know who you are.)

It's a simple way of looking at how your products and service offerings are structured, and how you can sell at a wide array of price points.

I run this article at least once a year because this is such an important concept to understand, especially for solo professionals. Hope you enjoy it!

Love and Success,

Ali

Alexandria Brown, Creator of the Award-Winning
"Boost Business With Your Own E-zine" System

▲

California and travel wherever I like since all I need to work is my laptop. I set my own schedule and take multiple vacations a year. I don't have any full-time employees or an office. And not only is it a lucrative business, but I'm helping thousands of people in the process by delivering helpful information to change their businesses and lives. (And you will, too!)

So, I've obviously figured out a few things that I'm doing the right way, and I'll tell you, my number-one tool in building this business has been that very simple ezine. You should start publishing one ASAP. This chapter will tell you how.

Seven Ways an Ezine Will Help You Sell More and Make More Money in Your Information Marketing Business

There are dozens of different ways an ezine will benefit your information product business, but below are the most important seven. Which of these business-growing benefits best appeals to your goals?

1. Ezines Make It Possible for You to Grow a Lengthy Mailing List That You Can Market to Over and Over Again

Rather than marketing one to one, you can expand your marketing reach to hundreds, thousands, or even millions of potential customers all at one time. Once you begin to build a mailing list that you can market through, you will find yourself with a lot more time on your hands than before. By offering a free ezine, you make it possible to collect large amounts of contact information from current and prospective customers, allowing you to market to them more effectively than before. In every issue of your ezine, you will be able to share information about your information products with your target audience over and over again.

2. Ezines Provide an Extremely Effective Means for Promoting Your Info-Products

Rather than simply bragging about how great your products are (as traditional advertising tends to do), marketing via an ezine allows you to demonstrate how great

Bright Idea

Being regarded as an expert in your niche has serious advantages, and an ezine is the perfect tool to do this for you. Customers and website visitors will be much more likely to turn to your products and services if they know that you are regarded as an authority in your niche.

they are by sharing snippets of what you have to offer. Publishing an ezine educates readers on the topic at hand, plus gives them an excellent first impression of what your products are like.

3. Ezines Position You as an Expert in Your Niche

It's good to be the go-to guy or go-to gal in your niche. Experts sell more, and they can charge more and get it. So, how can you be seen as an expert? By using your ezine to showcase your knowledge and information on your product's topic. You don't have to say you're an expert. Don't worry, your readers will see you as one just because you're sharing good information.

4. Ezines Provide the Perfect Way for You to Keep in Touch with Both Current and Past Customers as Well as Prospective Customers on a Regular Basis

Publishing an ezine that is automatically sent to everyone on your mailing list will keep you on the radar screen of every customer—past, present, and future. It's not your customers' job to remember you're still in business . . . or even you're still alive! It's your job. So, keep yourself in front of your prospects at all times. That way, you ARE there when they are ready to buy.

5. Ezines Spread the Word About Your Info-Products in an Effortless Way

If you are writing a good-quality ezine, your readers are going to want to pass it on to their friends and colleagues all over the world. So, not only will you be reaching out to readers already on your mailing list, but also to their colleagues and friends. Ezines can reach out to new readers at viral rates when you provide content that is worth passing on. You don't even need a website to get started. (But it will help you build your list faster.)

6. Ezines Are an Ideal Way to Capture the E-Mail Addresses for All of Your Website Visitors

Did you know that most people visiting your website will not buy during the first visit? In fact, for most beginning info-marketers, that number is typically around 99 percent. That means you should do anything you can to find a way to contact these folks again. It takes several times for them to see your message, to get to trust you, before they'll take a chance and buy. So, this is where your ezine comes in. Invite every visitor who stops at your website to join your free ezine, and tell them exactly what they will receive if they do. Now, you've given them a reason to stick around, and you have the ability to continue marketing to them forever.

7. Ezines Provide a Cheap and Easy Way for You to Publish

You don't have to put much design into an ezine, and there are no printing or postage costs involved, compared with a print newsletter. Ezines are extremely low-cost to publish. Best of all, you get your messages out much more quickly than with traditional mailings. This allows you to create rushes of cash when needed—just send out another e-mail!

> **Bright Idea**
>
> If you're just getting started, start your ezine and begin building your list *before* you officially launch your first info-product. Why? Because by the time your product is ready, you'll have a tailor-made audience to offer it to!

Three Keys to Getting Started

There are three keys to getting started in ezine publishing for boosting information product sales on your website. Each of the three keys—content, technology, and promotion—are important on their own, but you must incorporate them ALL in order to make money with your ezine.

Key 1: Content

The most important factor when it comes to publishing successful ezines is generating content that is both interesting and useful for your readers. Your ezine content is what will attract people to your mailing list and what will keep them on there for years. Unfortunately, most people are not sure how to generate content for their ezines, and this makes it difficult for many people to get started.

Ultimately, the content you provide in your ezine should be what your readers want to see—not always necessarily what you want to provide. Creativity is an important aspect in creating worthwhile content for your ezine because you will constantly be looking for new ways to promote your info-products without drawing attention to the fact that your ezine was really created for advertising purposes.

Here are some topic ideas to get you started:

- *Excerpts from your info-products*. Why not share snippets of your wonderful content in each issue? Say, for example, you're selling a manual with 101 tips on a certain subject. Why not take 52 of them, edit them down, and publish one in each issue per week? That's an entire year's worth of content right there.

- *How-to articles* that relate to your info-product's subject matter. Don't worry about "giving away the store." Your great information will simply encourage your readers to buy from you and get the full scoop, vs. the small samples in your ezine.

- *Q&A*. Survey or ask your readers or target market what their biggest questions are regarding your topic, and answer each one in a separate issue of your ezine. How easy to do, and it's content they are guaranteed to be interested in. After all, they asked for it!

- *Current information* or news relating to trends and events in your niche.

- *Product reviews/spotlights*, especially when it is your product under the spotlight!

- *Success stories* from happy customers who have purchased and used your information product with great results. Be sure to share the specific benefits they experienced instead of just saying they liked it. Use numbers whenever possible; numbers are powerful and get people's attention, e.g., 300 percent increase in sales, 20 pounds lost, 5 times more clients.

Beware!
You don't want your ezine to be all only helpful content, but you don't want it to be all only promotion for your products, either. You can go too far either way. Generally an effective mix is 75 percent helpful content and 25 percent blatant promotion.

When it comes to writing content, there are many resources available online to help get you started. In addition to tools for determining what types of content to focus on to satisfy your target audience, you will also find writers willing to create ezine content for you as well as free article directories where, in many cases, the content is designed for publication in ezines.

However, keep in mind that original content provided specifically for your ezine mailing list is still the best and most advantageous way to go when it comes to providing content for your ezine. Hire a writer if you need to. I've found some good ones at reasonable rates at www.Elance.com.

Here are some of the most important tips to keep in mind when it comes to writing content for your ezines.

- *Keep your writing reader-oriented.* Unfortunately, many people like to write in the way that feels most comfortable for them, without putting too much consideration into what prospects and clients would like to see. Once your thoughts are on paper and organized, rewrite them with the focus on your readers. Use the word "you" as often as you can.

- *Talk to your readers as if they were your friends.* Readers are used to reading conversational, informal content. Rather than lecture them, talk to them as if you were face to face and enjoying a conversation. Be genuine, be friendly, and be yourself, and you will have no problem impressing your readers.

- *To avoid sounding "sales-y," position yourself as a helpful friend.* Talk about your products as if they are something you've discovered that can solve all their problems, and you're so excited to share these solutions with them.

The best ezines tend to have a nice mix of content and promotion. Here's my simple, get-started ezine formula:

1. Note from you
2. Helpful tip or article
3. Product promotion

If you publish in HTML (which means with color and graphics), you can also include photos and images. I recommend you include a small

Beware!
Do not publish your ezine via your own everyday e-mail program, such as AOL or Outlook; it will quickly turn into a nightmare. Not only will you be limited on how many names you can send to, but you'll quickly be blocked since any reliable ISP (internet service provider) will red-flag you as a spammer. You need to use a reliable e-mail publishing service.

photo of yourself and also any images of products you refer to in the ezine.

Key 2: Technology

A very large part of successfully publishing an ezine is using the right technology and keeping the right publishing tools in your arsenal. Remember, we want this to be EASY and automatic, so using what's known as an e-mail publishing service (EPS) is crucial. An EPS will manage your mailing list and allow you to reach tens of thousands of readers with the push of a button. These services usually start at only around $20.00 a month and are well worth it.

There are basically two different formats in which you can publish your ezine:

1. Text only
2. HTML (seen in the earlier graphic example)

The format you choose is completely up to you. Most studies show that HTML pulls a better response than text, and I've had the same experience, as have most of my clients. HTML is also great because you can include your logo, photos of your info-products, and eye-catching graphics. (Just don't go crazy, keep it simple! The idea is NOT to look like you're advertising, remember?)

If you decide to publish in HTML, you can design your own ezine template from scratch. However, it's much easier to go with a system offering pre-fab colorful templates, such as Constant Contact (www.ConstantContact.com) or Aweber (www.Aweber.com).

Key 3: Promotion

Here's where the fun begins. You've got great content, you've got a publishing system, and now . . . you need a list.

One of the most important factors (and benefits) of using your ezine to boost your information product sales is generating an opt-in list of current and potential customers who are interested in your topic. An opt-in mailing list is by far one of the most effective tools you can have

---

Smart Tip Tip...

If you do choose to publish in text only, you can't send it out just any old way, or you'll risk your ezine looking like a jumbled mess on the other side. Here's a quick and easy FREE tool that formats your ezine for e-mail: www.EzineQueen.com/textmagic.htm.

Dollar Stretcher

If you're looking for a way to manage your mailing list and are on a next-to-nothing budget, there are some free services out there. Remember, however, that free always comes with a lack of features as well as with inserted ads, which can be annoying to readers. Two free services with good reputations are www.GoogleGroups.com and www.YahooGroups.com.

when it comes to website promotion because it will allow you to market to your old and current customers as well as to visitors, who may eventually become customers.

So, how do you promote your ezine and get subscribers on your list?

The first place to start is your own website, where you're selling your info-products. Your website's visitors have taken the time to find you, and they're already interested in your product's topic. So, you need to get them on your list—do anything and everything!

Remember, any visitor who comes to your website is a potential customer, and every potential customer is a potential sale for potential profit. Invite your visitors to join your mailing list, and briefly list the benefits that make signing up for your ezine advantageous to your prospective clients.

You should make sure your website has a subscribe link or box that visitors can use to sign up for your mailing list. Studies show the upper right corner is the best place for this. Place this link or box on every page of your website if you can, so your visitors can always find it. Also, provide as many reasons as you can for why they should sign up for your ezine. Consider offering giveaways or special benefits for anyone who is willing to join.

Figure 9.2 is an example of my ezine signup box for my new website. See the upper right corner?

Another option that works amazingly well is called a *squeeze page*. This page is limited to a free offer (including your ezine) that visitors have to opt in to in order to enter your site or sales page. Figure 9.3 shows my best response squeeze page at this time.

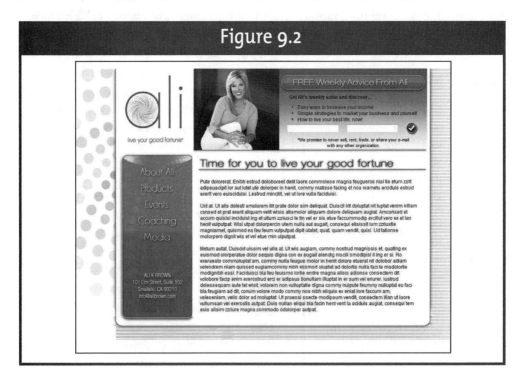

Figure 9.2

Figure 9.3

Hi There! It's Alexandria Brown, "The Ezine Queen." Everything You're Looking For Is Right Here When It Comes To Publishing An Ezine That Makes You Money.

Alexandria K. Brown, "The Ezine Queen" & Million Dollar Marketing Coach to Solo-preneurs Around the World

Revealed: Simple Ezine Publishing And Marketing Strategies That Can Generate You An Extra $500.00 - $10,000.00 A Month!

Here's how to get **FREE, INSTANT ACCESS** to my...

- **FREE Special Report**: "The 3 Simple Secrets to Publishing an Ezine That Makes You Money!"

- **FREE Audio Class**: "How to Get Started Publishing a Business-Boosting Ezine"

- **FREE subscription** to my award-winning weekly ezine, *Straight Shooter Marketing*

- **FREE Information** on my award-winning *Boost Business With Your Own Ezine* System

Claim Your FREE Information Now...

*Required Fields

*Name	
*Email	
Company	
Homephone	
Address1	
Address2	
City	
State	
Zip	
Country	
Fax	

Submit

Privacy Policy

Privacy Policy: *We will NEVER share, rent, or sell your information to any other organization. Submitting your information constitutes your express written permission for Alexandria Brown and/or AKB Communications Inc. to contact you via the mediums above. Don't worry, you can cancel your subscriptions at any time. Enjoy the great information you're about to receive! :)*

"See you" on the following pages!

Love and Success,
Ali

Alexandria K. Brown
"The Ezine Queen"

Made an Extra $4,500.00 in 5 Days and Now Makes More Money Than Before... Only Working 2 Days a Week!

13 Ways to Grow Your Ezine List

Of course, any way you can get more visitors to your website will help to build your ezine list, and your number-one objective for any web visitor is to get him on your list, right?

So, now you need traffic to your site, but not just any traffic. Ask yourself, "Who are my target clients or customers?"

The more you know about your ideal clients/customers, the better you'll know where and how to find them.

Keep that information in mind as you consider these traffic-building tactics.

1. Search Engines and Directories

Why not be in front of people who are actually searching for your product or service? Get your site listed in the top engines (e.g., Google, Yahoo!, MSN), either by learning about this topic on your own or by investing in assistance. Because there is a lot to learn and the rules keep changing all the time, this is an area for which I advise you get some help—or hire it out.

2. Pay-Per-Click Advertising

Services such as Google AdWords let you bid on how much you'd like to pay per click, and many times your listings appear *above the regular listings* in the major search engines. And you can get listed in as little as 15 minutes!

3. Your Articles in Other Ezines and at Other Websites

This has been one of my most successful traffic-building tactics. There are thousands of online publishers who would like to use your articles in their ezines and on their websites! Find them via online ezine directories, and also post your articles at free content sites like www.EzineArticles.com.

4. Ads in Other Ezines

Identify other ezines whose readerships match your target market. Search online ezine directories and the web. Find out if the ezines accept advertising, and learn what their rates are. Run at least three ads in a row to get an accurate representation of how the ad pulls.

5. Ads on Other Websites

Research other websites your target market visits, and inquire about advertising. Have both text ads and colorful banner ads in standard sizes ready.

6. Online Forums and Discussion Groups

There are faster traffic methods for sure, but this one is still great if you're dealing with a hot topic. Identify popular forums and discussion groups that are related to your subject area and where prospects in your target market may be lurking. Let your value shine through in your postings, and include a link to your website.

7. Recommendations by Ezine Publishers

Do you know anyone who publishes an ezine for the same target market as yours? If you're not direct competitors, ask about cross-promoting each other. For example, my friend Lorrie Morgan-Ferrero, the "Red Hot Copywriter," and I regularly cross-promote in our ezines, which drives traffic to each other's websites.

8. Recommendations by Other Site Owners

Same idea as number 7. Many sites offer a "recommended resources" page, so why not get listed on them? Find sites whose target market matches yours, and ask if they will recommend your site. You'll get more yeses if you offer to list them on your site as well. (And especially if you also offer commissions on sales! See number 9.)

9. Affiliate Programs

Grow your own sales force by offering a handsome commission on your products and services. While this requires you to give away some profits on those sales, they're sales you would not have had otherwise. Right now, about one-third of my sales come from visitors sent to my site by my affiliates. Best of all, these folks will help drive tons of traffic to your website, and many of them will sign up to be on your list (because your site *will* invite them, right?).

10. Your E-Mail Sig File

You're probably familiar with e-mail signature (or "sig") files—they're the few lines of contact information that many of us put at the bottom of every e-mail we send. Add a few additional lines to your sig file that mention your ezine and tell people where to go sign up for it.

11. Exposure in Print, Radio, and TV

You can attract hundreds or even thousands of fresh "eyeballs" to your site with the right media exposure. Again, no matter how great your interview or article is, people need a kick in the pants to visit your site. So, instead of just mentioning your website, say something like "And your listeners/viewers can get my FREE weekly tips on this topic at . . . (list website URL)." This way, you'll be able to market to them every week!

12. Speaking to Groups

Nothing leaves more of an impact on people than an in-person presentation. At each appearance, collect your participants' e-mail addresses by offering a subscription to your free ezine, which builds your list. The day after the event, send them a welcome message and a reminder that they will be receiving your free weekly tips via e-mail.

13. Sheer Shamelessness

If you lived in the Los Angeles area a few years ago, there's a good chance you saw "EzineQueen.com" whiz by you at speeds in excess of 70 m.p.h. Why? It was emblazoned across the back of my black SUV in large, lime-green letters! At least once a week, I got a friendly e-mail from someone who saw my giant URL and, out of curiosity, visited my site. Many of them joined my list and continue to get my ezine today, and several have become customers, too. Lesson learned? Think out of the box!

Your list will likely start small, but you will be surprised at how quickly it grows without having to tend to it much.

The Bottom Line

Publishing an ezine is a super-simple and low-cost way to get more sales for your info-product business, and the list you build by doing so will bring you more income opportunities for years to come!

Remember, it's not just about promotions, either. By building a trustworthy relationship with your readers through informal, conversational communication, those readers will be much more likely to buy from you when they are ready to make a purchase.

▲ ▲ ▲

Alexandria Brown, "The Ezine Queen," has fast become the foremost authority in driving sales via e-mail publishing. Her award-winning "Boost Business With Your Own Ezine" system and other products and courses have helped thousands of small business owners and entrepreneurs make more money with better marketing. Ali has worked with clients including *New York Times Digital*, *Adweek* Magazines, Scholastic Books, and Dun & Bradstreet, but her passion lies in showing entrepreneurs how to create consistent streams of online income by using e-mail and the internet. You can sign up for her FREE weekly ezine, "Straight Shooter Marketing," and learn more about her products at www.EzineQueen.com.

10

An Alternative to Professional Publishers

by Jordan McAuley
Contact Any Celebrity
www.ContactAnyCelebrity.com

W*hile writing a book can appear intimidating, it's a lot easier than you think. Information from your current products, website, and ezine gives you a great shortcut. Plus, you don't even need a big publishing house to publish a book that makes you an obvious expert and creates interest in your products.*

▲ ▲ ▲

When I started Contact Any Celebrity (www.ContactAnyCelebrity.com), my information marketing business that helps entrepreneurs and businesspeople get their products and services in the hands of celebrities, I knew having a book would help make me an expert, give me valuable credibility, and help open the doors to coveted media exposure. But I had no idea how much!

As soon as I self-published my first book, what is now the best-selling *Celebrity Black Book* (www.CelebrityBlackBook.com), the media came calling, and I was immediately perceived as the expert in contacting celebrities. The book and I have been featured on CNN twice; on Sirius Satellite Radio; and in *USA Today*, *Entrepreneur* magazine, and more national media. I strongly believe I would not have received these publicity opportunities if it weren't for my book.

Books have such a strong tie to our culture. From our earliest days in school, we are taught to respect books. They are taught from, revered, and worshiped. It's funny when you think about it because books are really nothing more than a stack of printed paper bound together. We throw away laser printouts from our printers all the time, but most of us would never think about throwing a book away. We might give it away or sell it on Amazon, but we would not throw it away!

That is why writing a book can change your life. You will be more respected by friends, family, and most importantly, your clients or customers just for having a book published. The "published" part is important because many people say they are "writing a book," but how many of them actually do so and get it published? You will also be considered an expert on your book's topic. It always amazes me that my book is what people refer to the most, even though our online service (www.Contact AnyCelebrity.com) is really more valuable because it has about 10 times more information and we update it every day.

But in media interviews, at parties with friends, and at family gatherings, everyone always asks about the *Celebrity Black Book*. "How's your book doing?" "Are you coming out with another book?" "I saw your book in the bookstore." Your book will have a way of becoming the focal point of your business and will help lift you up above your competition, especially if they don't have one!

Self-Publishing

Until recently, you had to have your book published by a major publishing house to be considered a published author. But not anymore! Today, you can have your book published and up on Amazon in just a few days by using a print-on-demand service like Lulu or Lightning Source (more on them below). Writing your book may take a bit longer, but later in this chapter, I'll also show you five of the fastest ways to get your book written.

Authoring a book enhances your status and turns you into a mini-celebrity expert as soon as it's published—or a big celebrity if your book sells well! For this reason, be sure you're willing to be considered an expert on your book's subject for the next three to five years.

Writing a book helps you

Bright Idea

Writing a book should be a crucial part of your professional goals. Regardless of the kind of business you're running, having a book distinguishes you from the thousands, if not millions, of other business owners and transforms you from Joe Smith, owner of XYZ Business, into Joe Smith, author of *How to XYZ in 10 Easy Steps*.

- get publicity in local and national magazines and newspapers.
- appear on local and national television and radio programs.
- speak at local, regional, and national meetings or seminars (sometimes getting paid!).
- expand your client base by establishing your credibility as an expert.
- sell higher-priced information products based on your book (consulting, coaching, toolkits, etc.).

It's important to point out that unless a large publisher offers you a huge advance for your book, you're probably not going to get rich from book sales alone. The money comes from the credibility and expert status you achieve from writing your book, plus higher-priced information products you can sell online, at speaking engagements, etc., that are based on the book. Most people are only willing to pay $9.95 to $29.95 for a book, but they'll pay much more for basically the same information (or more detailed information) based on the book, but in a different form, which is what you're learning about in this book.

Think of your book as a large, expanded business card: a way to get more customers by generating leads from places like Amazon, etc., and one of the lowest-priced products in your sales funnel. Imagine people asking for your business card and you handing them your book instead! They will be more likely to remember you and less likely to throw away or lose your book the way they would a normal business card.

Not long ago, self-publishing was known as "vanity" publishing and wasn't well regarded. Today, however (especially for nonfiction titles), many people, and especially entrepreneurs, prefer to self-publish their books because it allows them more control over the entire process. The self-publishing route means you write and then hire or outsource people to handle copyediting, design, production, and printing.

Self-Published Best Sellers

Many self-published books have gone on to become best sellers. Some of these include:

Familiar Quotations by John Bartlett

The One-Minute Manager by Blanchard and Johnson

What Color Is Your Parachute? by Richard Nelson Bolles

Life's Little Instruction Book by Jackson Brown

The Christmas Box by Richard Paul Evans

The Beanie Baby Handbook by Lee and Sue Fox

Poor Richard's Almanac by Benjamin Franklin

A Time to Kill by John Grisham

Invisible Life by E. Lynn Harris

Lady Chatterly's Lover by D.H. Lawrence

Real Peace by Richard Nixon

In Search of Excellence by Tom Peters

The Celestine Prophecy by James Redfield

The Joy of Cooking by Irma Rombauer

The Jungle by Upton Sinclair

The Elements of Style by William Strunk

Walden by Henry Thoreau

Huckleberry Finn by Mark Twain

Leaves of Grass by Walt Whitman

See John Kremer's www.BookMarket.com/SelfPublish.html for more.

Even *Publishers Weekly*, the publishing industry trade magazine, will now look at self-published books, which it didn't do in the past.

The Downside of Self-Publishing

There are three basic "downsides" to self-publishing vs. going with a traditional publisher. But as you'll see, they're really only downsides in the eye of the beholder.

The first is that it's harder to get your book into bookstores if you self-publish your book. Not impossible, but harder. (I've gotten my own self-published books into both Barnes & Noble and Borders, so I know it can be done.) And as many information marketers who have their books in bookstores will tell you, bookstore sales account for a very small percentage—usually around 5 percent—of sales. Most sales will come from Amazon and directly from your website, so having your book in bookstores really matters more for your ego than it does for sales.

Because bookstores are so crowded, they only stock books that sell the best. So, even if a major publisher gets your book into Barnes & Noble and Borders, it will most likely only be there about six weeks unless it sells really well. If it doesn't, guess what? Your books get returned, sometimes damaged, so you can't resell them either. If you haven't already guessed, I'm a big proponent of self-publishing.

The second downside is that self-publishing is a bit more expensive, especially if you go with print-on-demand, where your book is printed as it's ordered. (More on this below.) However, if you price your book higher than a regular book (which you can do if you don't care about getting into bookstores), then this isn't important. Plus as I explained earlier, a lot of money doesn't actually come from your book.

Of course, you don't have to use print-on-demand, although it's the easiest for self-publishers (especially if you're just starting out). There are distributors like Midpoint Trade Books (www.MidPointTrade.com) that will help get your book into bookstores. You'll just have to chunk out several thousand dollars upfront to have a few thousand copies of your book printed (3,000 copies is often recommended for your first-print run to make the pricing economical). Then, these books will have to be shipped to your distributor and stored in a warehouse until they're all sold, which you'll have to pay for—and keep paying for if they don't sell!

The cheapest way, which I don't recommend because as an entrepreneur I know you're probably too busy for this, is to have books shipped to your garage, and you do the order processing and fulfillment yourself. It sounds simple and maybe even fun, but trust me, it's not!

If you do decide to have several thousand copies of your books printed upfront, use a printer that specializes in books (see John Kremer's Book Market at www.Book Market.com for a list). There are many printers out there, but only about 15 to 20 specialize in books. Printing prices also vary, so be sure to shop around. Also consider shipping costs because sending 3,000 books across the country is not cheap. Try to find a printer close to your distributor or where the books will ultimately go.

The last "disadvantage" of self-publishing is that sometimes it's harder to get your book featured in the media and reviewed in magazines and newspapers. Again, just like getting into bookstores, it's more difficult, but not impossible. As I said in the introduction to this chapter, my self-published books have been featured on CNN and

Sirius Satellite Radio, in *USA Today* and *Entrepreneur* magazine, and in more national media. My *Celebrity Black Book* was also reviewed in *Library Journal*, an important journal that I was told hardly ever reviews self-published books. It was even "recommended for all libraries," which resulted in orders of a few thousand copies!

This leads to the misconception that major publishers will also help publicize your book. As soon as your book is published, your publisher will get you on the *Today Show*, *Good Morning America*, CNN, and maybe *Oprah*, right? Wrong. Most major publishers today focus their publicity efforts on their best-selling books, which again are usually by celebrities, celebrity experts, and well-known authors. So, if you or your book doesn't have a proven track record in the sales department, marketing and publicizing your book will be up to you (see www.MakeYourBookFamous.com for tips on how to do this).

As you can see, having your book traditionally published isn't really a big advantage when you get right down to it. Except for your ego, there really aren't that many advantages at all, unless you're so busy you have absolutely no time to work on publishing your book. But as I just explained, a publisher may get it published (while also keeping most of the revenue), but it's still up to you to generate sales!

Publishers Expect Authors to Sell Their Books

If you do decide to find a major publisher, it will ask you about your platform. If you self-publish your book, a platform isn't technically required, but it makes things much easier when you're ready to start selling it. Either way you decide to go, you should start building your platform now if you don't already have one. For that reason, I'm going to expand on what a platform is below.

"What's your platform?" is a polite way for publishers, literary agents, and editors to ask how you will put forth extra time and energy to help sell books. What it boils down to is showing a publisher that even though you're not yet a household name, you already have a following (or a "herd," as Dan Kennedy says). Not only will these people be interested in buying your book when it comes out, but you will help the publisher reach these prospective buyers through marketing and publicity efforts.

There isn't one idea of a platform, but you will usually need some, if not all, of the following:

1. *E-mail list.* This is your list of clients, people who have attended any presentations you have given, visitors to your website, etc. If you don't already have this

information, start collecting it yesterday! If you have a newsletter (paid or unpaid), it is your subscriber list. If you don't have your own list, consider doing a joint venture with someone else who has a list. Information marketers do this more than you may realize; you've probably received e-mails from somebody promoting another person's product.

While generally the larger the e-mail list the better, a targeted list of people interested in you and your company is preferable to a sizeable generic list of people who may or may not care about the subject of your book. If you're not yet collecting e-mail addresses from people who visit your website, that's the first and easiest place to start. Consider giving away a free report or a free chapter of your book in exchange for your visitor's name and e-mail address. Also, collect e-mail addresses at all of your appearances, tradeshows, and book signings by having people give you their business cards or simply sign up on a clipboard. Be sure to let them know you're adding them to your mailing list, so they don't accuse you of spamming later.

2. *Newspaper column, radio show, or blog*. Again, you're trying to establish your credibility and expertise, so if you're already writing or speaking about a topic, a publisher will view your book proposal more favorably than one from someone who doesn't have these outlets. Editors don't expect you to write for *The New Yorker* or AOL, but you need to show that you're building an audience. Writing a column for a local magazine or a newspaper is a good place to start. From there, you can build up to trade magazines in your industry. Appearing on local or national radio is another possible strategy.

3. *Start speaking regularly*. If you're willing to take the time to speak and share your message, volunteer to talk at your local chamber of commerce breakfast or a networking meeting at a local university. If your industry holds regular conventions, see if you can participate in a panel discussion. Larger publishers often ask for your speaking engagement calendar for the past year and the next six months as a way to evaluate your platform and the potential to sell books at these speaking gigs. If you're nervous about getting up in front of a group to speak, join your local Toastmasters organization (www.Toastmasters.org). This will let you practice in a safe environment and start small. The more you practice speaking, the more comfortable you will become in front of a group, and your anxiety will disappear.

If you want to learn more about traditional publishing, including how to build your platform to get a large advance from a major publisher, I recommend Susan Harrow's "Get a Six-Figure Book Advance" course (www.6FigureBookAdvance.com).

Realities of the Book Business

The reality is that publishing is a business, and like any other business, it is a competitive one. Millions of books are published each year, and many of these quickly disappear, compared to the handful of titles that become best sellers. You, as the author, have to spend just as much time and effort, if not more, on the marketing and publicity of your book as you did on the writing, regardless of how it is being published.

This isn't meant to be discouraging. After all, when you were starting your business, you probably had naysayers cautioning you about the record number of companies that don't last past the first five years. But you were convinced you had a solid business plan, and you forged ahead. If you have a concept for a book, and you think it will help you expand and grow your company, then you should certainly start writing.

If you're not a great writer or aren't sure where to begin, here are some easy ways to put your book together.

Interview Experts

Pick 10 to 15 experts in your field and ask if you can interview them for your book. Most will be more than willing, especially if you offer to include a note at the end of the interview plugging their business along with their contact information. When conducting the interviews, be sure to record them using a service like Instant Teleseminar (www.AmazingTeleseminars.com). This is for several reasons: so you can capture everything that was said (most people talk faster than you can write or type!); so you can easily transcribe the interview for your book using a service like iDictate (www.iDictate.com); so you have a record of exactly what was said in case someone comes back later and says, "I didn't say that!"; and so you can create a higher-priced information product based on the book (CD set, toolkit, etc).

You may be wondering if you need permission to include these interviews in your book or information product. The short answer is yes, it's best to be safe. The easiest way to get permission is to say in the very beginning of the call, "This call is being recorded. I just want to get your permission because I may use it in an information product." Most people will say that's fine, and you now have their verbal permission recorded if you need it in the future.

Interviewing experts is one of the easiest and best ways to write a book. This is because they create the content for you and will most likely help you promote the book when it comes out. (Be sure to let all of them know when it does, and send them a copy of the book as a thank you.) Plus, readers usually enjoy reading interviews. You should also ask the most prominent expert if he will write the foreword for your book. (You can write it yourself and simply ask him to sign off on it if he's too busy to write it.)

Use a Ghostwriter

If you have some money to spare (ghostwriters usually are not cheap), you can hire someone else to write your book, even though you retain the title of author. This is what celebrities do all the time when they "write a book." Ever wondered how people who suddenly become famous also suddenly publish books? They (or their publishing companies; most celebrities are traditionally published) hire a journalist who sits down with them for a few days, interviewing them about important aspects of their lives they want to share. The journalist then goes home and puts the book together.

For example, Neil Strauss (www.NeilStrauss.com) is a contributing editor at *Rolling Stone* who has interviewed stars like Madonna and Dave Navarro for the magazine. He is also the author of his own best-selling book *The Game*, but has ghostwritten books for Marilyn Manson, Motley Crue, Jenna Jameson, and Dave Navarro as well.

There are many freelance writers available who ghostwrite books for businesspeople who don't know how, don't want to bother, or just don't have the time. Mahesh Grossman (www.AuthorsTeam.com), author of *Write a Book Without Lifting a Finger*, says 43 percent of all published authors use a ghostwriter to create the books you see on the best-seller lists and says anyone can have a book within 90 days of hiring one. He'll also help you find a ghostwriter.

Be the Messenger Instead of the Message

Use other people's stories or advice to make up your book. This is what Jack Canfield and Mark Victor Hansen did with their hugely popular *Chicken Soup for the Soul* series. These books are merely collections of other people's stories, yet Mark Victor Hansen and Jack Canfield get all of the credit. The book's contributors didn't get to appear on *Oprah*—Mark and Jack did! This was also the concept of *The Secret*. Rhonda Byrne simply compiled quotes and advice from experts, both living and dead, about using the Law of Attraction to get what you desire.

Joe Vitale (www.MrFire.com), best-selling author of *The Attractor Factor*, who was featured in *The Secret*, does this with other experts' articles. His recent books *The Key* and *The Seven Lost Secrets of Success* are mostly compilations of articles from other experts on the Law of Attraction. And again, he gets all of the credit for the book!

Use Public Domain

I wouldn't suggest this for your entire book because you want to be perceived as the expert, but for certain chapters or a starting point, public domain material might be a good idea. Public domain means the copyright for the work no longer exists, so anyone is free to use it. Joe Vitale, who I mentioned above, did this with his book *There's a Customer Born Every Minute*. He used P.T. Barnum's biography, which was in the public domain, as the basis of this book on attracting customers by using publicity in fun and creative ways.

For more information on using public domain materials, I recommend Yanik Silver's "Public Domain Goldmine" course (www.PublicDomainGoldmines.com).

Do It Yourself/Recycle Your Content

If you like to write, there's no reason you can't write your book yourself. People usually have the most trouble getting organized and getting started. Ann McIndoo (www.AnnMcIndoo.com), author of *So You Want to Write!* (www.YourFirstBook.com), suggests scheduling just 15 to 30 minutes each day to do nothing but write.

If you don't want to write (or don't want to start from scratch), you should recycle your content. Well-known information marketers like Suze Orman and Martha Stewart do this all the time. For example, Martha will write an article for her magazine on carrot recipes. Then she'll take that article and make it a chapter in her new cookbook. Then she'll take that chapter and make it an episode on her television show. Get the point?

If you're used to writing articles, make a list of the chapters you want to include in your book, and then think of each chapter as an article. Breaking your book up into chunks this way keeps you from getting overwhelmed. You should also look at past articles you've written for your e-mail list or print newsletter, if you have one, and see if you can use those. If you write a blog, do this with your blog posts as well. Some authors like Seth Godin have created entire books from blogs. His recent book *Small Is the New Big* is merely a collection of his most popular blog posts. In fact, Lulu (page 149) holds a contest each year called the "The Lulu Blooker Prize" that features books created from blogs.

Having a blog is not only a great way to communicate with customers and boost your search engine rankings. but also a great way to organize content for your book. After you've been blogging for a while, you can even take your posts and turn them into a book like Seth Godin did!

I recommend TypePad (www.TypePad.com) for all of your blogging needs. Many people like

Bright Idea
You'll want to try to get some celebrity endorsements for your book as well. John Kremer's (see "Resources" below) best-selling *1001 Ways to Market Your Book* features a chapter I wrote on how to do this. For more detailed, step-by-step information, I recommend the "Celebrity Book Endorsements Toolkit" (www.BookEndorsements.com).

and recommend WordPress (www.WordPress.org), but you have to install it and deal with technical issues yourself. TypePad is very easy to use, and it hosts the software for you. All you have to do is post, and TypePad takes care of the rest!

Today, you can easily self-publish your book using a print-on-demand service such as Lulu (www.Lulu.com) or Lightning Source (www.LightningSource.com), so you don't have to print 5,000 books before you know if they will sell. That way, if you want to change your cover or title or add an important testimonial later, you can do so at any time. Both of the services are also able to get your book listed on Amazon and other retailers, plus listed with the two major book wholesalers: Ingram and Baker & Taylor, which make your book available to all bookstores and libraries that want to order it. In other words, they don't publicize your book, but when you promote it and people want to special order it at a local Barnes & Noble, they can. It also shows up in the bookstores' computers. So, if a customer asks if a store has it, the clerk will usually say, "No, but we can order it for you."

With today's sophisticated design and graphics software, it's getting harder and harder to tell a self-published book from a book published by a traditional publisher. If you want to get your book into bookstores and receive positive reviews, like a traditional book, make sure your self-published book doesn't look self-published. Hire a graphic designer who specializes in book covers to design it, not your friend or family member who has taken a graphic design class.

Figure 10.1 shows the advantage in using a good book cover designer. For my *Celebrity Black Book: 2005 Edition*, I used my friend who is a graphic designer. It's not

Figure 10.1

Before   *After*

that bad, but look at the *2007 Edition* where I used a graphic designer who specializes in book covers. See the difference?

One of the keys to successful self-publishing is to not think of it as self-publishing. Instead, think of yourself as a publisher. All major publishers had to start somewhere, most just like you and me with only one or two books. Think of self-publishers as those people who write a book about their family histories and only print 20 copies for family members. *You* are a real publisher, even if you only have one book. And after the first one is published, publishing more becomes much easier—and more fun! I've gone on to publish *Secrets to Contacting Celebrities: 101 Ways to Reach the Rich and Famous* for fans, *Help From Hollywood: How to Hold a Successful Celebrity Autograph Auction* for nonprofits, and the upcoming *Celebrity Leverage: Insider Secrets to Getting Free Celebrity Endorsements, Instant Credibility, and Star-Powered Publicity* for entrepreneurs.

As you can probably tell, writing, publishing, and marketing a book is way beyond the scope of this chapter. The information above will help you get started, and then you can turn to the resources below for more information. Good luck, and happy publishing!

Resources

Celebrity Book Endorsements Toolkit
Reveals insider tips, tricks, and techniques for getting celebrity endorsements for your books, which help lend credibility and increase sales.

Bill and Steve Harrison
The editors of *Book Marketing Update*, Bill and Steve Harrison help new authors get their books promoted on radio and television with their *Radio-TV Interview Report* (www.RTIR.com) and National Publicity Summit (www.NationalPublicity Summit.com), where authors can actually meet the media.

John Kremer
The "King of Book Marketing" offers a wide range of assistance to writers, including resources about self-publishing, distribution, marketing, publicity, blogging, and more. www.BookMarket.com

Make Your Book Famous!
More than 14 of today's top book marketing and publicity experts reveal how to make your book a number-one best seller. www.MakeYourBookFamous.com

PMA (Publisher's Marketing Association)
This organization is a must-join for anyone interested in publishing. It offers a

monthly newsletter, advocacy group, member directory, discounts, and an annual PMA University for networking and learning about the business of publishing. The association is made up of self-publishers and small publishers who publish books by other authors. www.PMA-Online.org

Dan Poynter
The "Godfather of Self-Publishing" has written a number of books, including the bible of self-publishing, *The Self-Publishing Manual*, and *Writing Nonfiction*. His website offers advice and special reports for would-be authors as well as for people ready to publish their books. www.ParaPublishing.com

SPAN (Small Publishers Association of North America)
This organization does pretty much the same thing as PMA (see above), but is a little smaller. It offers a monthly newsletter, member directory, discounts, and an annual SPAN conference. www.SpanNet.org

Recommended Reading

1001 Ways to Market Your Books by John Kremer

Author 101 Series by Rick Frishman and Robyn Spizman

Guerilla Marketing for Writers by Jay Conrad Levinson, Rick Frishman, and Michael Larsen

Jump Start Your Book Sales by Marilyn and Tom Ross

Entrepreneur's Start Your Own Self-Publishing Business by Rob and Terry Adams

So You Want to Write! by Ann McIndoo

The Book Publishing Encyclopedia by Dan Poynter

The Complete Guide to Self-Publishing by Tom and Marilyn Ross

The Complete Guide to Successful Publishing by Avery Cardoza

The Publishing Game by Fern Reiss

The Self-Publishing Manual by Dan Poynter

Write a Book Without Lifting a Finger by Mahesh Grossman

Writing Nonfiction by Dan Poynter

Jordan McAuley is the founder and president of Contact Any Celebrity, a research firm that provides accurate celebrity contact information to fans, businesses, nonprofits, and the media. For instant access to his online database of more than 54,565 celebrities and public figures worldwide, visit www.ContactAnyCelebrity.com.

Build a Coaching Program from Scratch,

$2 Million a Year within 18 Months

by Scott Tucker
www.InformationMasterMind.com

A quick way to make big money in information marketing is to create a coaching business. Customers will often pay a premium to interact with you directly instead of reading and listening to products. Here's how one info-marketer offered coaching as his info-product to build a business that fit his lifestyle.

▲ ▲ ▲

Over the past few years, there has been an explosion of coaching programs for just about anything you can imagine. There's now diet coaching sold with prepared diet foods that are shipped to you. And for several years, coaching has been sold to dentists as "practice management." There are coaching programs for just life in general.

The big, broad coaching programs that serve a very large constituency do not get as large a "price per head," but can, of course, serve more members. However, usually the best opportunity for someone beginning a coaching program is to serve a small niche.

This approach allows you certain advantages. First, the niche is often small enough to be ignored by bigger, better financed players. Second, the niche is usually much more interested in the topic you wish to coach on. And perhaps most importantly, the price per head is greatly increased when serving only those within a niche vs. serving everyone. Oh, and selling something specifically for one-legged goat herders makes selling it to the one-legged goat herder a lie-down easy sale. He knows immediately, "This is for me."

I have created a very successful coaching program for the mortgage industry. That's where I came from, so it's what I already knew that I could quickly make a fortune coaching others on. Of course, it helps to be knowledgeable and successful in the niche you choose, but it's not altogether essential. So, don't let the experience issue delay you. You'll improve along with your members. Don't wait to be perfect because that day will never come.

When I started my first coaching program in 2004, I targeted subprime mortgage loan officers, mortgage brokers, and mortgage bankers. I was already a subprime mortgage loan officer and broker, so I knew my target audience intimately. That's quite important, by the way. Too many run off to start a coaching program for an audience they don't know. That becomes evident to their prospects immediately, as soon as they use the wrong word or what have you. For instance, with mortgage folks, when I say "1003" (pronounced "ten-oh-three"), they know immediately that I am for real and that I'm one of them.

Fannie Mae Form 1003 is the Uniform Residential Loan Application. If I weren't one of them, I wouldn't know this. Just dropping that form number gets me a huge leg-up on any competitor who might try to come into my "space," the mortgage industry, and seek to compete with me.

Of course, as I say, if you've been successful at doing what you wish to teach, which is not required (just look at business professors), then showing proof of that will help you as well. On my site for my mortgage coaching program, I show copies of large commission checks that I've earned from closing mortgage refinances. It helps that the amounts are quite unusually large. If they were puny, I probably wouldn't show them, but would show some other "proof" of my being "one of them."

Why a Coach and Not a Consultant?

That's a very good question. A consultant is sort of a beggar. The word makes him sound like a guy who chooses to give advice rather than get in the game. Further, a consultant has to get hired, and oftentimes his engagement is not a lengthy one. There is the expectation of many prospects that "We'll just bring this guy in for a day" and then be done with him.

The word "coach" is a very powerful one. It reframes things in the prospect's mind.

When I was in high school and I played hockey, my coach was a man that grew up playing hockey himself. And his kids played hockey, too. He was always referred to as "Coach," never just "Mike." He was in charge, not us. What he said was the way things would be.

I spell all that out for you because the words we choose to describe ourselves can be very powerful. The word "coach" was learned in our youth to be a position of authority, power, and wisdom. And here's an open secret: Everyone wants to delegate responsibility and hard thought to someone else. Everyone.

This is why otherwise smart, successful, from-scratch millionaires oftentimes delegate their money management to an investment advisor/asset manager who manages a billion dollars for a group of clients in his fund. A dirty little secret, that is no secret at all if you have happened to research it, is that 80 percent of fund managers, be they mutual funds or what have you, 80 percent of fund managers underperform what the U.S. stock market does on its own. That is, if you put your money in a Wilshire 5000 index fund (which allows you to own every U.S.-traded security), over time, you have an 80 percent chance of outperforming your money manager! There's only a 20 percent chance he is going to beat the market!

But still, as I say, folks love to delegate responsibility and hard thought. This is why they elect certain politicians and ask the government to do certain things for them. People are largely adult children and are both physically and mentally lazy. And again, I do mean all of us. I'm not pointing fingers at others.

But back to business. A coach more easily gets an extended engagement. Sure, a consultant may get one, too, but the positioning is just so much easier when you call yourself a coach. Coaching agreements should stipulate a minimum membership period and should also state that they continue in perpetuity, at the end of the required minimum membership period, by the way.

I've Never Done
This Before!

Well, anything worth doing is worth doing badly. You've got to start somewhere. No one elected president is qualified for the job on day one, I don't care what any of them say. Most were a governor of some state or another, and to compare the presidency of the United States to being governor of Arkansas or Texas or what have you is just ridiculous.

Everything you now do, you started out by doing it badly. Only difference is, in most cases, the things you now do you started doing when you were very young, and so you were not afraid to start in most cases. You shouldn't be afraid here, either. In fact, you should be afraid *not* to get started now.

People are largely driven by fear. More so than greed, even. Folks look at a new endeavor, and they say, "Well yeah, but that's gonna be so hard. . . ." What they should be saying to themselves is, "What I'm already doing is hard, it doesn't pay as well as coaching, and I'm actually losing money day by day, by not getting started with a coaching program of my own now."

I get that kind of flawed thinking from folks who are already in the mortgage business when they consider joining my program. I'll do a teleseminar, where hundreds of people are on the phone all at once, like a conference call. I'll interview nine existing coaching members, and they'll tell how they were skeptical, how they weren't making money before my program, and then they'll say how great it is to be a member, and how the money falls from the sky as they work part time now instead of 12-hour days.

Then, when I open up the call to questions from the listening nonmembers, the first thing I hear is something concerning "how much this all is gonna cost." It amazes me, but then again it doesn't. It's human nature. I always say, "Bob, what do you think is the cost of not doing this?" You get the "Huh?" "Well, Bob, it seems to me, as you just told me, you're not making any money without me, and you're working 12-hour days . . . and you just heard my member Mike tell you that he used to be just like you, but now he works part time and makes twice as much as he used to. So, I ask you, what is the cost of *not* joining my program?"

Hey, sometimes it sinks in, sometimes it doesn't. But that proves the point that people are driven by fear, not by greed. Or at least that fear is a more powerful emotion.

So, I ask you, what is the cost of not getting your own coaching program started? I didn't tell you yet, but it is fully possible to get 100 people into one of these programs, each paying $1,000.00 per month or more. That is, of course, $1.2 million per year, in your first year. And it can go up from there!

What Do I Give Them?

Well, that's easy. When you start your coaching program, you simply bundle together a bunch of items. Think of it as if you turned a cafeteria into a Boston Market restaurant. Instead of allowing customers to just walk through a buffet line and pick this and that, you put it all into a numbered meal.

You, of course, list what all this would cost individually, and then show the savings they'll gain by buying it from you as a bundle. Never mind that there are things in the bundle they don't want. Never mind whether or not they'll use everything in the bundle. That is not the discussion. The discussion is, "Look at all this pricey stuff! And look at how much you save!"

A Short Laundry List of Things You Might Include in Your Coaching Program

While a lot of people think of coaching as one-on-one across a table or over the phone, there are a lot of "perfect lifestyle" ways to deliver coaching. Choose the ones that give you the lifestyle you need while providing the information your customers want.

Three Times a Year, In-Person, Mastermind Group Meetings

You can have these wherever you choose. In your out-of-the-way hometown, a nearby city with a decent/not-so-decent airport, or a domestic/international vacation destination. It is up to *you*! These meetings should be for two days, so that folks will see the value in traveling to them. I don't know why, but folks do not like to travel for a one-day meeting, no matter how valuable. Foolish, but true.

Monthly Group Coaching Calls

Some coaches choose to do one-on-one calls. The problem with this is that the members of the group don't get to learn from one another. For the most part, all members ask the same questions anyway. They all need to learn/re-learn the same stuff. Also, a group call gives them a sense of community. And your retention rates will be higher the more you can gather everyone together. They won't want to leave the new community you've formed for them. This is true of the two-day meetings as well. That's why you need to get your members to those meetings! Oh, another problem with individual calls is that a single member more easily gets into gripe mode when they're one-on-one with you. They're better behaved and more positive on the group calls. Also, if you don't do a group call, you'll be spending a day or two a month talking to everyone individually. Doesn't sound so bad until you do it once!

Members-Only Online Forum

You can set up a "membership website," using affordable membership website software available by simply "Googling" to find and choose one. Or you may simply choose to use a "Google Group." Members love to have this sort of online interaction with one another. What's funny is that they'll ask each other questions and largely coach themselves! Also, leaving your group would mean loss of this online community. This is called *pain of disconnect*, and it's very important in retaining members.

Weekly Group Coaching Fax

They need weekly reinforcement anyhow. And when you send them something by fax, not only is it timely, more so than the mail, but it is tangible. Too many make the mistake of sending their members e-mails. This is unwise. It is not a physical thing. E-mails are not valued.

24/7 Fax Access to You

Allow them to send you faxes, day or night. Tell them that the faxes will be returned within two business days or whatever is your choice. Do not promise immediate response. Promising to be their slave does not elevate you in their eyes. Also, do not give them e-mail or phone access to you. If you allow e-mail access, you'll get hundreds of e-mails from your members, with every ill-thought-out question that pops into their minds. By making them send you a fax, many members will find that they'll crumple up the paper, having better thought out the question and even given themselves the answer. They will/should find value in that alone: getting the right questions asked of themselves. Of course, do not allow phone access either, or you'll be taking phone calls at all hours and will have no time for anything else.

Monthly Calls or CDs with Others

There are folks that will license their generic coaching materials to you for a monthly fee. The calls and/or CDs they can do for you and other coaches might be on proper mindset, etc. This gives your members more information, without taking up more of your time.

Access to Your Secret Vendors

In my mortgage coaching program, I use certain vendors for very specialized, unusual marketing pieces. I give my members license to use my mortgage marketing in their local areas, but also give them disconnectable access to my vendors that get the pieces in the mail, etc. This license and access to disconnectable vendors provides you with huge pain of disconnect should a member choose to leave.

What Should I Charge Them?

Well, that depends. Is your coaching going to help them lose weight? Then it only has a value of what folks will pay for coaching on that topic.

Or is your coaching for a profession? And is it going to make them more money? Well, if it's going to help them make more money, then you can make the argument I did earlier: "What's it going to cost you *not* to do this?"

People will pay dearly for things that don't give them financial benefit. Surely no one likes being overweight. Everyone would like effortlessly or more easily to be at the proper weight. But what can you get them to pay for that?

What if your weight-loss prospect is a secretary who makes $22,000.00 a year? What can she afford to pay you? Although losing weight might increase her income somehow, it's unlikely. She has no financial reason to join your coaching. Well, I guess there's the marriage argument, but that's a stretch as well.

Now, if you choose to help restaurant owners make more money, then you can get them to pay more for that than you can get the $22,000.00 per year secretary to pay for weight-loss coaching.

The restaurant owner already has significant capital investment in his restaurant(s). He also has spent a lot of time and emotion on his business. But I think most importantly, there's the money invested, the looming corporate and personal bankruptcies if he fails to make more, and the opportunity to get quite rich if he's able to make more money with your coaching. It's for these reasons that the restaurant owner is a far better prospect for you than the secretary.

Many coaches find that men are better buyers than women. Well, it's still the case that, on average, men make more than women. That right there makes it a likelihood that male prospects will be better for you. But it's not a drop-dead certainty.

Many coaches find that business owners are better buyers than employees. This is almost always true. So, that's a big tip for you in selecting your target audience.

Sometimes, folks from certain states buy your coaching more easily. For me, in the mortgage category, California is a hotbed of mortgage activity. Also, because loan amounts are higher, so are commissions, and so California brokers can more easily afford to pay me.

I currently charge $4,997.00 to join the program, plus 24 months of coaching at a minimum of $1,797.00 per month. That's $48,125.00 over 24 months. If I tried to get the $48,125.00 up front, I would be unlikely to get it. Sure, some brokers could write me a check for that amount, but I'm much more likely to be able to get $4,997.00 to start plus $1,797.00 per month.

Using what I teach, my members can do just one loan that they wouldn't have gotten otherwise each month and make an extra $10,000.00 per month, on average. So, even if they only get that one additional deal, they pay me $1,797.00 per month and get $10,000.00 per month in return. Most get far more than that, but even if they barely work, they come out $8,000.00 better off each month. It's hard not to join a program that puts an extra $8,000.00 in your pocket each month, even in spite of yourself.

Who Else Has Created a Successful Coaching Program Like Yours?

Well, coaching programs can take many forms. One friend of mine who has a very interesting business is Stephen Snyder. Stephen's affinity with his audience is that he was once bankrupt. That might not sound like a qualification to you, until I tell you that Stephen coaches the recently bankrupt!

He gets car dealers all over the country to sponsor his seminars. They sponsor them without putting their names all over them. The seminars are all about going to see Stephen the guru.

The car dealers pay for his marketing expenses in each town. Stephen puts together a mailing and pulls courthouse records of the recently bankrupt to mail to, and the car dealers bear the expense of the mailers.

When folks get to the seminar on "Life After Bankruptcy," they are taught all of the ins and outs of how they can get credit again, instantly . . . at the seminar. Stephen will sell 300 cars at a seminar. Well, that is, they'll have 300 Fords in the parking lot, and Stephen will do a talk on how "you can drive this car for only this much a month, even though you're recently bankrupt!"

Of course, they're not so picky about the car. The sale is made as soon as they're told they can drive home today in a new car.

Stephen will sell them many other things, but one thing that gives him continuity income is selling the seminar goers into a law firm's credit repair service. Stephen receives monthly income for each new person he puts into the credit repair service, and the folks he puts into the service receive coaching from the law firm, without Stephen having to do the coaching himself!

Stephen's business now does hundreds of seminars a year, now with folks simply watching him on a screen in hotel ballrooms all over the country each weekend. And it's a $30 million per year business!

And there's my friend Ed O'Keefe. Ed used to be a dead-broke bartender. Then he figured out that he needed to start a coaching program, but not for bartenders! He selected dentists instead.

But what can a dentist learn about dentistry from a bartender? Well, Ed offered several dentists in his area the opportunity to work with him, for free. Ed would design effective direct-response marketing for their practices, with the doc footing the bill for the marketing, but not having to pay Ed a dime.

He got one doc to take him up on the offer. Ed started playing guinea pig with that doc's practice and with his marketing. With that dentist's help, Ed very quickly got an understanding of the business side of the practice. He gained a very basic understanding of the dentistry being performed, but he most certainly didn't have to go to dental school to go into that niche.

With the deal he made with that dentist, he had the dentist proofread his marketing pieces, and because they were going to consumers of dental services like himself, Ed was never far off in what he wrote.

Very quickly, Ed's marketing was making that dentist a fortune. Then, Ed quite easily was ready to roll out his marketing system and coaching program to dentists all over the country. Not only did he have proof that it worked, but he had a really great testimonial from a dentist! He never had to show up and say, "Hey, I'm just a bartender, but I think . . ." He got to show up with his "credentials" already made irrelevant. Dentists want the outcome and will ignore that Ed's not a fellow professional. Today, Ed's business does $6 million per year!

The Biggest Mistake to Avoid

Probably the biggest mistake you can make starting out is to promise too much access to you. I covered this earlier, but don't think that customers will pay more just for more of you. In fact, you need to manufacture some scarcity in order to get them to pay top dollar. They need to get what they need, but not everything they want. People don't value others who are too available.

What You'll Need to Pack
into Your Toolbox

There's just no way of getting around the fact that you're going to need a website. This website can be, and probably should be, constructed solely for the purpose of *selling* your coaching program to your prospects.

A couple of good examples are my sites www.MortgageMarketingGenius.com and www.InformationMasterMind.com. You'll notice that both sites have what are called *squeeze pages* at these addresses.

Squeeze pages promise the benefits of what's inside and squeeze visitors for their information in return for the information you promise to give them in return. Usually, you'll want to promise your "free report," which will be nothing more than a sales letter, testimonials, proof of results, and ordering information.

Your squeeze page also needs to perform the function of getting the visitor's permission to be contacted by you with follow-up marketing. The sale is almost never made upon the first visit to your site, so you'll need to get various forms of contact for each visitor, not just e-mail.

You'll need to do follow-up marketing to prospects via e-mail, direct mail, fax broadcast (if targeting professionals in an industry niche), and perhaps the occasional voice broadcast message to answering machines and voice mails.

A really great way to get your coaching program started is to book a date with a hotel to use its meeting room and to guarantee a small number of room nights under your block. The hotel will give you a reduced room rate for your folks, even cheaper than they could get from hotels.com or what have you. In return, when you fill your room block, your meeting room will be free!

When you sign that hotel contract, the motivation to fill your hotel room block, so you don't get stuck with a bill for the meeting room, will serve as motivation to start promoting your seminar. The purpose of the seminar will be to sell coaching.

As part of the promotion to fill your seminar, you'll use e-mail, fax, voice, direct mail—some have even used messenger—to promote your event. You'll then promote your free teleseminar (like a conference call for all of your prospects) that you'll hold maybe four weeks before the actual seminar. You'll tease your prospects in your teleseminar promotional marketing to them for about seven or ten days before the teleseminar with all of the stuff they're going to learn on the call. "You'll learn the seven deadly secrets of 'x,' and how to avoid them." "Learn how to do x, y, and z without ever leaving the house, putting on a tie, or driving to meet with another prospect again." "How to lose more weight/make more money/etc. than you ever thought possible, while still eating cheesecake everyday/working from home/etc."

Also, in the promotion of your teleseminar, promise them that they'll hear from folks on the call that have used your coaching successfully. This is great if you've got 'em. Oftentimes, even if your coaching program is new, you have someone in your life you've already helped on the topic you wish to coach on, and you can use that person on the call for the testimonial interview.

You'll want to promise your prospects that you'll also take live Q&A (questions and answers) on the call from them for free. That will help get them onto the call. I recommend you do this last on the call, and keep reminding them that it is coming up, to keep them on for the entire call.

Right before the Q&A, you need to give your pitch for your upcoming event. And of course, you should have done mini-pitches throughout the call up to this point. Now, you'll find that many of the questions you'll get from folks will be buying questions about attending your event!

When you hold a teleseminar and/or seminar for nonmembers, you'll need to remember that you need to tell them *what* they should be doing to get the promised results, but not *how* to do it. You might need to read that sentence again! It's important!

They will gain insights from you simply telling them what they should be doing. This will give them the illusion of information. Sure, some info is being given, but they won't be able to leave the call and do the things you have described without your help! And they'll kinda feel this on the call. Their reaction will be "Gee, this all sounds great! But I don't think I can do it without attending his seminar/joining his coaching."

Now you've got 'em right where you want 'em, and closing them on the seminar/coaching shouldn't be hard at all!

How Do I Get Prospects to My Website?

If you're targeting folks in your profession, teaching them how to make more money, which is a great way to make money with coaching, you can use trade magazine ads to drive prospects to your website for your free report. If targeting consumers, you can use magazines that are niched to the interest you wish to coach on.

You can also use Google AdWords. These are paid placement listings on Google that appear along the top and along the right-hand side of the Google screen when someone searches for your search terms. I buy "mortgage marketing," for instance. Whenever someone searches Google for that, they see my ad.

You can do direct mail to compiled or response mailing lists. A compiled mailing list is simply a list like "men with dogs." A response list would be "men with dogs who subscribe to *Dog Lover* magazine." See, the response list has RESPONDED to a commercial offer, indicating likelihood to do so again.

With businesses, you can voice broadcast to their answering machines and voice mail while they are closed. (This is not legal advice.) Business phone numbers are not protected by Do Not Call regulations.

In summary, there's absolutely no reason to wait to get rich in coaching! Waiting to do things just delays them or makes it so you never get to them! Use my plan, and simply get started today!

▲   ▲   ▲

Scott Tucker is a successful coach to the mortgage industry. He shows members of his mortgage coaching program how to make much more money in the industry, while working far less. Scott also teaches people new to the coaching business how to get their programs started and how to make an already started program much more profitable. More information on Scott can be found at www.InformationMasterMind.com.

A Coaching Program Making

Millions with No Affinity, No Money, and No Experience in Info-Marketing

by Ethan Kap and Brett Kitchen
www.DoneForYouInfoMarketing.com

*I*t's easy to think you can only create an info-marketing business if you have a lot of experience. What do you do if you don't have experience? Here are two info-marketers who created a coaching program in a niche where they'd never operated before. Follow their steps to create your own.

▲   ▲   ▲

Our story started close to five years ago. We were insurance agents selling insurance to businesses.

At that time we were bitter enemies. We hated each other. Our boss, Mark, thought that competition was a good thing, so he lied to us about each other to fuel the fire. Behind our backs he would tell us about what the other was doing, just to make us dislike each other. Stupid.

Overall, insurance was a good opportunity, good in a painful way. It was nice to be able to grow our income based upon our own production, not some corporate hierarchy. But as we quickly realized, making cold calls every day for a living is a frustrating experience.

When we started at the agency, Mark walked up to the cubicle, slapped a ten-pound Yellow Pages phone book down and said, "Start calling."

After several years of pounding the phones, driving all over the state, and getting ripped-off by customers, we decided there must be a better way. We looked for ways to get customers to call us . . . instead of us chasing them. (Novel idea!)

Luckily, we were blessed to come across direct response marketing.

We spent thousands on products, books, seminars, and coaching. We started to apply the principles of direct response marketing, and soon we were flooded with phone calls from new clients. *It was really a beautiful thing*. Since that day, we have not made another cold call. Nor will we . . . ever again.

While our life was better, our heart wasn't really in it. We saw the potential info-marketing businesses held, and we wanted to pursue that opportunity. We wanted out of the agency and ended up finally leaving insurance behind because we got tired of working for tyrants and snakes.

Luckily, we had seen the power of information marketing when attending seminars. During one memorable seminar, we looked at each other and said, "I don't want to be down here listening, I want to be up there teaching!"

We decided to get in the info-marketing game. It would have made sense to do it in the insurance industry, but due to some legal issues at that time (we were afraid our ex-bosses would sue us), we didn't.

So, we started looking at other industries that we could build an information business in. In this chapter, we're going to show you exactly how we, with no affinity and no money, built an information business for furniture retailers that went from 10K in credit card debt to $1 million per year in continuity income within 11 months.

It's been a fun ride! Buckle up.

Let's get started with the first thing that we did, which you should do when you are looking at getting into information marketing. Keep in mind that you don't need experience, you do not have to be a certain age (we are in our 20s), and you don't even need a lot of money to get started and ultimately be successful. (But it sure makes it easier when you have some dough.)

All you need is something of value. That may be marketing help, sales training, financial expertise, advertising, business operations, etc. It doesn't have to be in the niche you are pursuing, but you've got to add some type of value.

The Five Criteria You Need to Use When Evaluating a Niche

We understand that searching for a niche among all of the possibilities is like searching for land after getting dropped into the open sea. We had no jobs and had to create an info-business quickly to support our families. These are the steps we used to research and evaluate niches before we selected furniture retailers. We recommend you follow these steps to identify a great opportunity for yourself.

1. Is There Competition in the Niche?

There are two ways to look at this. The first is this: If there is competition, you need to look at how they are marketing—if they are making any money, how much money they are making, and also how you are going to be different from them. There is no sense in going into an industry or a niche offering exactly the same service for the same people. You are going to have a hard time selling that. So, you have to make sure that you are different.

If there is no competition in the niche, there is a good and a bad side. The good side is, you have the marketplace to yourself. The bad side is, it might mean that people have been unsuccessful in that arena. You've got to find out why there isn't any competition there. Is it because somebody has already tried and failed? Or is it because it isn't profitable? Perhaps, you are just the first to try.

The other positive thing about seeing competition is that at least you know that there is money to be made there. So, if there aren't any competitors, be leery. Do a little more research and find out if someone has offered a similar product and has failed.

A secret to getting this information is the trade journals. Look in trade magazines for the past year or two and visit their websites. Search for the type of services that you are offering. Find out all the research about your competitors, or the lack thereof.

2. Does Your Product Help Them Make More Money?

This is a really big deal. It's not essential, but we can promise you, your job is going to be much easier if you are selling something that is going to help your customers make more money. Let's take sales training, for example. If you are able to help someone increase closing ratios by 25 percent, that is a significant dollar value increase directly from what you are offering. If you charge $500.00, and you can increase sales to the tune of $1,500.00, then they'd have to be flat out stupid not to see the value. This is the type of sale you want to create if at all possible, the "you are stupid if you don't buy my product" sale.

You *can* sell information products in any niche. You can sell karate or weight loss or speed reading courses. All that stuff can be sold, but if you are talking about the easiest and best way to get into information marketing, it is with a product that helps your customers make more money. You want to find a niche with business owners or/and entreprenuers looking to make more money.

3. How Large Is Their Transaction Size?

That means, how much money do they make when they sell an item. Take, for example, McDonald's, where the average sale is $5.00, vs. high-ticket retail, like ATVs for $6,000.00 or $7,000.00 or home sales where they are several hundred thousand dollars.

The larger the transaction size, the better chance you have to convince people that investing with you is a good move. They will justify to themselves, "Just one sale and I'll make it all back." That's what you want them thinking.

4. Do They Currently Spend Money on What You Are Offering?

A colleague of ours helps used car dealers improve their marketing. One BIG problem with this. Used car dealers don't typically advertise. A lot of them think they can do mostly word of mouth, put their little classifieds in AutoTrader.com, and that's it.

In our niche, they spend a lot of money on advertising (which is our specialty), and that is one of the MAJOR reasons we decided to start in this industry. It's compelling to tell clients we can cut their advertising cost by 10 percent, and increase sales. If they are spending $100,000.00 a year, then we just saved them $10,000.00. They're only paying us $5,000.00, so it's a no-brainer. Find a niche where they are currently spending money on what you sell, and you'll find it much easier to get started.

5. The Most Important Item on This List: Are They in Pain?

Are these people happy with their status in life? If so, you might be wasting your time. It's difficult to get large numbers of people to take action if they are all happy with the status quo.

Now, don't go find a niche where everybody is going out of business. Obviously, that spells doom for your company. But find a niche where people are in pain. They want solutions. They want to increase sales. They want to make more money. And they are not happy where they are right now.

Expertise Is Everything!

Another important thing that you need to do to get into the coaching or information marketing business is to position yourself correctly. Below are seven ways to position yourself as an expert even if no one has heard of you before. Now obviously, it is in your best interest if people have heard of you before, but that's not what this chapter is about.

If you are in a niche where people do know you, take these suggestions and make an even stronger case for yourself. If no one knows who you are, you're still in luck!

The following are seven ways to position yourself as expert, even in a niche where you've never been heard of before.

1. Get Specialized Knowledge

The first thing you want to do is develop an area of expertise. Basically, you want to come in and have specialized knowledge. This comes back to the principles of *Think and Grow Rich*. (If you haven't read that book, you must.)

2. Proclaim Yourself the Expert

Come out and say, "I am the expert." People are looking for someone to follow, and if you position yourself as a leader with a strong message they resonate with, they will follow you. You must overcome the fear that you aren't adequate. We don't care who you are or what you've done, you have to have faith in yourself and in what you can do for people. Just come out strategically, and show your expertise. (For a deeper understanding of this principle, read *To Be or Not To Be Intimidated* by Robert Ringer.)

Expertise Tip

Create a public persona in your industry. We are known EVERY-WHERE in the industry as "The Traffic Guys."

Our bobblehead graphic goes along with the name, and everyone recognizes it.

(You can get your own made for $50.00 by going to www.mydavinci.com.)

To paraphrase a quote from Micheal Korda's book *Power*, "You have to step up and take your power. Relying on others to give you power is inherently a powerless position because if they gave it to you, they can also take it away." The same is true with expertise. No one will anoint you an expert; waiting for that to happen will be a long, fruitless endeavor.

3. Attach Yourself to an Existing Celebrity/Expert

One of the things that we did that really helped was going to tradeshows and industry events to meet other people. We handed out material, articles that we had written, etc. If you have self-published a book, that is something to hand out at these events (not to clients, but to other associates). Make connections, be in the limelight, meet people, and start to make relationships.

This is where it all starts. It's a relationship game. Nothing more, nothing less. Don't be intimidated. Be proud, strong, on the verge of cocky. People are attracted to confidence. Once you build these relationships face to face, follow up with these big names in the industry and interview them, co-market your products, and co-author articles. This is very effective in transferring their credibility to you.

4. Self-Publish a Book in Three Hours!

It is very important and very easy. Fast, too! The easiest way to get it done is to use a service like idictate.com and talk out the content. It's very easy to talk about a subject for one or two hours and have 50 to 100 pages from that. Then, contact a printing house like West Press

Smart Tip

You can get a 100-page book dictated in one to two hours. Clean it up and then get a printer to print it for you! Don't make it any more complicated than that!

and get it printed. It is very inexpensive. You can create 100 copies and hand them out at tradeshows to prominent members of the industry.

5. Create Miracles

The appeal of the info-marketing business to many is limited customer contact. Customers can come to your website or see an ad, they can fax in an order, and you can ship it without ever speaking with them. However, when you begin your info-marketing business, this is the WRONG strategy. You want to help the first couple of clients one on one, so you can be sure they implement and create success stories. Use the testimonials from those people in your marketing. Splash them on your trade magazine ads, direct mail pieces, and e-mail blasts. Use them wherever you can! Those miracles will spread, and they will become your strongest form of advertising. People will come to you just because of your miracles.

6. Write Articles in Industry Magazines

This is A HUGE trick to instant expert status and free publicity. You must nurture, build relationships with, and find ways to get published in industry magazines.

Bright Idea

You'll find magazine editors much more interested in your articles after you've spent some money with them. Even if you are just starting out, spending a little in each issue, even on classified ads, says a lot about your commitment to their magazine.

Much of this comes back to taking the time to build relationships with magazine editors. They want to know you are credible. Meet them face to face if possible, and introduce yourself. Let them know you have new exciting content you'd like to share with their readers, and you agree not to write the same articles in any other magazines.

Soon, you'll be writing for several magazines, and that is the best exposure you can get.

"One of the biggest reasons for our success was writing in industry magazines!"

7. Take a Stand Against Industry Norms

This will irritate some, but will do a lot to bring you notoriety and status in the industry. In our industry, everybody was doing brand-building advertising. We made a splash when we came out and said brand building is dead. You must change to survive. In your industry, find out what the norm is and position yourself against it.

The Secret Weapon Responsible for One-Third of All Our Sales!

Here's a tool everyone needs to be using, it's called *teleseminars*. You can create a single teleseminar, and it will make you more money than just about anything else you can do. We used to travel and speak. It's good exposure, but it is TRULY a pain in the neck. In testing, we've found that we convert just as many clients, if not more, doing a simple teleseminar from our office.

Within a teleseminar, we use a teleseminar service company that gives us a telephone number and a pass code for our guests. Then, we have a separate phone number and pass code for ourselves as moderators. Through e-mail marketing, ads in trade publications, and direct mail, we advertise a free call about marketing your furniture store, with the guest phone number and pass code. During that call, we give them a presentation that lets them know what our product did for other retailers and explain how they can get the same results for themselves.

It's really quite simple. About a year ago, we did a very successful teleseminar with four testimonials on it, and we rerun it twice a month for new prospects. Every time we did the call, we recorded it. That way, once we had a good call recorded, we could replay it over and over again without us having to prepare and do the call ourselves.

Every time we run it, we convert 34 percent of those prospects into our coaching program. So, if we get 30 people on the call, we're virtually guaranteed to get 11 or 12 customers out of that deal. You might hear big numbers from marketers saying, "We get 500, 600 people in our teleseminars." (First, keep in mind that most marketers are lying to you anyway when they quote numbers like that.) We used to feel bad when we only got 30 or 40, but then we'd get 10 new members and say, "Wow, this isn't so bad after all!"

Never get discouraged if you don't have those numbers. We have never had anything over 100 prospects on a teleseminar. In fact, our average is probably more like 25 or 30, and we did one where we only had one guy on the line, and he hung up!

But we kept after it. Now, we run teleseminars twice a month, and every time we get another 30 to 35 percent conversion.

Here are some tips on running effective teleseminars:

1. *Spend time beforehand to identify all the doubts that customers are going to have when faced with your sales proposition.* What is going through their minds? What are all the doubts they might potentially have, excuses for not buying? Then you must strategically eliminate those doubts one by one throughout the call.

2. *You must have testimonials.* Success stories sell better than anything else. Get two, three, or four of your most successful clients, and let them talk about the changes your products have made in their lives. You want to do a little bit of background work with them before the call, so they know what to expect. Make sure that they are prepared for your questions, and help them give the answers you want.

3. *To encourage people to stay on the line, tell the listeners up front about a great offer they will get at the end of the call.* There are more resources on teleseminars on our website at www.DoneForYouInfoMarketing.com.

Four Cheap or Free Tools to Get You Off the Ground!

This next section will save you hundreds and thousands of dollars as you get started. These tools helped us build our business without spending a fortune on overhead.

1. *A teleconference line that is very inexpensive (free).* One of the best ones that we have used is free conferencing.

   We first signed up for a teleconference line when we were sitting in a hotel late one night working with Tom Orent. We just pulled the trigger, signed up, and started messing around with it. It was one of the best decisions we made.

> **Tip...**
>
> **Smart Tip**
> Make sure your conference line can record the call and let you download it afterward. This will turn into gold for you and give you tons of great content.

2. *Use a 1-800 number.* One of the best sources that we have found is www.TollFreeExpress.com. We actually have used that service for the past two years. It is very inexpensive. It allows people all over the country to call you, and even international callers with the right plan.

▲

Four Cheap Tools We Used to Build Our Information Business

1. www.NoCostConference.com
2. www.TollFreeExpress.com
3. Cheap autoresponder like www.Aweber.com
4. Use an outbound, commission-only salesperson

It's critical if you are taking leads and orders over the phone to have a toll-free number. You want it to be as easy as possible for people to give you money. Plus it will help you look like a legitimate business, which you should be. It is very good to use and very inexpensive.

Another benefit is the flexibility of forwarding the number to an outsourced receptionist, virtual assistant, etc. We've had to hire and fire five different VAs, and it's been awesome to be able to keep the same number and forward it to a different location.

3. *Use a cheap autoresponder, and do it everyday.* AWeber, www.Aweber.com, is a good place to start. It's only $20.00 a month to set up an account. It can help you get started on collecting e-mails from websites and building campaigns to send out e-mails, so you can start communicating with your customers through e-mail.

4. *A commission-only salesperson.* This tool is very unconventional and very effective. (In fact, we don't know many marketers who use this tool.) Many people shudder when we say that. They are afraid that it is going to be hard to find someone to do this dirty work. We have found just the opposite.

In fact, the most effective people we've found have been college students within our spheres of influence: friends, family, friends of family, etc. Cast your net broadly and see what turns up. We generate at least 20 percent of our new members through outbound salespeople who don't cost us a dime until they sell something! It has given us a dramatic increase in our business for a small amount of effort.

Case Study: The $2,700 Blunder That Started Us on the Wrong Foot and Made Us Look Like Fools in the Entire Industry

You can see the copy of the first ad we used when we launched our program (below). We flipped a coin and Brett won, so we put Brett's picture in the ad. Underneath it, we put the following: "Home Furnishing's Marketing Guru." Now, there are a couple of reasons why this was such a terrible idea. The first reason was that it was totally unbelievable. Here we were, totally unknown in the industry, with a picture of Brett that looked like a 19-year-old kid—and the majority of our prospects are 45, 50, even 60 years old.

Special Advisory for Home Furnishings Retailers…

At Last—The nation's most successful adviser to the Home Furnishings industry reveals in this exclusive Free Report 7 Hidden Secrets To Doubling Your Customer Traffic AND Exploding Your Profits

Brett Kitchen
Home Furnishing's Marketing Guru

"How To Simply and Easily Double the Traffic Walking Through Your Door In 9 Minutes... Guaranteed!"

This is a tested and proven shortcut that is working right now for other Home Furnishing Retailers to bring in customers by the droves. It's fast, it's simple, it's easy…and you're about to discover how to do it yourself. For *free*

Not only will this advisory reveal how to have truckloads of new traffic bombarding your store, but you'll ALSO learn the little known secrets of making sure your customers are begging to give you Their Money.

What I'm going to share with you is NOT,

Regurgitated advertising advice you've heard 100 times before. While most businesses spend **countless hours** struggling only to <u>increase traffic by minuscule amounts</u>…I will show you step-by-step how YOU, as a Home Furnishings Retailer, will **Actually use "killer" marketing tactics to …**

- ☐ Explode your business traffic and Explode the response of Every Ad you run by 147% or more. (This will work with ALL types of advertising—even radio and TV!)

- ☐ Put "Customer Loyalty" in place that will place your bottom line on steroids and bring in more customers than you ever thought possible.

- ☐ Discover the **hidden goldmine in every single month** that will have customers pounding down your door waiting for you to open.

- ☐ Make your customers feel **obligated** to buy only from you and feel guilty and humiliated for ever stepping foot in one of your competitor's stores.

"Frankly I was skeptical, but this industry advisory turned out to be the most important and useful business building information I have ever learned about putting tons of customers in my store." –Morgan Garrett, Garrett Mattress Outlet, Salt Lake City, Utah

Act Now and Request This Free Retail Industry Advisory Titled "How To Simply and Easily Double The Traffic Walking Through Your Door…Guaranteed."
In Just 9 Minutes Increase The Traffic Walking Through Your Door, Returning Again and Again, Spending More Money Each Time!
CALL NOW 1-800-393-2054!
For the first 29 who request This Free Advisory, I will also send you:
FREE Audio CD Titled "7 Deadly Sins of Advertising" AND a FREE E-book titled "Science of Getting Rich" by Wallace D. Wattles!
<u>Call Today 1-800-393-2054</u> or email me at <u>info@furnitureprofitsystems.com</u>
www.furnitureprofitsystems.com

Case Study, continued

Right out of the gate, they see a picture that looks like we are about the age of their kids or even their grandkids. Plus, they've never heard of us before. These guys are a skeptical bunch to begin with; then we come out and say, "I am the home furnishing marketing guru."

Just a stupid, stupid way to start out. Just destroyed our credibility. This was our first full-page ad. Luckily, it was in a small magazine, so it didn't kill us. But be careful when you come out and proclaim yourself to be the expert that you do it in a way that it is believable.

If you are going to be the expert, act like the expert. Do not act like a flash-in-the-pan, fly-by-night company. Make a claim that people can get behind and believe.

It cost us $2,700.00 to put that ad in the magazine, and we got virtually no response. It really hurt our credibility in the industry.

As you go into an industry that you do not have any affinity with, you need to understand who you are talking to. Do a good job of speaking their language. If you are significantly younger than they are, don't show your picture right out of the gate.

Two Ways to Maintain Authority and Control Over Your Members Even If You Are Half Their Age and Have No Affinity

The first way to control your members is by being tough on them. We have found the nicer you are to your clients, the more uncontrolled access you give, etc., the worse they behave. They think they can abuse your time, they value your services less, and they drop out earlier. Being the "nice guy" is terrible positioning.

Be tough on them. What we mean by that is, you must establish the rules of the game up front. You expect them to implement, and if they are not going to accomplish anything, you might kick them out of the program. Use words like "Hey, if you are not going to get this done, then you should not really be in our program."

The second thing that you want to do is to tell them what to do. People are looking for someone to tell them what to do. They want authority. Do *not* use wishy-washy words with your members. That is death. Don't use "I think" or "My opinion." Say, "Here's what you should do." "This is the way it works." "This is what you need to do to be successful." In the end, that is why most people joined your program. They are looking for someone to guide them down the path to success. They want you to wave the magic wand, to give them success, riches, and all the things they want in life.

Like Pedro in *Napoleon Dynamite* said in his speech for class president, "If you vote for me, all your dreams will come true."

The info-marketer must preach, "If you follow my program, all your dreams will come true."

You can actually download our scripts on how to handle your customers when they first join your programs by going to www.DoneForYouInfoMarketing.com.

The Fastest and Best Way to Sell High-End Coaching Programs

Now, let us talk about the fastest way to sell high-end coaching programs. Let's be honest, the real reason why all of us are doing this is to make money and make a lot of it, fast.

As you know, we have an incredible story. We built a million-dollar business in 11 months with no affinity, no experience, and no money. We literally financed the company from personal credit cards. Maxing them out and getting more.

It was crazy, maybe stupid, but we were determined to be successful. The reality is, if we can do it, then anybody can do it. We had no experience in info-marketing or in furniture retail, which was our niche. We had no joint ventures. Had no help from anyone inside the industry. Yet, we were still successful. *All that means is that you can be, too!*

The fastest way to sell high-ticket coaching programs at $1,000.00 a month or even higher, without spending a fortune or putting people in seminars (which is how many of the info-marketers do it), is by selling done-for-you products. Many marketers spend a fortune doing seminars, and then they sell their $1,000.00 a month coaching programs.

Our way is totally different; we do it all through mail and teleseminars. The reason that we can do that is because we sell done-for-you products. We developed a system that has about seven to ten done-for-you products on an ongoing basis, such as done-for-you marketing promotions, done-for-you e-mails, direct mailers, etc.

The reality is, *people don't want information anymore*. They don't want to learn anything. They are lazy slobs who want money with no work. So, that's what we have to give them today. We used to be able to sell education. Not any more.

Now, you can get into the done-for-you business, quickly and affordably. To learn more and to get a tour of our done-for-you center, go to www.DoneForYouInfoMarketing.com.

Therefore, we developed our system of done-for-you programs. This offer is very appealing to people. It's a trend that will continue. To be successful quickly in the info business, you need to include done-for-you services and products as part of your offering.

Is there work on your end? Yes, we won't lie . . . but the rewards monetarily can be much higher. For example, selling a $1000.00 per month program with just coaching/masterminding may take tons of cash to market and several years to get a sufficient number of members. We had more than 50 members within five months of launching our Platinum Program, and it was all done through the mail. Done-for-you is an easier sell, and you can charge more for it.

The Dark Side of Done-for-You Products

Sell done-for-you, but explain that it works better if they put their own touch to it. That way, you aren't on the hook for all the results.

Once you get the initial groundwork set, done-for-you can be just as easy as coaching if you can get good partner vendors. *There are some downsides*. You are on the hook for actual performance of your system. If you are running a coaching program and somebody does something that doesn't work, you can always blame it on them: "You did not follow my advice." People accept that. But when you do it for them, you are on the hook for it. *It better work*. This is the real downside to done-for-you services and products.

The Worst Mistake So Far . . . Read This Even If You Miss Everything Else in This Chapter!

The one major mistake we made nearly cost us everything and nearly destroyed our business. It had to do with our merchant account. When we started, we opened up a merchant account and grew our business slowly. We developed the relationship with our provider.

After about a year, we received a phone call saying another company could save us over $2,000.00 per month. That's a lot of dough, so we switched over to it without sitting down and really thinking it through. We told it what we were doing, and it promised us, "Everything will be OK. We understand what you do."

It was all B.S.

To make a long story short, the salesperson was blowing hot air. The fraud department held our money. It thought we were doing something fraudulent.

Miraculously, someone at the company made a mistake and released our funds. I was told by the company, *"Someone will be fired over that."*

This mistake literally almost cost us our business. We needed that $35,000.00 to pay bills, pay ourselves, and keep running. It was incredibly stressful.

The point here is this, do everything in your power to maintain strong relationships with your merchant providers. Give them the proper documentation that they need; make sure when you are signing up customers that you collect agreements, signed documentation that defines what you are charging and when, etc.

Then, be in contact with the merchant account regularly. Show it your growth plans, and always be ahead of the game. Go get a higher limit before you need it. The relationship with a merchant account is essential to grow business. A bad relationship almost cost us ours.

Resources

Two Merchant Services Providers. These providers are experienced with working with info-marketers. They are a good place to start:

www.InfoMarketingMerchant Services.com

www.ChargeTodayInfo.com

The Secret

Now, on to positive things like the number-one tool that built our business, keeps members in, and practically eliminates refunds. *This tool is one-on-one coaching calls.* Some people get into the info-business because they do not want to talk to anybody ever again. That is an option with this type of business. But if you really want to build a significant business with a high income and do it quickly, *then you will talk to your members on the phone on a regular basis, especially when you are starting out.*

When we started, we structured one-on-ones to our members as a bonus. They bought the package, and as a bonus, they got a one-on-one call with us and 20 minutes per month ongoing. We would walk them through the process, help them implement, help them create marketing pieces, *and most importantly, build a relationship with them on a personal level.*

We still have many of our members from the very beginning because of the relationship we developed with them in the beginning. We're not saying be an open door. In fact, you can't let them abuse your time: Don't let them call at any time and talk to you, and don't let them talk for hours. Just schedule it for 40 minutes, and stick to the 40 minutes. Then, you move on. The best way to end a call is simply to say, "I've got another call right now, so I have to run." If you really, truly want to build a relationship with your custumers, then you WILL spend some time with them on the phone, especially if you are just starting your program.

> ## Resources
>
> Two free resources to run your coaching program:
>
> Run your conference calls for free with www.NoCost Conference.com.
>
> Create a free mastermind group with Google Groups.

The Structure of a Million-Dollar Coaching Program

Here are some points on how to structure a coaching program that only takes a couple of hours per week to fulfill and yet produces a six- or seven-figure income.

1. *Two teleseminars per month.* Do these calls using your free teleconferencing service, so they are totally free. The first call of the month can be a critique call, where you help members with advertising pieces, or it can be a strategy call to teach a concept. The second call should be an interview with one of your members who has a great success story or with an outside expert.

2. *An e-mail group.* You can find this for free on Google or Yahoo!. There are also other services you can use, but these are free. Create an e-mail mastermind group where people share information with one another. They can only have access if they are a part of your program. This really helps build a strong relationship with your customers. And it happens without your having to be there.

   Now, it is critical that you review each one of those messages. You have to do this to make sure the content from the members isn't negative. It should be positive content to help people grow their businesses and grow themselves.

   It's also a powerful way to get testimonials. Many people get on the Google Group and share an exciting success they had using your strategies.

3. *A members' website.* Members can visit to download and upload information. They can learn, get access 24/7, and see who else is part of the program. You can get examples of good membership websites just by going to Facebook or

MySpace to see what they are doing there. Membership websites create a strong sense of community and the pain of disconnect if members want to cancel your services.

So, there you go. You just got our success map on how to build a million-dollar information marketing business with no affinity, no money, and no experience. We went from $0 to $1 million in 11 months . . . and following our model, you can, too. For more information, visit www.FoneForYouInfoMarketing.com.

▲　▲　▲

Ethan Kap and **Brett Kitchen** declared themselves "The Traffic Guys" and created a successful information marketing business helping furniture retailers get more customers into their stores. As former insurance agents, they didn't have experience with retail. Their strategies help anyone looking to research a niche, identify a market, and create a successful information marketing business.

Speed Implementation

How to Get Your Info-Marketing Business Up, Running, and Profitable Quickly

by Melanie Benson Strick
Million Dollar Lifestyle Business Coach
www.SuccessConnections.com

Most info-marketers create a new business while trying to run another business or while already employed at a job. It's easy to get overwhelmed and too busy to get your business started. Here are the strategies you need to balance your life and launch your info-business.

▲ ▲ ▲

Have you ever tried to carry a small child when your hands are full? You've been shopping for hours, and every arm, hand, and finger has a bag attached to it. Your focus is on getting those bags into the house quickly, so you don't drop anything.

But standing in front of you, the child (with an imploring look, much whining, and a persistence that won't quit) is insisting on being picked up. You try to move faster toward the house, but the child is unrelenting. He needs attention right now to avoid a total meltdown. So, now what? You already have your arms full . . . there's no room for anything else, but you love this child and want him to have your attention. How do you balance both?

Starting a new venture is like trying to pick up that child when your arms are full. You already have a million things to do all day with your current business or career. Now, you have this whole new venture with a to-do list a mile long that needs attention in order to get your business up, running, and profitable.

John was in this very situation. John had heard about the world of information marketing for years. Studying the likes of Dan Kennedy, Alex Mandossian, and Armand Morin, the allure of making millions by marketing information to others had piqued John's interest, and he was ready to start his own information marketing business.

John joined one of my coaching programs and very quickly realized that he had a big problem. He was still spending 40 to 60 hours a week in his current role. By the time he finished all of his current responsibilities, commuted home, ate dinner, and tried to be a part of his family for a few minutes, there wasn't much energy or time left to pursue other goals. Frustrated, disappointed, and disillusioned, John had come to a crucial point in his journey: he had to learn how to leverage his time better.

The Greatest Obstacle to Success

After coaching entrepreneurs for more than seven years, I have found that the greatest obstacle to a successful business is action, or more specifically, *the lack of it*. Many great businesses fail—more than half according to the Small Business Association—due to the entrepreneur's inability to take the right action at the right time.

There are many reasons why entrepreneurs exhibit a lack of action. I'll list a few of them. Mark any that apply to you.

- ❏ Too many distractions
- ❏ Lack of knowledge of what to do
- ❏ Competing priorities

- ❏ Lack of planning
- ❏ Inappropriate mindset or attitude
- ❏ Poor habits
- ❏ Do-it-myself mentality
- ❏ Opportunity addiction
- ❏ Deficient time management
- ❏ Lack of proper systems

When these obstacles arise, it forces the entrepreneur to move at a speed that is not optimal for success. Here is a simple formula that I want you to use going forward:

Knowledge + Speed = Massive Success

Have you ever noticed how some people accomplish so much, while others seem to be slower than a turtle? The turtle-speed entrepreneurs are the same people who complain about not having enough money, results, and success. Then there are the people who are like a bull in the china shop, moving fast and furious, leaving a wake a mile wide as they race to the finish line.

The funny thing is, neither the turtle nor the bull ever accomplishes real success. Yes, speed is essential to getting your business profitable. But let's be clear about what speed really works for the long term.

When I was in my coach training program, I was like that bull. I was determined to get things done quickly. I wanted money coming in the door, and I was willing to get it at any cost. I'd jump in with both feet and make things happen. I was puzzled by this paradox: it seemed

Beware!
A strength over-used becomes your greatest weakness.

that even though I was moving quickly, my results were in quicksand. The world around me wasn't keeping up; nothing changed fast enough, and I was mad as heck!

To overcome this issue, my wise mentor showed me three implementation styles.

1. Slow Implementation

Slow implementation is where things seem to take weeks, months, or even years before results show. Often, this is a result of the entrepreneur's inability to make decisions, surrounding himself with naysayers and doubters, so his confidence is low or he has so many distractions that he cannot focus properly. Or, he just doesn't know WHAT to do . . . so he does nothing.

Slow implementers, just like the turtle, are excruciatingly slow to achieve their goals. And the buildup of too few results is often combined with lots of money being invested in learning more. More information doesn't necessarily make for more success. Actually, too much information can inhibit your ability to take action quickly.

A strength overused can become your greatest weakness. If you find yourself compelled to continue to focus on learning, but with few results, it may be time to shift your priorities to being in action mode.

2. Reckless Implementation

The reckless implementer is always running around like a chicken with its head cut off. He wastes time, money, and precious resources doing things over and over again because he doesn't have the plan or systems to leverage his time better.

Reckless implementers, like the bull in the china shop, appear fast to the outside world, but are really moving forward very slowly, sometimes just running in circles. They typically are unprofitable, don't retain customers, and tend to have massive up and down sales.

3. Speed Implementation

A speed implementer has the ability to integrate the better of two worlds: attaining enough information to make quick, high-payoff decisions, while taking massive action on a daily basis. Speed is about being focused and clear, taking calculated risks, and knowing what works.

In this chapter, I will show you how to become a speed implementer. I'm going to help you uncover some of the secrets that six- and seven-figure information marketers know that make the difference between making it big and making a mess. Let's start with a secret formula.

The Secret Formula for a Speedy, Profitable Startup

Think about a high-performance car in a race. To operate it at high speed, so it arrives at the finish line in good time without getting into any accidents, the car's systems all must be working optimally. Not only does it have to have high-performance oil and gasoline, it also needs a tune-up, and the driver must be able to pay attention to and handle the car's power and speed. There will most likely be some obstacles that the driver has to proactively negotiate.

Moving your success forward with speed is like driving a race car. As the driver, if you are not operating optimally, you will crash. If your business doesn't have the proper systems and structures in place, it will slow down, putter, or give you less than ideal results.

So, how do you ensure optimal speed performance?

It's called the inner and outer game of speed. Have you ever heard these sayings?

Your inner game dictates your outer game.

What you focus on expands.

Your attitude dictates your altitude.

These quotes are reminders of how important our thoughts, clarity of vision, and beliefs are in influencing our daily habits and actions, which in turn determine our results.

To be able to operate at lightening speed, without crashing, it is vital that we understand what our inner and outer game formula is. I developed a tool called the Millionaire Success Compass™ to help you (see Figure 13.1).

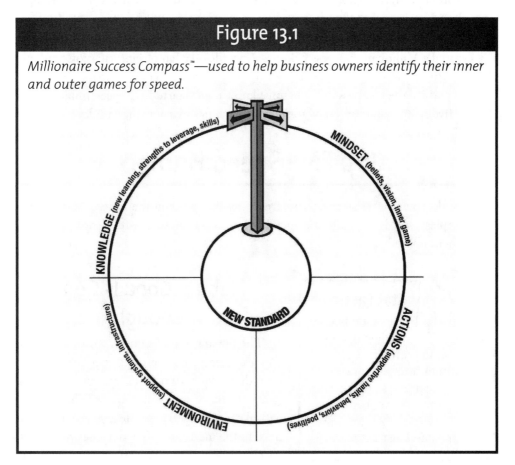

Figure 13.1

Millionaire Success Compass™—used to help business owners identify their inner and outer games for speed.

- *Mindset.* The thinking, attitude, beliefs, and vision that happen inside your head all day long. Your mindset is often very unconscious and can wreak havoc without you even knowing why. Getting your mindset aligned with what works for this kind of business is essential to eliminating sabotaging habits and doubts and making bad decisions.

- *Actions.* Your habits, activities, and tasks that you choose to act on. We often do things from a place of comfort versus a place of effectiveness. To be a speed implementer, you must do what works every day.

- *Knowledge.* Knowing what to do when can be the missing link for this business. Once you know what and when to do the right things, you can move into a speed that many never can achieve.

- *Environment.* This includes the systems, structures, and support for you and your business. Can a car racer win without a pit crew? Can a pit crew be speedy if it doesn't have a system for replacing a blown tire in 30 seconds? Your environment must support your end goal and the pace at which you are working.

Learning to use the Millionaire Success Compass™ could be a chapter in itself, so I can only give you a small taste here. If you'd like to learn more about how to use it, I've created a Millionaire Success Compass™ profile on a famous information marketer that you can get free at www.FastTrackToLifestyleBusiness.com/compass.

Two parts of the compass that you must know to get started as a speed implementer: the top five speed habits and how to strengthen your environment with leverage.

Top Five Speed Habits

How do you know that what you are doing will get you the fastest, best results? The simplest way is to study the speed habits of other successful people and start doing them immediately.

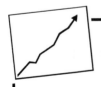

Stat Fact
There are two million bytes of information coming at you every minute. Our brains can effectively process only seven (plus or minus two) bytes at a time. No wonder we get overwhelmed and distracted!

Habit 1: Good Is Good Enough

The pursuit of perfection is a dream killer. If you are trying to make things perfect and have everything figured out, or are on your fifth review to make sure you got all of the typos, it will take you years to generate results in this business. In the meantime, someone else will capitalize on the void in the industry and get rich first.

What you must practice is knowing that "good is good enough." You might make small mistakes, people might find typos, and you might decide to do it differently in the future. But at least you are making money. If you don't get out there, you won't learn what works and what doesn't work, and you certainly won't be making any money.

Habit 2: High-Payoff Focus

A habit that can make or break you is the ability to focus your time and energy first on the things that get you results quickly. Knowing the difference between a distraction and a high-payoff opportunity is like money in the bank.

About three years ago, I worked with a top information marketer on what she considered a motivation problem. She had some very lucrative opportunities that she was procrastinating to implement. Instead of working on the deliverables, she was spending her time rollerblading at the beach, hanging out with friends, or surfing the net.

I took her through the exercise in the ULTIMATE Success Generator™ on high-payoff focus, and immediately she realized that these opportunities were really distractions from her priorities! Within just a few months of getting refocused on her priorities, she launched her live event series and broke $1 million in revenue.

Habit 3: Power Planning

An idea in your head is probably exciting, but it isn't profitable. Surprisingly, more than half of business owners don't plan. No wonder they are reckless or moving too slowly. First of all, keeping the plan in your head doesn't allow others to effectively help you. Second, you can't identify the weaknesses of your plan in your head. So, you will inevitably run into a lot of roadblocks and breakdowns.

Step 1. Map Out the Basics

Planning is easier than most people think, if you know how. If you follow the On-Time Results™ model, then the first step is to map out what needs to be done, when it needs to be done by, and what resources to use.

Step 2. Break Down Into Bite-Size Chunks

You can't eat an elephant in one bite, and the trunk is actually too big, too. Our brain comes with an "it's too big" radar screening system that literally causes us to search out something more fun to do if a task seems too big or overwhelming.

To overcome this "it's too big" issue, break down each task into activities that can be done in a two-hour segment of time. For instance, a task called "complete website" is an elephant-sized chunk. "Write sales copy for website" is an elephant's trunk-sized chunk. "Write first draft of home page sales copy" is probably the right size chunk for an action.

Habit 4: Speed Decision Making

Another habit shared by speed implementers is making decisions quickly. I worked with a man who wanted to build an information marketing business around his knowledge, but he was working full time. Even though we had a well laid-out plan, nothing ever seemed to get accomplished. We finally identified the road block as not enough time, and decided he needed a virtual assistant to build his website, edit his writing, and update his blog while he was at work. It took him six months to hire the virtual assistant!

Making decisions quickly is another habit essential to the speed implementer. But to make decisions quickly, you must know what criteria and facts you need. Three of the most common facts you need are:

1. How much money will it cost?
2. How much time will it take?
3. When and how do I make my money back?

Your criteria will be based on your values and priorities. Values are like your compass; they are standards or ways of being that must happen. Priorities are the needs that must be met in your life and business.

Let's say you are evaluating a marketing opportunity like advertising in a newsletter. It costs $100.00 per month, it will take you an hour to create the ad, and you make your money back when you sell your $97.00 product. An example of criteria might be that you market in ezines that promote programs or products that complement your offerings to your target audience, rather than directly compete.

Once you have the knowledge gathered, your job is to make the decision quickly. Flip-flopping, procrastinating, and dragging your feet only generate bad energy that will sap your momentum.

It might also help to put a decision threshold in place. Any decision less than $500.00 gets made within 24 hours. (P.S., This is also a great speed strategy for delegating to your team: Any decision less than $250.00 doesn't need my approval.)

Habit 5: Ruthless Time Management

Of the five habits, this one is probably the most important. Without it, nothing else will work. Ruthless time management is about your having a crystal-clear focus on what's important and implementing boundaries, so you won't get distracted from it.

A few ways I use this strategy include:

- *Time blocking.* I block time in my calendar every week for the priorities and tasks that must be accomplished. I also block out the time in my calendar when I handle administrative stuff (Tuesdays) and when I am available for coaching (Wednesdays and Thursdays).

- *E-mail and phone call support.* My assistant has systems, templates, and scripts to handle people's incoming questions, so I don't get distracted responding to routine questions.

- *Information management.* Every piece of marketing, education, or reading I need to review is collected in a special folder until I have my time block to review it.

- *Urgency control.* From my family to my friends and clients, I practice extreme self control to manage their urgencies. I will often say, "I'm available to answer your question after 5 P.M." or "I'm only available on Tuesday, Wednesday, or Thursday for a session this week." I also practice the mindset of "Your poor planning does not constitute an emergency on my part."

The only person who can make sure things happen with speed is you. If you aren't in control of your time, then someone else is.

The Power of Leverage

Another trait of speed implementers is recognizing the power of leverage. Leverage is being able to apply a little bit of effort to achieve a big result.

We will explore three leverage techniques here (there are many more for the world of information marketing that have been covered in other chapters).

Systemize

To systemize is to do something once, capture the "system" (or preferred process to accomplish your desired results), and then follow the system over and over again. When you implement systems, you are, in essence, creating checklists, templates, and scripts that enable someone else to replicate you—so you can do something else. Systems also ensure that the job is completed the way you would do it, so that quality control is in place.

Without systems, many recreate the wheel over and over again. People forget the steps, look everywhere to remember access codes or special scripts, or make up their own way of doing things. A business without systems is inefficient, losing profits, and is probably losing clients, too.

Systems You Must Have

- ○ Incoming prospect scripts
- ○ New client intake templates
- ○ Monthly bookkeeping checklist
- ○ Product fulfillment checklist
- ○ Marketing strategy implementation procedure
- ○ Written job descriptions
- ○ Customer service and refund policies

The easiest way to create systems is to go through the process the first time yourself, document each and every step you take, and then write it up in a procedures guide. If this project is too big, then you might want to hire a systems specialist like Process Prodigy (www.ProcessProdigy.com) to help you create a systems package for your business. Another option is to leverage other people's systems and customize them to your business. One way to get access to systems for an information marketing, consulting, and speaking business is through the Virtual Team Building Tele-Bootcamp (www.VirtualTeamBuildingTeleBootcamp.com).

Automation

Automation is using technology to replace human effort, so tasks are accomplished automatically. With automation, you may need to create the process initially, but once it is up and running, the machine takes over, and you are freed up to do your job.

Some examples of automation in action:

- *Recorded calls*. Record your conference call when training a new team member, so that it's always available for any new person going forward.

- *Training videos*. Using Camtasia or GoToWebinar.com, you can host a new member training call, record it, post it to a website, and always have it for new members to access going forward. This really cuts down on customer service questions and keeps customer retention high.

- *Auto responders*. Create a sequence of e-mail communication that can be delivered to a new customer, a prospect, or even a lost client and that is automatically sent on a predetermined timeline. I recommend and use www.CartSolutionsSuccess.com shopping cart system.

- *Prospect follow-up*. A great way to automate follow-up (which, by the way, is the single greatest neglected marketing technique) is using a system that distributes a preprogrammed sequence that includes direct mail. There are many technologies that do this. Two that I'm familiar with are Infusion (www.Infusion.com) and Send Out Cards (www.SendOutCards.com).

- *Live chat.* Live chat is a feature that you install on your website that allows a viewer to click a button and get instant access to someone on your team. This technology allows you to leverage technology to minimize your customer service expenses as well as give your clients the perceived value of instant help.

- *FAQ sites.* By identifying the most commonly asked questions and the typical answers given by you or a member of your team, you can create FAQ pages on your website. This gives readers instant access to the answers they need, while freeing up your team for other tasks.

These are just a few of the thousands of automation opportunities available to you. Once you have identified your systems, you can begin to evaluate more automation opportunities. You may also encounter situations where you or a member of your team is deluged with monotonous work, at which point exploring ways to automate the work can speed up your timetable for results.

An important comparison to make as you explore automation is the expense of the technology vs. how much the manual labor, mistakes, and missed opportunities are currently costing you. You will find that the technology wins almost every time.

Delegation

Delegation is the ability to outsource tasks to others who can do it faster, cheaper, and possibly better than you. As entrepreneurs, often we feel that we have to wear ALL of the hats to save money (or because no one can really do it as well as we can, right?).

This "Lone Ranger" mentality keeps you stuck, stuck out of the speed mode. You'll either be moving as slowly as the turtle or be the reckless bull in the china shop, running as fast as you can to keep up with everything. Neither is optimal for results (see Figures 13.2 and 13.3).

About two years into being an entrepreneur, I continued to struggle with getting everything done. I was overwhelmed, frustrated, and struggling to accomplish it all. There was one week in which I put in over 100 hours. I remember having to say no to multiple social engagements, and at the end of that week, I was really grumpy. My sister, one of the people I turned down, wisely asked me, "Didn't you quit your corporate job, so you could have freedom in your life?" Ouch. She was right. But I didn't have freedom. I had recreated a job for myself.

I happened to be coordinating a small business seminar with wealth builder Loral Langemeier, author of *The Millionaire Maker*. During the seminar, Loral said something

Figure 13.2

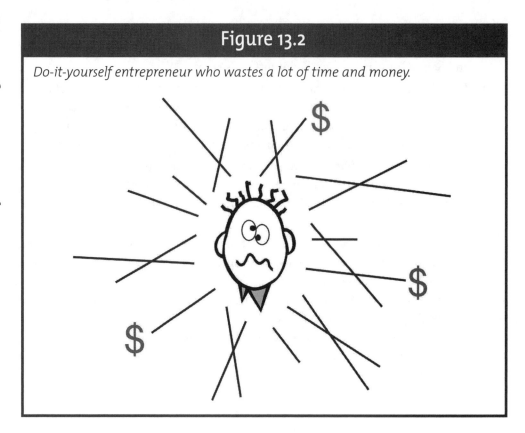

Do-it-yourself entrepreneur who wastes a lot of time and money.

that really stuck with me: "When someone presents me with a great idea, I say to myself, 'Great idea, now, who is going to do it?'" Loral is crystal clear on what her job really is—making millionaires. She doesn't allow herself to get distracted by the administration, tactics, and low-payoff opportunities that most people focus their attention on.

Timothy Ferriss, in his book *The 4-Hour Workweek*, shares one of his biggest tips that got him on the speed implementation track. Timothy evaluated what he did every day that generated 80 percent of his results. The realization was that only 20 percent of the tasks he performed on a routine basis actually generated 80 percent of his results. He quickly got rid of or outsourced the rest.

How to Kick-Start High-Payoff Delegation

Once you realize that delegating is a critical strategy in speed implementation for an information marketing business, then it's time to get started. Here are a few "rules of the road" for a delegation quick-start.

Figure 13.3

Millionaire business owner who delegates, automates, and systemizes.

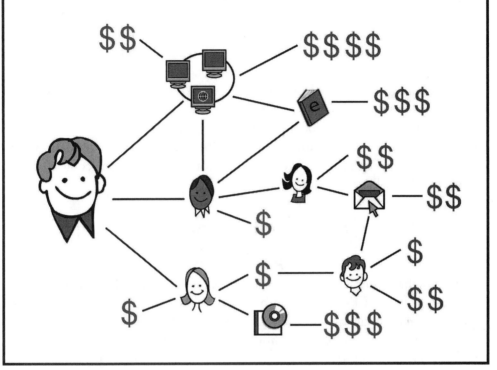

Top Six Virtual Team Resources

- ○ www.AssistU.com ($35.00–$75.00 per hour for trained VAs)
- ○ www.MultipleStreamsTeam.com ($25.00–$45.00 per hour for information marketing specialists, ten-hour trial available)
- ○ www.TeamDoubleClick.com ($20.00–$40.00 per hour, specialty is real estate, pays for two hours for training)
- ○ www.Elance.com (technically oriented, rates vary based on job)
- ○ www.CatchFriday.com ($8.00–$15.00 per hour for overseas assistants, can be slower to respond)
- ○ www.CraigsList.com (local community posting board, many virtual and on-site resources available)

Determine the Delegation Opportunities on Your Plate

The most important place to start is identifying what is on your plate that you can take off. This is an exercise that every member of the Virtual Team Building Tele-Bootcamp starts with. First, write out all of the jobs you are currently doing. We suggest you break it into three categories: what you love to do, what you do because you have to, and what you have to do, but hate. (You find yourself procrastinating, making mistakes, or feeling drained when you have to do the jobs you hate.) Bookkeeping is typically a job that shows up on the last list.

Being new to the information marketing world, you may not know all of the tasks you need to be doing. I've created a list of "101 Ways to Triple Your Income by Outsourcing Your High Payoff Activities." You can download your copy of it right now at www.VirtualTeamBuildingSecrets.com/101ways.

Identify Your High-Payoff Delegation Opportunities

Once you have your list, it's time to do a little bit of research. For the sake of making this step simple, let's assume that most of the tasks that you can outsource to a capable virtual assistant will cost you $30.00 per hour. First, focus on the "have to do but hate" column. Second, knowing how much you are worth per hour (if you don't know, I've included a little formula), identify three to ten tasks that if you were to get them off your plate, you would save time, money, and sanity for yourself.

Your Hourly Worth Formula

Decide how much money you plan on making this year (Let's say $100,000.00).

Divide by 45. (I'm giving you seven weeks' vacation. I take more, but let's start with that.)

Divide by how many hours you wish to work in a week. (Let's say 20 hours per week, realizing that at least half of your "working hours" aren't generating a direct income.)

You are worth $111.00 per hour ($100,000.00 ÷ 45 ÷ 20 = $111.00).

Let's consider bookkeeping for a moment. Let's say you wrote in your "hate to do" list the following:

- Paying invoices/bills on time
- Balancing bank statements
- Tracking and paying affiliate payouts
- Creating client invoices and tracking payments
- Preparing tax documents
- Matching receipts to categories in QuickBooks

If these things are being done at all, they probably aren't done very well. (Typically only the bare minimum is done until tax season, at which time everything else in your life stops while you spend hours and hours getting caught up.) Bookkeeping is not your core talent, is it? No, probably not. So, not only does it wear on you to do the bookkeeping, but you also aren't doing it very well, which can lead to costly mistakes.

Now, let's assume that a virtual bookkeeper charges around $30.00 per hour and can complete your monthly bookkeeping in about 10 hours per month. That's a $300.00 per month cost to your business.

If you were to free yourself from the chains of something you hate, how much more energy and time would you have to devote to high-payoff activities? My guess is it takes you longer than 10 hours to do your bookkeeping, probably more like 16 to 18 hours (remember, you aren't that great at bookkeeping).

Let's assume for the sake of this discussion that you are worth $100.00 per hour. And let's assume out of 16 free hours, you are actually productive four of those hours

Ten Highest Payoff Outsourcing Areas

1. Handling incoming e-mail and phone calls
2. Client billings, general invoices, and bill paying
3. Online article submissions
4. Website updates
5. Setting up auto-responders
6. Sales copy writing and ad creation
7. Customer service
8. Product fulfillment
9. Office filing
10. Contact and prospect follow-up

and turn those four hours into a client opportunity or sell more of your product. You've just generated $400.00 in revenue. You have created a profit!

$ 400.00 in revenue
– $300.00 cost for bookkeeping
= $100.00 profit

Not bad!

Adopt the "Instant Delegator" Mentality

An Instant Delegator is someone who practices the habit of getting things off their plates immediately to someone else's. Often what happens is the entrepreneur gets stuck trying to learn it the first time or has the erroneous thinking that "It won't be that hard; I'll just do it real quick." Next thing you know, you've spent five precious hours messing around with something that your assistant could have done in an hour.

To be a masterful Instant Delegator, there is a little formula that might help. I call it my "On-Time Results" model. This model, which is explored in detail in the ULTI-MATE Success Generator,™ is the key to rerouting things quickly so you can eliminate distractions and stay focused on the important stuff. Figure 13.4 shows how it works.

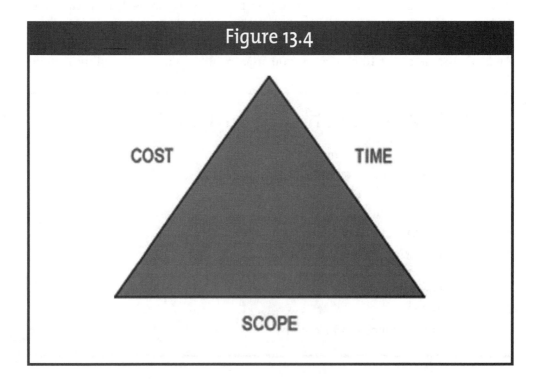

Figure 13.4

COST

TIME

SCOPE

Scope

In any project, whether it's a simple request of a team member or a detailed contract with a client, it's important to define the scope of the project.

Here are some key questions to ask:

- What do you expect it to look like when it's complete?
- How does this project or goal relate to the rest of your business and life?
- Does it make sense to break this project or goal down into smaller parts? If so, what would they be?

Identifying all of the details up front, in writing, ensures that everyone's expectations are met at the end. The number-one reason vendors lose money on their contracts is because they don't define the detailed expectations of both parties.

Time

Identifying the agreed-upon completion time is one of the most important, and most often overlooked, elements. It's simple. Everyone needs to be clear about the deadline. Even if you are just asking your assistant to complete a task, make sure he understands the expected date of completion.

Cost/Resources

It's important for everyone involved to understand the budget and what resources are available. It's very easy to slip into being the bottleneck if your team members have to ask you every time they need to make a decision involving money. Give trusted team members a budget to work with, and watch things get done in record time.

A great example of a system for resources that we use in my company is a WIKI. A WIKI is accessible to everyone on my team via a website and provides a list of every resource we have, from contact files to passwords. This really minimizes confusion and lost time searching for things.

Being a speed implementer means making a commitment to surround yourself with a team that can make things happen. Speed requires that you to stay focused on high-payoff activities. But if you are letting yourself get distracted with administrative minutia and task-oriented things, then you will never be able to maintain speed.

If startup costs are a concern, then you may want to consider a "bootstrapping team" that is comprised of low-cost resources. A few you might consider are:

- *Interns.* A college or a high school student who is learning about business from you.
- *Apprentices.* Someone new to your field who wants to learn from you.
- *Retirees.* Willing to work for less just to have something to do.
- *Stay-at-home moms.* Sometimes they just want to be part of the "grown up world."

- *Barter or trade.* You give your product or service in exchange for someone's work on your projects.
- *Overseas contractors.* There are tons of new outsourcing firms in countries like the Philippines, India, and Russia.

A team can fit any budget, business size, and work style. The key is to determine what kind of team you need to kick-start your results, stay profitable, and keep your sanity.

The Bottom Line for Speed

The real point about speed is that moving fast isn't the only thing that matters; it's HOW you move forward that matters. Adopting the inner and outer game of a speed implementer will give you the innate tools to do things quickly and get results the first time.

Now is the time to put things to the test. Pick one or two concepts and make a commitment to put them into action right away. Don't delay, don't procrastinate, and certainly don't put this book down until you've gotten clear on your two action steps. It's time to be a speed implementer!

▲   ▲   ▲

Melanie Benson Strick, Million-Dollar Lifestyle Business Coach, teaches entrepreneurs how to stop feeling overwhelmed so they can create more money, more freedom, and more prestige. Co-author of *Visionary Women Inspiring the World: 12 Paths to Personal Power* and contributing author to *Entrepreneurial Spirits,* Melanie is creator of "Virtual Team Building Secrets," which teaches entrepreneurs how to hire, fire, delegate, and manage a virtual team, catapulting them into 6+ and 7+ success. Listen to an interview at www.VirtualTeamBuildingSecrets.com/5steps.

Appendix
Info-Marketing Resources

One of the toughest parts of the information marketing business is finding vendors who understand what you are trying to accomplish and are able to get you there. Too many fail to deliver. An info-marketer must be able to act quickly. Once you get new customers, incompetent vendors can kill a business.

Here are vendors who understand info-marketers and are ready to help you become successful.

Customer Service
Turn-Key Customer Service, Marketing Implementation, and Product Fulfillment

To streamline their businesses, smart info-marketers have outsourced all of this time-consuming work to Sheiff Services. Randy and Camille Sheiff are in the office each day, supervising a call center, managing an InfusionSoft ManagePro CRM system for their clients, and making sure orders are fulfilled and customer service questions are handled promptly.

In fact, because they are doing all of this, their info-marketer clients are able to start up their businesses more quickly, get more marketing steps implemented, and generate a lot more money without any additional effort. In addition, they don't have to deal with the dozens of customer questions that come in each day.

For more information about how Randy and Camille Sheiff can take over the administrative hassles of your info-business, call Randy at (512) 353-5037 today.

Event Management
The Easy Way to Minimize Liability, Reduce Stress, and Increase the Profitability of Your Events

There are thousands of dollars of potential liability when you sign a hotel contract for your boot camp or event. Plus, the document is so long, it's difficult to figure out what it even says.

Bari Baumgardner has been negotiating hotel contracts and managing events for her clients for more than 15 years. Her clients benefit from her experience and the volume pricing she is able to negotiate with hotels. Because Bari works with several infomarketers, hotels make concessions to her, so they will be considered for other future business.

Hotels have experts who negotiate with event planners every day. You need an expert on your side. Outsourcing the complicated and time consuming event management work to Bari, so you can focus on marketing and on-site sales, can add tens of thousands of dollars in new revenue to your event.

For a complimentary meeting evaluation, phone Bari at (704) 334-0909 or e-mail BBaumgardner@SageEventManagement.com today.

Business Marketing/Management System
A Software System That Puts Your Info-Marketing Business on Autopilot by Automating Your Marketing, Sales, and More

Are you tired of never being in control of your prospect and customer information? Does your business suffer because you use three, four, or five software programs to manage your business? We understand your pain, and we have a web-based CRM Software program built specifically for your info-marketing business.

ManagePro CRM is your customer relationship management system. Finally, you will be able to put your customers at the center of your business where they should be. All of your customer interaction via e-mail, phone, fax, or in person is tracked and managed in one place, so you can close more sales and maintain better relationships with your existing customers.

No more trying to track which leads are in which step of multiple marketing sequences. ManagePro CRM lets you SUPERCHARGE your follow-up sequences. In addition to sending follow-up e-mails, ManagePro CRM will send direct mail pieces, faxes, voice broadcasts, and more—automatically.

For a free product tour, auto responder test drive, and online demonstration, visit www.InfoMarketingCRM.com.

Legal Services

Build Your Business, Protect Your Assets

Contact Nevada Corporate Planners Inc. at (888) 627-7007 for information and fees on helping your information marketing business get off to a fast start! Or e-mail us at NCP@NVinc.com.

Successful Info-Marketing Business Startup

Garrett Sutton is a corporate attorney advising small business owners. As one of only three Rich Dad's Advisors, he teaches corporate formation and business finance strategies to thousands of new business owners each year. He has written several best-selling books, including *Own Your Own Corporation* and *How to Buy and Sell a Business*. He also hosts a syndicated internet radio show, "Wealth Talk America" (www.Wealth TalkAmerica.com). His firm provides asset protection and business-building services to thousands of clients around the country and internationally. For more information, visit www.BusinessCreditSuccess.com.

The Business Growth Lawyers

In the speed of today's business world, actionable information creates opportunity. Opportunity creates a position for unique revenue streams and fast, high margin profits to the individual or company that controls the flow of information. Naturally, opportunities of this magnitude get the focus of government regulators, and enterprising info-marketers need sound legal advice to navigate the complex mix of legal disciplines.

Info-Marketing Law is a legal practice that connects the diverse disciplines of intellectual property, contract law, franchising, business opportunity, consumer protection, FTC regulation, corporate securities, business law, and internet law, blending them into a specialty for the information business. Go to www.NickNanton.com.

Publicity Tools

Free Publicity, Drive Traffic to Your Website

When you use PR LEADS, we'll put you in touch with reporters who need to quote experts like you. That's right. We get approximately 100 requests a day from reporters who are writing stories for major publications who desperately need to find experts to quote in their stories. We'll give you their names, their e-mail addresses, and their story angles, so you can contact them! If you have the information they need, they'll feature you and your books in their publications. We're talking big name publications and media outlets like the *Wall Street Journal*, *CNN*, and *Newsweek* as well as *Redbook* and *Glamour*. For more information, visit www.InfoMarketingPR Leads.com.

Media Duplication

These companies handle duplication for all of your follow-up mailings, product fulfillment, or duplication jobs. They can produce the duplicates and deliver them to you or ship directly to your customers when you receive orders.

- CD duplication
- DVD duplication
- Cassette duplication
- Complete line of packaging

Corporate Disk Company

Joseph Foley, (800) 634-3475 x233 or visit www.disk.com.

McMannis Duplication

Tony Wedel, (620) 628-4411 or visit www.McMannisDuplication.com.

Merchant Services

Finally, a merchant services provider that appreciates info-marketers, understands the business, and wants to help you make more money.

Info-marketers everywhere are shocked to learn that their merchant services provider considers them to be a liability. Even after these providers unconditionally accept your business, they can impose six-month holds on your money without notice, refund your customer charges, or cancel your account altogether.

Now, there is an alternative. One merchant services provider likes info-marketers and wants your business, too. For a free, no-obligation evaluation of your current merchant services needs and your future opportunities, visit www.InfoMarketingMerchant Services.com. Complete the quick form, and someone will contact you right away.

Merchant Services with Info-Marketers in Mind

Info-marketers, let Charge Today provide you with full-service merchant accounts and credit card processing solutions for today's demanding marketplace. From merchant accounts, ACH/check services, secure gateways, and virtual and physical terminals to shopping carts, ChargeToday.com is the info-marketer's premier partner for credit card payment and processing solutions. For more information, visit www.ChargeTodayInfo.com. Complete the brief form, and Charge Today will be in touch with you within 24 hours.

Info-Marketing Technology Tools

The Shopping Cart Used by the Most Info-Marketers to Take Orders Online, Follow Up with Prospects, and Run Affiliate Campaigns

All of the shopping cart and marketing tools that info-marketers need to automate a successful online info-marketing business. With 1ShoppingCart, info-marketers have the ability to take orders online, accept credit cards, e-mail customers, use automatic ebook delivery, use ad tracking tools, have unlimited auto responders, discount/update modules, and have access to a built-in affiliate program. www.Info MarketingShoppingCart.com

Create Products Fast

We help info-marketers uncover quick-profit niches and discover what their prospects and customers want to buy "most." With the Ask Database, you can create new products from scratch, effortlessly grab more testimonials from members, uncover new market niches using Google AdWords, and quickly determine winning teleseminar content. www.InfoMarketersAsk.com

Easy Follow-Up Messages and Ezines

With AWeber, info-marketers can configure follow-up and newsletter messages with name personalization click-through and open rate tracking, attachments, RSS, and split testing at no additional cost. Messages can include HTML using our 51-plus predesigned templates, or you can create your own with the integrated easy editor and images or plain text. www.AWeberEmail.com

Audio/Visual Production

Bayfront Productions

Turn to Bayfront Productions to create high-quality audio and video products. After working with info-marketers for many years, it knows what info-marketers need to create products and marketing materials. Miroslav Beck at (813) 810-6241 or visit www.VideoMarketingExpert.com

Leading Experts TV

One stop to creating a broadcast-quality 30-minute show highlighting you as an expert. Use your video on your local television station, or exhibit booth, or broadcast it as part of sales presentations. Visit www.LeadingExpertsTV.com for more information.

Printing/Mailing Services

McClung Companies

Tom Trevillian at (540) 949-8139 or visit www.McClungCo.com

City Print (Division of City Blue Print)

Steven Harshbarger at (316) 267-5555 or visit www.CityBlue.com

Handy Mailing Services

Vergil Esau at (316) 944-6258 or visit www.HandyMailing.com

Advantage Media Group

Adam Witty at (843) 414-5600 or visit www.AdvantageFamily.com

Datum Direct

Dave Brady at (312) 492-8822

Pete the Printer

Pete Lillo, visit www.PeteThePrinter.com

Packaging/Promotional Products

American Retail Supply

For advertising aids, product packaging, or items to insert into mailings to grab your prospects' attention, contact American Retail Supply at (800) 426-5708 or visit www.MakeYouHappy.com for ideas.

Information Resources

The Ultimate Shortcut for Success and Profitability in Information Marketing

Every month, hundreds of startups turn to the Information Marketing Association to get their businesses started quickly. With its two monthly newsletters, Best Practices in Information Marketing monthly call, and a monthly Get Started Quick coaching call for those just starting out, there is no better tool to make your business profitable. And, for a limited time, it's FREE.

Readers of this book can join the Information Marketing Association for FREE by visiting www.GetIMAFree.com today. You may cancel your membership at any time. There is no obligation. Over the next two months, you will have the opportunity to enjoy all of the membership benefits that our members already enjoy.

Info-Marketers' A–Z Blueprint Seminar

For anyone who is in or wants to be in the HIGHLY PROFITABLE business of providing information.

Here's a partial list of topics discussed by Bill Glazer at the Information Marketing Business Development Blueprint Seminar:

1. Seven Decisions the New Info-Marketer Needs to Make
2. How to Evaluate a Niche or Subculture Market
3. How to Thoroughly Profile the Prospective Customer
4. How to Leverage the Affinity You Have With a Niche
5. How to Create a Relationship With a Niche You Have NO Affinity With
6. How to Get Testimonials When You Just Start Out in a Niche
7. How to Get GREAT Testimonials From Customers/Members
8. How to Use Your Lead Generation Strategies to Give You a Whole Lot More Information About Your Market Than JUST New Leads

9. A Close Look at a Beginning, Simple Marketing Funnel

10. An Inside Look at the Six-Year Evolution of Bill's Marketing Funnel

11. An Inside Look at Bill's 2004 Marketing Funnel

12. How to Create Joint Ventures that Produce Good Leads @ Bargain Cost

13. How to Work Effectively with Trade Journals and Associations

14. How to Systemize and Automate the Entire Marketing Funnel

15. How to Grow Rapidly with Minimum Staff

16. How to Find the Right Staff for an Info-Marketing Business (#1 headache I hear!)

17. When to Give Up the Front End and Concentrate on the Back End

18. The Easiest Ways to Create Back-End Products

19. Different Coaching Program Models to Consider

20. Outside-the-Box Lead Generation Strategies (like "The Industry Survey")

21. Successful Uses of Audiotapes and CDs as Sales Tools

22. How to Sell via Tradeshows, Seminars, and Speaking Opportunities

23. How to (Legally) Use Broadcast FAX

24. How to Mine Unconverted Leads 12 to 36 Months After Acquisition

25. How to Build the Most Saleable Info-Products/Kits

26. How to Minimize Refunds

27. How to Maximize Referrals

28. THE COMPLETE BUSINESS BLUEPRINT—Used for Bill's BGS Marketing Business

29. How to Maximize Profits AND Customer Value With "Forced Continuity"

30. How to Front-End a Newsletter

31. How an "Offline Guy" Uses the Internet Painlessly and Profitably

32. An Inside Look at the Financial Truths of Info-Businesses: Actual Revenues, Costs, Profits, etc. (Real Case Histories)

33. How to Identify Missed Opportunities in Your Info-Business Plan

34. Seven Most Frequently Made Mistakes to Avoid

35. How to Expand from One Niche to Multiple Niches—How I'm Doing It Now

36. How to Negotiate With Media to Make Sure You Get the Best Deal—Even After They Already Said You've Got the Best Price

37. How to Analyze New Vendors to Avoid a Business Nightmare

38. Copywriting Formulas and Shortcuts—Bill will give you his own copywriting questionnaire that he personally uses before he writes any copy for a client or himself. Frank Discussion on Outsourcing vs. Doing It In-House (The Pros and Cons)

39. When Do You Give Up on a Niche?

For more details, visit www.InfoMarketingAtoZ.com for a special limited time offer just for buyers of this book.

Champions of the Info-Summit

Who Else Wants to "Pick-the-Brains" of the Sharpest Information Marketers in the World?

Imagine . . . Just ONE IDEA Can Make You Independent for the Rest of Your Life! This program includes:

- Big Breakthroughs in the Information Marketing Business
- How a Successful Info-Business Was Increased by 500 Percent in 12 Months
- How Agora Did It
- Copywriting Secrets from the Pro
- How to Most Successfully Market Your Million-Dollar Seminar or Boot Camp
- How to Sell High-Priced Coaching
- Integrated Media Magic: How to Crossbreed Online and Offline Marketing for ANY Information Business
- How to Sell Information Online . . . Even If You're a Total Computer Dunce!
- Secrets of Online Copywriting
- Teleseminar Selling Secrets
- How to Turn Unconverted Leads into a Flood of Extra Profits by Adding Inbound and/or Outbound Telemarketing to Your Marketing Funnel
- The Five Gold Rings of Wealth Production from Info-Entrepreneurship
- How to Turn Your Info-Products Into a Lot of Extra Cash, Automatically, on eBay

For more details, visit www.InfoMarketingChampions.com for a special limited time offer just for buyers of this book.

Creating Copy that Sells

A Step-by-Step System that Removes all the Guesswork, Waste, and Frustration from "Creating Copy that Sells" Once and for All . . . GUARANTEED!

The info-marketing business requires a lot of salesmanship. Quite frankly, no matter what business you pursue, there is no more important skill you can learn than effective sales copywriting. Today, it's never been easier to learn.

▲

Bill Glazer created a groundbreaking web-assisted product that puts at your fingertips all the tools you need to become an expert copywriter. In addition, it walks you through the entire process step-by-step, so by the time you finish the program, you have produced high-quality sales letters, just like the marketing pros.

In part, this system includes:

- The **"11 Building Blocks"** that must be incorporated into just about every piece of copy you write.

- The **"20 Critical Copy Concepts"** that will take your work to the next level. Many of these are tools that only very successful pros think about. In fact, they are the tools (and tricks) that often separate the good copywriters from the professional copywriters.

- **"Kopy Kryptonite."** These are the BIGGEST MISTAKES that people make when writing copy that will kill your results the same way that Kryptonite affects Superman. I've identified seven of them, and believe me, you need to know what they are and avoid them like the plague.

- The **"Step-by-Step Questionnaire"** I use the questionnaire to get organized before I write copy and also how to get the right "raw material" to mold into great copy.

Visit www.InfoMarketingCopyThatSells.com for more information.

Seven Newsletters that Unlock Your Vault to Riches in One Easy Package for Your Convenience

Matt Furey's *Internet Marketing Money-Generator*. Each month, the Zen Master of the Internet® gives you hard-hitting real facts of what works in internet marketing.

Psycho-Cybernetics—The Newsletter. Monthly teachings of Dr. Maxwell Maltz permeating the subconscious minds of achievement-oriented entrepreneurs worldwide to program yourself for success.

Eddie Baran's *Website Critiques*. How would you like to get inside the mind of **THE MAN** who has been responsible for creating ALL of dozens of money-generating websites since the year 2000?

Pete the Printer's *Client Newsletter with Direct Mail Secrets*. When it comes to anything having to do with print marketing, Pete Lillo, aka "Pete the Printer" is the man top marketers call on time and again.

Pete Lillo's Dynamic NEW *SUCCESS AMERICA Newsletter*. Monthly stories proving that anyone can become a Success in America (or elsewhere) with hard focused work and a determination to focus.

Matt Furey's *Maximum Health & Fitness*. Matt's international best seller, *Combat Conditioning*, continues to give everyone from martial artists to traveling businessmen the keys to getting fit and staying fit.

Dan Kennedy's *Look Over My Shoulder Program*. Dan Kennedy, aka "The Millionaire Maker" and the world's HIGHEST paid copywriter (his typical fees are now $100,000.00 plus royalties), allows you to see the projects he is working on and how they develop into finished magnetic marketing.

For a limited time, this collection of newsletters is available on a 2-for-1 Special, limited to 98 people. For the details, visit www.InfoMarketingGoldCrown.com right now.

Glossary

Here are common terms you will hear within the information marketing business.

Affiliate: A relationship in which there is an agreement between two people to sell a particular product. One individual has customers he wants to market the product to, and another one has the product or service he wants to offer to customers. Typically, the individual who has the product will create an affiliate program. Many of these are executed online, and most of the popular shopping cart software programs today have this feature built in. The affiliate completes an application. Upon approval of the affiliate relationship, the affiliate is assigned a unique website address and given access to the affiliate toolbox that has e-mails, websites, ads, and other things the affiliate can use to help sell the program. Then the affiliate uses the link, uses those sales techniques to help sell the product, and an affiliate commission is paid on those products. Commissions vary substantially by the different products and services sold. Very often the terms are negotiable for individuals who are able to sell a lot of affiliate programs, but for most folks, you normally have to earn a higher commission rate by performing well for a particular affiliate.

Affinity: A measure of your relationship to a market. If you have been a member of a market for a number of years, perhaps having established a career there, then you would have a high affinity with that particular market. If you are new to a market (for example, if you are going to sell to Harley Davidson owners, you have never owned a Harley Davidson, and you do not know anyone who owns a Harley Davidson), then you would have very little affinity with that market.

Alexa.com: A website that allows you to gather information about competitors and about websites within a particular market. It provides a lot of information about the site, including how much traffic it is receiving from the internet.

Back end: The most profitable part of an information marketing business and what distinguishes info-marketers from all other types of information publishers. Info-marketers are able to sell coaching, consulting, seminars, automatic implementation products, and newsletters, and offer other people's products to their customers as additional revenue opportunities.

Churn: The number of new members joining a market at a given time. For instance, the real estate agent industry is a market where there is a lot of churn. Many individuals join that market in hopes of making lots of money as a real estate agent. In contrast, the funeral director industry has very little churn. Most of the entrants in that market have been in family-owned businesses for many years or they are large corporations buying the family-owned businesses. There are not a lot of new companies jumping into the funeral director business that were not in it 12 months ago. The real estate agent industry has lots of churn, and there are lots of new customers to sell to. The funeral director industry has little churn. The customers in it today are pretty much the same ones who will be in it 12 months from now.

Claims: The benefits you are telling potential customers they will receive from using your product. Income claims refer to the amount of income you state others have received from using your product.

Coaching: An arrangement where you provide advice and counsel to customers to help them implement their own problem solutions. You may have already provided them the information they need, but through a coaching program, you are able to give them specific information for their particular problems as well as specific case examples to help them solve the problems. This is generally distinguished from consulting. Consulting is actually doing it for them, whereas coaching is helping them to get it done for themselves.

Continuity: A program where on an established interval, usually monthly, customers are charged a set fee for a given level of product and service. Most programs are on a monthly continuity. This entire concept was pioneered and made popular by the

Book-of-the-Month program, where customers trusted a publisher to send them a book every month related to their interests. This created an ongoing continuity relationship between these customers and the publisher. Info-marketers have used continuity to completely revolutionize their businesses and add many more subscribers vs. using the annual subscription model. (See *Forced continuity*.)

Ebook: A book in a digital file that communicates information to your prospects and can be delivered electronically over the internet. Rather than printing a product, weighing it, putting postage on it, and mailing it, you are able to instantly deliver an ebook and put your product in the customer's hand immediately.

Endorsed mailing: A mailing where an individual is given a letter of endorsement, usually a brief letter that is added to the front of his sales message, that gives credibility and recognition to the offer and sales message that it would not have gotten if it had to stand on its own.

Forced continuity: An arrangement where the customers are provided a free trial period of a program, and then at the end of the free trial, they are automatically added to the continuity program. It does not require customers to act in order to opt into the monthly continuity. Customers can always opt out if they choose to; however, they do not have to act to opt in. (See *Continuity*.)

Front end: Marketing your products and services to new customers. It is the first step of your info-business. After you are able to obtain customers through your front end, you can develop the back end of your business by selling additional products and services to the customers who have already made a purchase from you.

Group coaching: A model where, instead of the coach interacting with one student at a time, the coach interacts with many students at one time. In general, a coach is providing advice and counsel, examples, and encouragement to students and is not performing actual services for them. In the group coaching environment, there are many students interacting at the same time with one or more coaches.

Guarantee: Your assurance to your customers that your product is everything you say it is. You promise to stand behind your product and send their money back if your customers are not satisfied with it.

Guarantee, conditional: A guarantee where you force the customers to go through certain hoops in order to receive their money back. They may have to implement certain features within your product to demonstrate they have tried some things before you will give them a refund.

Guarantee, unconditional: A guarantee where the customers can simply ask for the refund, and they are given the refund without any conditions whatsoever.

Herd: A term Dan Kennedy coined to refer to an info-marketer's customer base. Expanding on the herd analysis, Dan teaches info-marketers to build a fence around their herds to protect them against poachers and to prevent customers from escaping.

Joint venture: When two or more individuals get together to create and market a product to a particular industry. In many cases, one of the joint venture partners has a list of customers, and the other joint venture partner has a product or will develop a product or service for those customers. The partners work together to sell the product and then split the proceeds.

Kit: A collection of materials you are delivering all at one time to your customers.

Lead generation: The process of identifying individuals within a market who are interested in more information about the product or service you are offering.

Market: A collection of customers who have something in common and most importantly, have a common problem you can solve as an info-marketer.

Mastermind meeting: The ideas of the mastermind alliance and masterminding grew from Andrew Carnegie, Henry Ford, Harvey Firestone, and Thomas Edison as reported in books like the popular best seller *Think and Grow Rich* by Napoleon Hill. One of the factors successful people share is a group of people they can work with to help solve problems. By working together to solve each other's problems, each of them benefits. Many information marketers have been able to duplicate the benefit of mastermind meetings through their coaching programs.

Monthly CD: An audio program or other program offered through podcast and other means that individuals subscribe to. They can be provided by one person as a monologue, or they can be in a conversation or interview format between an expert and a host.

Multipay: An arrangement where the info-marketer helps customers afford the product by putting it on a payment program. It can be two-pay, three-pay, five-pay, etc., and it helps lower the initial price of the product and decreases the risk that customers may perceive from the sale. For example, if a customer looks at an offer that is $250.00 a month for four months, that may be more acceptable to him than paying $1,000.00 all at once, even though he could probably self-finance that $1,000.00 through a credit card. It feels like $250.00 is all he is risking, so he is more apt to participate in a multipay program than in an all-up-front sale.

Newsletter: A publication that is published, usually monthly, by an information marketer to communicate with customers, to provide ongoing help and information, and to reinforce what the info-marketer has taught them in the past.

Niche: A group of individuals with a like interest or a similar demographic. Normally these niches are defined as business oriented—the customers could be plumbers, restaurant owners, chiropractors, doctors, or accountants, for example.

Offers: What you are agreeing to provide your customers for a fee. Most teachers within the info-marketing world will tell you your offer is the most important part of your marketing campaign. You should create your offer before you create a product or anything else. You should create a compelling offer, a collection of resources, tools, techniques, manuals, CDs, videos, coaching—whatever you want to package in your offer. You should decide what your offer is going to be first, and then you can go about the job of creating the product and offering it to the marketplace.

One-step sale: A process in which you go straight from introducing yourself to the customer to asking for the sale within one marketing piece. This is contrasted to lead generation marketing, where you first generate a lead through a lead generation ad and then create a sales sequence to sell to that lead. Through one-step sales, you are trying to sell at the point of first contact.

Online marketing: A method in which you use the internet to communicate with a large population of people using automated software to handle the lead capture, marketing, and sales process as well as, many times, the product delivery.

Order form: Also called a *response device* or an *application*. It is a piece of paper, the document, or the web form the customer uses to make a transaction. This is where the customer fills in his name, address, and credit card information. The order form is mailed, faxed, or completed online or on the telephone. If completing a telephone order, the person taking the order usually has an order form to fill out for the customer.

Prerecorded message: A message, usually through a toll-free number, that you offer within your lead generation ad to encourage your customer to leave his name and contact information, so you can deliver the rest of your sales message to him.

Reachability: A term referring to a niche that describes the amount of ease with which you can put your marketing message in front of your prospective customers. If a niche already has several magazines, others already marketing there, or its own cable television channel, then that market is highly reachable. If there are no magazines specific to that niche, then its reachability is low.

Response device: See *Order form*.

Risk reversal: A marketing term for a guarantee with which you ease a customer's fear of making a purchase by taking on all of the risk of the sale. As the customer evaluates whether or not he wants to buy your product, he is deciding whether he can trust you. By offering a refund of the purchase price and to pay for return shipping if the customer returns the product, you are taking on all of the risk of the sale. This will help your customer buy from you with confidence.

S&D: A term coined by Bill Glazer that means "steal and distribute." Rather than reinventing new ways of doing business or new marketing programs for a particular niche, you should be adapting programs that have proven themselves successful in other areas and implementing them within your own market.

Self-liquidating leads: When your lead generation ad charges the potential customer a fee to receive the rest of the marketing sequence. For example, the ad will have an offer, invite people to respond, and charge them $9.95 to get the rest of the marketing sequence. This type of lead has two benefits: 1) it provides income from the lead generation process that helps pay for more lead generation ads; and 2) it increases the quality of the lead because even though it is a nominal fee, only the most motivated individuals will be willing to go through the work necessary to respond. When you use a free lead generation system and all people have to do is pick up the phone, you are going to dramatically increase the number of leads you get and the number of opportunities you have to sell to individuals, but you are also going to increase the marketing cost.

Squeeze page: A web form that captures a name and address from a prospect before you allow the prospect to see the rest of the sales message.

SRDS: The acronym for the Standard Rate and Data Service, which is a manual that has details about every list commercially available for sale. From the SRDS manual, you will be able to learn about markets based on the types of lists available for them and to evaluate how easy it will be for you to reach this market through direct mail.

Subculture: A way of evaluating a potential market. Whereas niches are based on professional designations such as doctors and plumbers, subcultures are based on hobbies and interests of particular individuals. Golfers, fishermen, hobbyists, Star Trekkies, bird lovers, fish lovers—all of these are subcultures you can market to.

Subniche: Specialties within a particular niche. For example, a plumber could be a commercial plumber who only works in 30-story buildings, or he could be a residential plumber. There are many subniches for doctors: dermatologist, surgeon, gynecologist, anesthesiologist—all of which are subspecialties or subniches within the niche of medicine.

Telecoaching: A process of delivering coaching services over the telephone, rather than in person or by mail.

Telemarketing: A process of delivering a sales message over the telephone.

Teleseminar: A seminar delivered over the telephone. Most teleseminars offered by information marketers are free and designed to provide a sales presentation. The sales presentation can be for a telecoaching program as a back-end product, and many info-marketers also use teleseminars to convert sales on the front end. So, not only will they offer printed sales letters and CDs, but they will also invite their leads to call into a teleseminar to hear a sales presentation.

Tollbooth position: Once you have developed a list of customers, there will be other individuals who want to sell products and services to your list. Because you have a relationship with your list, you are in a position to charge others for access to your customer list, either through an affiliate program, JV opportunity, endorsed mailing, or some other agreement.

Try-before-you-buy: Often called a *puppy dog close* because it was borrowed from the pet stores that allow you to take a cute and cuddly puppy home for the evening. Once you have taken a puppy home, gotten used to him, shown the puppy to your neighbors and friends, and taken him for a walk, the likelihood of you bringing that dog back to the store is extremely low. An info-marketer very often may offer a try-before-you-buy where the customer is able to complete an order form, fax it in, receive the product, examine it for 30, 60, or 90 days, and then the charge goes through automatically if the customer has not returned the product.

Wordtracker.com: A website that allows you to find out exactly how many people are searching for particular key words and phrases. When you are trying to determine how to position your product within a market, you can examine the types of key words and phrases individuals are searching for on the internet. That will give you a hint of what you should be offering them.

Index

How to Jump Start Your Information Marketing Business with Additional Business Templates, Business Building Tools, and Ongoing Support

Now you have the tools you need to start your own highly profitable information marketing business. As you build your business, if you want to tap into other professionals and obtain additional tools, the Information Marketing Association may be for you.

Receive Bill Glazer's A to Z Info-Marketing Blueprint for FREE

As a special bonus for readers of *Entrepreneur* Magazine's *Start Your Own Information Marketing Business*, you can receive the complete A to Z Info-Marketing Blueprint for FREE when you join the Information Marketing Association.

As a new member, you'll receive another module of the A to Z course each week. The audio is available to listen to on your computer or through a simple MP3 download. Also, you receive all of the PowerPoint slides and handouts. Plus, it's archived on the site for your future reference. To see a partial list of topics covered by Bill Glazer in his Information Marketing A to Z Blueprint, see the list on page 207.

With your IMA membership, you'll receive a license to access the online version of the course. You are welcome to access the course at any time, review the handouts, and listen to the program. If you like, you can download the audio and create audio CDs for your personal use. You'll receive your user ID and password with access to the A to Z Course within 24 hours.

In addition to this great course, you'll also receive all of the benefits of the Information Marketing Association:

1. *Educational Resources*
   - Info-Marketer Profiles and Detailed 'How-To' Check Lists with *Info-Marketing Insiders' Journal*
   - DAN KENNEDY'S NO B.S. INFO-MARKETING LETTER & ULTIMATE INFORMATION ENTREPRENEUR SPECIAL REPORTS
   - Info-Marketing Best Practices Teleseminars

2. *Help with Your Business Issues*
   - Jump Start in Information Marketing Business
   - Information Marketing Expertise, When You Need It

3. *Online Networking*
   - Newsletter and Jump Start Coaching Call Archive

- – Member Discussion Forum
- – Joint Venture Opportunities

4. *Free Content for Your Newsletters, Websites, and Products*
   - – Easy Content CDs
   - – Gallery of Experts
   - – Easy Content Archive

5. *Showcase of IMA Member Products and Other Promotional Opportunities*
   - – IMA members are invited to submit articles, reports, tip sheets, and other content to be included in the Copyright-free Content CDs (see item above) provided to all IMA members
   - – Sell your products and services through the IMA's Joint Venture Directory
   - – Encourage other info-marketers to sell seminar seats by including your seminars in the Information Marketing Industry Calendar
   - – Include yourself in the Gallery of Experts
   - – IMA members may submit proposals to offer discounts on certain of their goods/services to other IMA members
   - – Product Showcase to sell your products through the IMA

6. *Increased Credibility with an Industry Identity*

7. *Members Only Discounts and/or Preferred Services*

8. *Special IMA Banking Services from Family Merchants Bank*
   - – Special Bank Financing Programs for High Price-Point Coaching Programs, Seminars, Courses, Lifetime Memberships, Business Opportunities, and Franchises
   - – Credit Card Processing Services and Support Specifically Designed for Information Marketers
   - – Exceptionally Competitive CD and Money Market Rates ... Assistance with Self-Directed IRAs and Other Retirement Accounts ... and Unlimited Federal Deposit Insurance (above $100,000.00)

9. *IMA Member Gatherings*
   - – FREE Regional Member Networking Roundtables
   - – Annual Member Gathering with Dan Kennedy and Bill Glazer

10. *Representation of Industry*
    - – We will make ourselves heard on everything from postal rate increases and internet use taxes to do-not lists.

For more information, visit www.FreeAtoZBluePrint.com.

Other Books by Entrepreneur Press and the Information Marketing Association

The Easy 9-Step Process to Wealth and Riches
Welcome to the information marketing industry—a little-known industry of entrepreneurs, most working only part-time hours and netting seven-figure profits.

Info-marketers gather information and sell it in convenient forms to people who need it. The topics include everything imaginable, from better sex, to teaching parrots to talk, to gardening, to investing in real estate, to running businesses. In addition to an easy 9-step process for you to create your own info-business, this book profiles 30 info-marketers, and reveals their businesses strategies, marketing materials, and business documents, so you can have the tools you need to duplicate their success.

- **How One Ex-Salesman, Ex-Law Enforcement Officer, Ex-Company Owner Turned Surplus Junk Into a Million-Dollar Info-Business .... Page 28**
- A Direct Sales Process That Turned Into an Info-Business .... Page 35
- **The Quick Way to Determine the Selling Price of Information Products .... Page 43**
- What to Say to Get Customers to Believe That You Really Do Offer High-Quality Products .... Page 121
- **How a Simple Change Multiplied a Product's Sales Price by 4 Times .... Page 51**
- How a Professional Speaker Got Off the Road and Built a Million-Dollar Business She Could Run From Her Home Office .... Page 53
- **How a Mom From New York Built a Business From Her Home That Kept Bill Collectors Away and Gave Her Family the Extra Money for a Great Lifestyle .... Page 101**
- What a Successful Veterinarian Did to Get Veterinarians From Around the World to Buy His Marketing Strategies .... Page 62
- A High School Kid Built a Business and Earned More Than His College Professors .... Page 32
- **How an Info-Marketer From a Small Town in Kansas (population 565) Built an International Business .... Page 72**
- Someone Who Teaches Men How to Get Women to Approach Them for Dates .... Page 76
- **An Australian Built a Business Teaching Salons How to Book More Appointments, and He's Never Owned a Salon Before .... Page 82**
- How an Info-Marketer Used His Products to Create a Professional Speaking Business Earning Him $10,000.00 per Gig .... Page 89
- **What an Info-Marketer Did With No Knowledge and No Customers to Build a Million-Dollar Business Within a Year .... Page 110**

- The 40 Ways to Make Money With Information Products .... Page 41
- **Blinded and Handicapped by Multiple Sclerosis, One Info-Marketer Overcame His Disability to Build a Successful Info-Business .... Page 59**

No other business provides the revenue, flexibility, and lifestyle that information marketing provides. And now, you can create your own million-dollar business—in just 12 months or less.

Dan Kennedy

Dan is widely acknowledged as the leader in developing the modern information marketing industry. Certainly more people have gone from zero to multimillion-dollar info-businesses under his guidance than by any other means or mentor, and virtually every significant breakthrough in this industry in the last decade has come from Dan and his clients, including the now common continuity and forced continuity approaches, the ascension model, every means of selling high-priced coaching, boot camp add-on days, contests to promote coaching, and on and on and on. To learn how to use Dan's most recent breakthrough, info-marketers each paid $12,000.00 to attend a three-day briefing. Four different info-marketers pioneering this newest business model each went from zero to more than $1 million in income within 12 months. Dan is the author of nine business books, including his newest, *No B.S. Time Management for Entrepreneurs*, available in bookstores or from online booksellers. Additional information and free chapter previews are available at www.NoBSBooks.com. Included with the book is a coupon for a free kit of peak personal productivity tools. Dan is also a busy entrepreneur, consultant, speaker, and direct-response advertising copywriter. Info is available at www.DanKennedy.com.

Bill Glazer

Bill entered the information marketing field at Dan Kennedy's urging. As a famously successful owner of menswear stores, Bill began in that niche and quickly built his BGS MARKETING into a million-dollar-plus information business. Today, BGS provides "advertising tool kits," marketing, and training to 47 different retail niches, and its *Outside the Box Advertising* newsletter has more than 3,700 subscribers throughout the United States, Canada, and 16 other nations. Bill so adeptly and thoroughly mastered every aspect of information marketing, and ran such a well managed info-business, that in 2004, Dan handpicked him as his successor and sold the *No B.S. Marketing Letter* and the membership business to him. Bill has multiplied its size; instituted the most progressive forced continuity marketing systems, online marketing, and affiliate programs; and now manages the original newsletter, a second newsletter—*Gold+ telecoaching*, Internet telecoaching, and this year, three coaching groups.

Robert Skrob

For 13 years, Robert has created and promoted trade associations and has consulted within that industry. His business, Membership Services Inc., is a successful association management company that directs the operations of dozens of associations serving different industries. His experience in multiple industries has given him unique insights into building info-marketing businesses, and he has created several info-businesses within different industries. In addition to running his businesses, he provides coaching, marketing, consulting, and copywriting services to info-marketers. Purchase this book at your local bookstore, BN.com, or Amazon.com today. Or visit www.Info MarketingBook.com for more information.